# Good Words for the Young

## A Child's Devotional

Edited by
Rebekah Choat
& Jess Lederman

**Good Words for the Young: A Child's Devotional**
is a production of
The Works of George MacDonald (worksofmacdonald.com)

Edited by Jess Lederman and Rebekah Choat
Interior design by Tracy Wilson
Cover art by Melissa Alvey


ISBN: 1539618439
ISBN 13: 978-1539618430
Library of Congress Control Number: 2016918211
CreateSpace Independent Publishing Platform North Charleston,
South Carolina

For my son, David Elginbrod Lederman,
and his mother, my darling wife, Ling
Jess Lederman

For my daughters, Tabitha Leigh and Miranda Lynn
Rebekah Choat

For Kristina, Jon, Megan,
and Zach,

Merry Christmas! I'm
so thankful for your
family :) I hope this
book brings you encouragement
and inspiration!
Many blessings on
the year ahead,
~Bethany

# Preface

*Good Words for the Young* was the name of "one of the finest magazines ever aimed at youth."[1] It was published from 1868 to 1877, and counted among its most prominent contributors a Scotsman by the name of George MacDonald. Some of MacDonald's greatest stories for children, including *At the Back of the North Wind*, first appeared in *Good Words for the Young*.

Who was George MacDonald? He was a poet, novelist, and minister, a mentor to Lewis Carroll—who first read drafts of *Alice in Wonderland* to MacDonald's children—a friend of Mark Twain, and an inspiration to countless Christians, including C.S. Lewis, author of *The Chronicles of Narnia*. Lewis' life was transformed when he discovered the Scotsman's writings, and he wrote that MacDonald has given readers "indispensable help toward the very acceptance of the Christian faith."

Small wonder, then, that many of the contributing authors to this daily devotional, whose title is inspired by the magazine published nearly 150 years ago, have included quotes from George MacDonald's novels and children's stories in writing their entries. Anyone interested in finding out more about MacDonald will find a wealth of information on george-macdonald.com, and on worksofmacdonald.com, the website of the organization which has sponsored this publication.

The creation of *Good Words for the Young: A Child's Devotional* has been a labor of love by eighty contributing authors, all of whom have written for the pure joy of helping to bring the word of God to children everywhere. I am grateful for their efforts, and thank each and every one! A special thanks also to Rebekah Choat, who, in addition to writing eleven entries, provided invaluable proofreading and editing during the project's critical final weeks.

1 From *Victorian Illustrated Books* 1850-1870, by Paul Goldman

And much appreciation to Tracy Wilson, whose creative interior design has helped to make the devotional so delightful, and to Melissa Alvey, for her inspired cover art.

This book is a non-profit production of *The Works of George MacDonald* (worksofmacdonald.com), and 100% of net proceeds are being donated to Hope Unlimited, Inc.'s *Teen Reach*. Founded in 2000, *Teen Reach* is committed to starting programs that bring hope and a brighter future to at-risk youth who usually reside in the state or private foster care system. Their camps and mentoring programs are spreading across the nation and globe, and now exist in seventeen states, the Philippines, and South Africa.

*Teen Reach Adventure Camp* (T.R.A.C.) is a three-day separate-gender program for teens, ages 12 to 16. At T.R.A.C., every activity is geared to teenagers having fun and being safe. Every teen receives a Bible, and their beliefs and life stories are respected. There is a challenge course, where they learn how to trust others and overcome challenges by working as a team. All volunteers are thoroughly screened, and camps are kept small, so the youth feel connected and safe.

T.R.A.C.*life* is a mentoring program for teens who participate in T.R.A.C. It is a vehicle to keep the special relationships that were started at camp going all year long, because mentoring relationships have been proven to change the direction of at-risk youth. For more information, see http://www.hopeunlimitedinc.org/.

Blessings to all,

Jess Lederman
onesimus@worksofmacdonald.com

# January 1

> For God so loved the world, that he gave his only Son, that whoever believes in him should not perish but have eternal life.
> **John 3:16** (ESV)

**I remember when** I was your age, and had to memorize Bible verses. Every week there was a new verse to learn at home and then say at Sunday School. At the time, I hated having to repeat those verses over and over again. I felt like it was a waste of time, and didn't get what the point was—not until a few years after I was done with school.

I was shopping with a friend, and we were in the food court eating French fries. I picked up a bag from a store and my friend said, "What is John 3:16?" I was shocked, because my friend did not know Jesus. I asked her where she had heard of John 3:16, and she laughed and said it was printed on the bottom of my bag! Sure enough, I flipped the bag over, and there it was. I could hear the verse in my mind, word for word, and told her it was one of the most important Bible verses ever written. I couldn't believe what happened next: she actually asked me what the verse was! I recited it to her, and then told her about how Jesus came into my heart.

I don't know if my friend ever asked Jesus into *her* heart—all we can do is plant the seed—but I was sure glad that I had memorized that verse, and many more. I have needed them at many different times, and you will too.

*Holly Van Shouwen*

# January 2

**As we enter** the New Year, let us remember to keep our words kind and uplifting towards others. Have you ever had a person make false claims against you? How did those words make you feel? The tongue is the smallest muscle in the human body, yet it can cause considerable damage to a person. Words that are spoken do one of two things: lift a person up or bring them down. Today, be conscious of your words when speaking. Do not harm or hurt another person with the use of your tongue. Remember, there are consequences for the words you speak, so speak kindly to others, just as you would want someone to speak kindly to you. If someone angers you and you are tempted to speak unkind words, just remember this verse and count to one hundred! The kindness that you show when you speak to someone today just may make a difference in that person's life, and you will be blessed in return.

*Laura Bennin*

The tongue can bring death or life; those who love to talk will reap the consequences.
**Proverbs 18:21** (NLT)

# January 3

Oh Lord God Almighty, who is like you? You are mighty, oh Lord, and your faithfulness surrounds you. You rule over the surging sea; when its waves mount up, you still them.
**Psalm 89:7-8 (NIV)**

**Water can seem** inviting and fascinating. But water can also be dangerous if we're not careful.

When we were six years old, my best friend Janie and I were on vacation with our families in a beautiful mountain area. It had a lovely blue lake that was fun for swimming for us children, and great fishing for the adults. We were allowed to swim in the shallow areas, but were told not to go any further. One especially hot morning, Janie decided to sit on the end of the dock and test the water with her toes. Before she even realized what was happening, she slipped into the water, which was much too deep for her. In her terror, she began thrashing around. Suddenly, she heard a voice saying, "Don't worry, I've got you," and felt a strong hand lifting her out of the water and back onto the dock. A stranger, one of the teenagers on the beach, had seen her distress and come to her rescue.

Like water, life can seem scary and even dangerous at times. But when the Psalm tells us that God "rules over the surging sea" and stills the rising waves, it isn't just talking about raging waters. It's giving praise to God for always being there for us, and for being in control, even in the scariest times when it seems that no one is there for us. We can *always* rely on the Lord, no matter what.

*Lisa Lynott-Carroll*

# January 4

> Let love and faithfulness never leave you; bind them around your neck, write them on the tablet of your heart. Then you will win favor and a good name in the sight of God and man.
> **Proverbs 3:3-4 (NIV)**

**One of the** things I love best about spring is being free of heavy winter clothing, particularly jackets with an attached hood. It's so hard to turn your head to look sideways because the hood is tied at the neck. It's a constant reminder that you have that hood on.

Well, that's the idea of this verse—binding love and faithfulness around your neck so you never forget to think of loving God and others, and being faithful (or loyal) to Him before anyone else. But that's not always easy, because sometimes we don't feel like being loving and faithful. We want to do things our own way. And that's where the next part helps us understand *how* to be obedient in this; that is, by writing it "on the tablet of our heart," because our heart is where love starts. Jesus helps us understand how love helps us to do the right thing in John 14:21: "Whoever has my commands and obeys them, is the one who loves Me." He is saying, when you love Him, then you will *want* to obey Him, not just because you think you have to.

So, reading our Bible each day helps bind God's Word to our mind, reminding us that God asks us to be loving and faithful. Then, the love we have for Him in our heart helps us to *want* to be loving and faithful to God always!

*Gwen Rushing*

# January 5

**Once there was** a very special little boy named Aaron, whose name meant "bringer of light." Everywhere he went, God's light was with him, for he loved God with all his heart, and God loved Aaron too.

One night, Aaron's mother tucked him into bed, praying over him, as always, saying, "Aaron, my little one, may the Lord's blessings and grace keep you always, may His face shine upon you, may the Lord's peace be with you all the days of your life. May the Lord give you sweet and pleasant dreams as you slumber, my little son." Aaron's mother then tenderly kissed his forehead before leaving his room.

Aaron fell into a deep sleep, dreaming that he began to explore the wonder of the living forest that lay behind his tiny home. As he entered the towering forest, its floor filled with ferns and flowers, and creatures great and small began to appear, welcoming him with playful expressions, delighted he had come. Exploring further, Aaron's wonder grew into excitement as he saw a lighted walking staff, something he had always wanted and needed. You see, Aaron's legs did not work just right, and walking was rather difficult. Aaron grabbed the staff joyfully, thanking God for His kindness and love. Surprisingly, the staff began to bloom with brilliant flowers and ripe almonds, of which Aaron heartily ate!

Then Aaron awoke, saddened to realize it was only a dream. But in the corner of his tiny room lay the lighted blooming staff he had received in his dream!

*Lisa Blair*

The next day Moses entered the tent and saw that Aaron's staff, which represented the tribe of Levi, had not only sprouted but had budded, blossomed and produced almonds.
**Numbers 17:8 (NIV)**

# January 6

I will do what you have asked, I will give you a wise and discerning heart, so that there will never have been anyone like you, nor will there ever be.
**1 Kings 3:12 (NIV)**

"There are good things God must delay giving until his child has a pocket to hold them—till he gets his child to make that pocket. He must first make him fit to receive and fit to have."
*Unspoken Sermons,* by George MacDonald

**There are many** goals to reach for in life, although your opportunities to achieve them may differ quite a bit from others due to your circumstances and your gifts. In God's eyes, one of the best gifts that one can possibly receive is *wisdom*. King Solomon had a heart for God when he was a young ruler, and he realized that what he wanted more than wealth and power was a wise and discerning heart. He asked God for this gift when he ascended the throne and, pleased by this request, God complied. To this day we speak with awe of the "wisdom of Solomon." God made him as memorable as he promised he would!

In our times, there is as great a need as ever for wisdom and discernment in how we live our lives, decide what we're going to do when we grow up, care for our families and friends, and deal with our pain and sorrows. We can take comfort in knowing that God loves to give us good gifts and honors our desire to grow in wisdom, no matter how difficult the journey may get at times.

*Lorin Hart*

# January 7

"More important than starting well in our walk with God is to finish well."
*In Search of True Freedom*, by Victor Manuel Rivera

**Everyone wants to** be successful; however, not everyone goes about it in the right way. It may seem easier to lie, cheat, or steal than to work hard to get ahead—but one day every person will have to stand before God and give an accounting for how they have lived their life. God has given us principles to follow which, when obeyed, will produce in us the peaceable fruit of righteousness. Following His ways may seem difficult at times, and people may not understand. But have courage to do what is right, even if no one else does! Be strong and set a good example that others can follow. Doing so will lay up treasures in Heaven, and cause you to grow "in favor with God and man." As George MacDonald said, "This is a sane, wholesome, practical, working faith: That it is a (person's) business to do the will of God; second, that God Himself takes on the care of that (person); and third, that therefore that (person) ought never to be afraid of anything."

*Laurel Shepherd*

Be strong and very courageous. Be careful to obey all the law my servant Moses gave you; do not turn from it to the right or to the left, that you may be successful wherever you go.
**Joshua 1:7 (NIV)**

# January 8

**All of the** animals of the earth are good in God's eyes and have his blessing. They please Him and bring him joy. When you look at bumblebees, dogs, snails, mice, whales, or dinosaurs, can you see how wonderful they are? God made them all out of nothing, and He loves them all. If you study them, you can understand the wisdom and beauty of God through them.

George MacDonald wrote, "God's creative hand is still at work in forest and field, in all the natural world." God's creative delight is still in all His creatures, as it was then in the beginning.

*Matthew Levi*

Then God said, "Let the waters swarm with swarms of living creatures! Let flying creatures fly above the land across the expanse of the sky." Then God created the large sea creatures and every living creature that crawls, with which the water swarms, according to their species, as well as every winged flying creature, according to their species. And God saw that it was good. Then God blessed them by saying, "Be fruitful and multiply and fill the water in the seas. Let the flying creatures multiply on the land." So there was evening and there was morning—a fifth day. Then God said, "Let the land bring forth living creatures according to their species—livestock, crawling creatures and wild animals, according to their species." And it happened so. God made the wild animals according to their species, the livestock according to their species, and everything that crawls on the ground, each according to its species. And God saw that it was good.

**Genesis 1:20-25** (TLV)

# January 9

> Two are better than one, because they have a good return for their work: If one falls down, his friend can help him up.
> **Ephesians 4:9-10 (NIV)**

**Maybe you play** a team sport: soccer, baseball, or volleyball. Maybe you play in the school band or belong to a scholastic team, racing to answer questions. Well, everyone belongs to some type of team, whether they know it or not. Your family is a team; your church is a team; you and your friends are a team.

God created us to be team players, to need one another. God gave each of us special gifts and skills. Some of us can run like the wind; others excel at math or science; still others have beautiful singing voices. God wants us to use these gifts to love and serve each other.

Even God works as part of a team. The Father, the Son, and the Holy Spirit worked together to create the world. Genesis tells us that God created the heavens and the earth and that the Spirit of God hovered over the waters. And John tells us that all things were created through Christ. Father, Son, and Holy Spirit working together created the world and everything in the world.

When we work as a team we share our gifts, and that makes our team strong. As a team, we all work for the praise and glory of God. God leads us; He is our team captain. And He gave us the Ten Commandments to show us how to work as a team. The commandments tell us to put aside jealousy, lying, and anger. We don't steal or hurt others. We work as a team.

And when we work as a team, we can all be winners. God planned it that way.

*Phyllis Hostmeyer*

# January 10

**Gibbie is a** young, innocent, speechless boy, and the main character in George MacDonald's novel *Sir Gibbie*. In his adventures, he is mistreated and twice almost killed by the mean-spirited gamekeeper, Angus. And yet, Gibbie has no interest in revenge. When an opportunity presents itself for Gibbie to retaliate, he instead frees Angus from the bonds that hold him. Here's how the story goes:

> "Gibbie saw his advantage. He snatched his clumsy tool out of the fire…and seizing with the tongs the rope between his feet, held on to both, in spite of his [Angus'] heaves and kicks. In the few moments that passed while Gibbie burned through a round of the rope, Angus imagined a considerable number of pangs; but when Gibbie rose and hopped away, he discovered that his feet were at liberty, and scrambled up, his head dizzy, and his body reeling… But Gibbie still had the tongs, and Angus's hands were still tied. He held them out to him. Gibbie pounced upon the knots with hands and teeth…The moment his hands were free, Gibbie looked up at him with a smile, and Angus did not even box his ears. Holding by the wall, Gibbie limped to the door and opened it. With a nod meant for thanks, the gamekeeper stepped out, took up his gun from where it leaned against the wall, and hurried away down the hill."

It is a great thing to not be overwhelmed by evil, and a still greater thing to overcome evil with good.

*Steve Fronk*
*For Caleb Gilbert*

Do not be overcome by evil, but overcome evil with good.
**Romans 12:21 (NIV)**

# January 11

One generation goeth, and another generation cometh; but the earth abideth for ever. The sun also ariseth, and the sun goeth down and hasteth to its place where it ariseth.
**Ecclesiastes 1:4-5 (KJV)**

"Afflictions are but the shadows of God's wings."

"I find that doing of the will of God leaves me no time for disputing about His plans."
George MacDonald

**I was having** a tough time. Things were not going well! I would sit in my car and think, "If only I had been born one hundred years ago," because I love the old time ways and books and how much simpler things must have been. Or I would think, "If only I had been born 100 years from now," because surely by then mankind would be better and science would have progressed.

Most important, the things that were bothering me would be far away from me, either in the past or in the future.

Then God put into my heart that He knew when I was made, what I was made for, and whom I was made to impact. It was no accident that I was here, now, and not at those other times and places! He put into my heart that my troubles were part of what was supposed to happen, to make me better able to help others! He showed me that the people and things I admired in those other times were what I could do, what I could be, for people right now!

You too were made for HERE and NOW! Look around you, see where God is leading you to be useful in your own place and time.

Life will get better, and you will be able to see the beauty around you.

*B. Daniel Speake*

# January 12

**Do you ever** feel like things aren't fair? Do you ever feel that others have a better life than you have or that things are easier and better for them? I think we have all felt that way at one time or another. Whenever I am feeling that things aren't fair or are too hard, I remember Gibbie. Gibbie is my favorite character from George MacDonald's book, *Sir Gibbie*. Gibbie was an orphan, alone, and was unable to speak. People abused and neglected him. But even though he could not speak, his love and kindness were a constant and clear song. His joy never wavered.

"To Gibbie, however, barelegged, barefooted, almost barebodied as he was, sun or shadow made small difference except as one of the musical intervals of the life that make the melody of existence. Hardy through hardship, he knew nothing better than a constant good-humored sparring with nature and circumstances for the privilege of being, enjoyed what came to him thoroughly, never mourned over what he had not and, like the animals, was at peace."

Instead of feeling sorry for himself, he spent his days thinking of ways in which he could help and be of service to others. Gibbie reminds me to be thankful for everything and to sing a new song to the Lord with every day, no matter what I feel like, or what I'm facing. Most important, I have learned from Gibbie that helping others is the best way to spend my day.

*Jolyn Canty*

Sing to Him a new song...
**Psalm 33:3** (NASV)

# January 13

"Be careful," Jesus said to his disciples. "Be on your guard against the yeast of the Pharisees and Sadducees"
**Matthew 16:6 (NIV)**

**Have you ever** heard someone say, "Be careful!" or "Watch out!" Such warnings indicate the presence of danger. Jesus said, "Be careful. Be on your guard against the yeast of the Pharisees and Sadducees." What is yeast? How is it harmful? Who are the Pharisees and Sadducees?

Yeast is a micro-organism that grows and expands under favorable conditions. Yeast is everywhere! Our world contains many different kinds. One type of yeast allows bread dough to expand and fill with air in a warm oven. The bread then becomes soft and *puffy* when baked. But the growth of harmful yeast can cause nasty infections that are hard to control.

Jesus warned his disciples against a *harmful* type of yeast growing within the minds of two groups of people who lived 2,000 years ago. The Sadducees were wealthy. The Pharisees were quite popular. Together, their wealth and popularity caused them to feel puffed up with the air of self-importance. In other words, they had begun to see themselves as better than other people.

The yeast that Jesus warned against isn't a real micro-organism. Instead, it is a yeast that grows bigger and bigger inside the human *imagination*. Feelings of self-importance present a spiritual danger called self-righteousness. When we become too puffed up with how wonderful we are, we can easily forget that other people are just as wonderful in God's eyes. So, Jesus says, "Be careful." Be on your guard against the yeast of self-importance or self-righteousness.

*Carol Wimmer*

# January 14

> I have hidden your word in my heart
> that I might not sin against you.
> **Psalm 119:11 (NIV)**

**When you are** a child your life is made of a lot of memories, good ones and bad ones. God has given each of us a brain that can remember a lot of information and events. That is why He tells us in Psalm 119:11 to hide His Word in our heart. Our "heart" does not mean the organ that pumps blood throughout our bodies to keep us alive. When this verse says "heart," it means the place where we hide God's Word: deep inside of our minds, which includes storing information in our brains. But just like the heart keeps us alive, storing God's Word in our minds and thoughts keeps us alive walking in God's ways. When we store God's Word in our hearts, when we make choices in our lives, including when we are tempted to sin, God's Word will help our minds make the choices that honor God. Spend time in God's Word, so that it can be hidden in your heart!

*Prayer*

*Father God, thank you for creating me. Thank you for the gift of a brain. Help me to use it to store Your Word in my heart and make good choices in my life. In Jesus name. Amen.*

*Jose del Pino*

# January 15

**Inside your heart** is a special room with a treasure chest in it. In the chest is a powerful tool that some might even call a super power. It can build bridges and tear down walls. It can help people get well when they've been sick. It can give people strength. It can heal broken hearts and make sadness go away. It can even find fun in the most boring of places. Do you know what it is? It is JOY!

George MacDonald knew the power of joy. Maybe his eleven children helped him understand how powerful it is. Many of the heroes and heroines in his stories use this power to overcome nearly impossible difficulties in their lives. My favorite use of this super power is found in the story *The Princess and Curdie,* when Curdie frightens away the goblins with singing and rhymes!

Joy is a powerful weapon and God wants us to know that it really does help us. King Solomon the Wise wrote,

> A joyful heart is good medicine,
> but a broken spirit dries up the bones.
> **Proverbs 17:22 (CSB)**

This has even been proven in hospitals! Patients heal faster when they smile and laugh. Your smile is a powerful gift; use it a lot.

*Annie Mae Platter*

# January 16

Then Jonathan made a covenant with David,
because he loved him as his own soul.
**1 Samuel 18:3 (NIV)**

**In George MacDonald's** tale *The Day Boy and The Night Girl,* two very different children meet because of amazing circumstances and become best friends as they travel together in life. Despite having grown up in very different environments, they learn to make the best of their differences and find comfort relying on each other's strengths. Each one teaches the other, and they grow to love each other as friends and later as husband and wife.

King David and Prince Jonathan had a similar friendship that we can learn a lot from and apply in our own friendships. David grew up as a poor shepherd while Jonathan was a prince in the palace. There were times when Jonathan's father Saul wanted to kill David, and Jonathan protected him no matter what the cost. When you are with your friends, sharing adventures and playing at school and at home, remember how these friends were loyal to each other even when they disagreed, had a big problem to deal with, or others tried to tear them apart. Friendship is a gift from God and each friend is a treasure!

*Holly Van Shouwen*

# January 17

"Some people don't know how to do what they are told. Because they are not used to it, they neither understand quickly nor are able to turn what they do understand into action quickly. But with an obedient mind one learns the rights of things fast enough, for it is the law of the universe, and to obey is to understand."

*At the Back of the North Wind,* by George MacDonald

**Here are a few** important things to know about obedience:

- It does not turn you into a robot or a zombie.
- It does not make you a prig. ("Look how good *I* am!")
- It does not make you less of a person.

Obeying and disobeying are habits. Habits can be learned and unlearned. You already do a lot of obeying – especially when it involves something you *really* like to do. Think about it.

You can't direct anyone else until you can direct yourself. That is to say, until you have learned to obey well, you simply can't lead other people well, even if those people are your friends.

When Jesus said, "Those who accept my commandments and obey them are the ones who love Me," He wasn't being mean-spirited or selfish. It's what you *do* that shows where your heart really is.

*Mary Lichlyter*

But those who obey God's word truly show how completely they love him. That is how we know we are living in him.
**1 John 2:5 (NLT)**

# January 18

**Was I happy** this Christmas when I got a magic kit from my uncle! I like magic, but it takes work and practice to learn the tricks.

That was good for Christmas break; now I am in school, and if my grades don't improve, I might have to go to summer school! And that's the truth, no smoke and mirrors here. I better put the magic kit in the closet.

My mom is OK with me playing with the magic kit, but she would really like to see me study more and to try talking to God. She tries to teach me about God, takes me to church, and prays with me at night. One night, before bed, she explained to me that it's great to get Christmas gifts, like my magic kit, but that *real* gifts come from God. All I have to do is ask God for what I need. How can that be?

I am not completely sure what Mom is talking about, but I am willing to keep trying. Before she turned off the light she said, "If you put as much time into prayer as you do with your magic kit, you might find answers."

For now, I am going to talk to God, study, and play on the weekends. And who knows? Maybe one day next summer, I can take out that kit and make some magic!

*Amy Adams*

Don't be deceived, my dear brothers and sisters. Every good and perfect gift is from above, coming down from the Father of heavenly lights, who does not change like shifting shadows.
**James 1:16-17 (NIV)**

# January 19

"Right is right even if nobody does it.
Wrong is wrong even if everybody is wrong about it."
*All Things Considered,* by G.K. Chesterton

And the people of Berea…searched the Scriptures day after day to see if Paul and Silas were teaching the truth.
**Acts 17:11 (NLT)**

**We live in** a time of *opinions.* Say something good – "That's *your* opinion." Say something bad – "Well, you're entitled to your opinion!" Nothing is *really* right or wrong, true or false—at least, that's the way the world thinks right now.

But attitudes change if you take my lunch or I take your wallet! They change when one person murders another. Then people start to talk of right and wrong. But not for long.

We don't like to be wrong! We don't even like to be thought right, because somebody might get mad, and getting somebody mad makes us wrong. (Large sigh.)

God didn't set the world up that way. Graciously, he laid out what's good and what isn't; he didn't make us have to guess. That's why we know not to steal, not to murder, not to be lazy. We know to tell the truth, to worship only Him, to love our families and friends (not to mention our enemies!), to treat people justly, to help those who need it. Whatever other voices may say, we know *rightness is what God says is right.*

Don't depend on people, even nice ones, to guide you as God does. Talk to trustworthy friends, but do your own work, too. Learn how to go to God's Word to find out whether what somebody says matches what *He* says about right and wrong.

*Mary Lichlyter*

# January 20

The eye is the lamp of the body. If your eyes are healthy, your whole body will be full of light.
**Matthew 6:22 (NIV)**

**One of my** very favorite books is *Sir Gibbie* by George MacDonald. Perhaps you will have the opportunity to read it one day. It is about a mute orphan boy who goes through some very tough circumstances in his life, but somehow always manages to see the best in everything and everyone.

Do you ever wish you could stop complaining and being negative?

Do you ever want to be unselfish and care about others? I know I do—but how?

One of the clues I found in the book was that Sir Gibbie firmly believed that there was always something good to look for, regardless of how bad things were.

He looked at things and people differently than everybody else. He wore different "glasses," if you will. I don't mean regular glasses; I mean a whole different way to look at life.

I want to find the good in everything and everyone too; don't you? So where do we get those glasses? They are given to us by Jesus, God's Son. In order to get your new glasses you must get to know Him through His Word.

How do we do this? By reading the Bible daily, your "vision" will begin to change. Over time, like Sir Gibbie, you will find yourself looking at life in a way that will focus more quickly on the good things He has given you than on finding ways to complain about your life. Try it!

*Alba Rice*

# January 21

"Well, please, North Wind, you are so beautiful, I am quite ready to go with you."

"You must not be ready to go with everything beautiful, Diamond."

"But what's beautiful can't be bad. You're not bad, North Wind?"

"No, I'm not bad. But sometimes beautiful things grow bad by doing bad, and it takes some time for their badness to spoil their beauty. So little boys may be mistaken if they go after things just because they're beautiful."

*At the Back of the North Wind*, by George MacDonald

**The Hooded Pitohui.** The Cone Snail. The Yellow-Bellied Sea Snake. The Cassowary. The Siberian Chipmunk. The Swan. The Poison Dart Frog. What do they have in common? They're beautiful (well, chipmunks aren't beautiful, but they're cute). They're also deadly – in themselves, in their actions, or by carrying deadly parasites. Seriously, they can kill you!

You can't blame the creatures. God decided to make them that way. However, you want to be wise enough not to think that their good looks make them friend material, more than the "plainer varieties."

Unhappily, that kid – or adult – who looks like a film actor, or has the cool clothes, or is the basketball star, or sings so well, or has charm, doesn't *always* have the beautiful character to match.

Do you know the saying, "You can't tell a book by its cover?" You can't tell people by their outsides, either. Don't be fooled. Give yourself time to know someone's character before you decide what kind of person he or she actually is.

*Mary Lichlyter*

There was nothing beautiful or majestic about [Jesus'] appearance, nothing to attract us to him.
**Isaiah 53:2 (NLT)**

# January 22

"Now, Curdie, are you ready?" [Grandmother] said.
"Yes, ma'am," answered Curdie.
"You do not know what for."
"You do, ma'am. That is enough."
*The Princess and Curdie*, by George MacDonald

Loving God means keeping his commandments, and his commandments are not burdensome.
**1 John 5:3 (NLT)**

**Do you have** anyone you trust completely, through and through? I hope so. When you esteem someone so much that you will do whatever that person asks, because you know it will be right, that someone is a treasure.

Not everyone has somebody like that. But there is One who wants your complete trust, your loyalty, your dependence. That's tough, because we want to be independent! We want to choose. We don't – or don't quite – trust anybody else.

But you can count on Him, entirely.

He has known you and loved you since long before you were born. He will never steer you in the wrong direction. He will never forget you or turn His back on you. He will never stop loving you and caring for you.

If you run away from Him, He will find you, because He loves you that much.

When He gives you something hard to do, or a hard way to go, He goes right along with you. He wants to be your boss, not your worker; your ruler, not your servant; your leader, not your advisor.

He says, "I have a plan for you that will do you good, not evil." He says, "Love Me, and do what I tell you to do." To Him you can completely say, "You know what I should do. That's enough."

*Mary Lichlyter*

# January 23

"'Come, young Curdie, what are you thinking of?'
'How do you know I'm thinking of anything?' asked Curdie.
'Because you're not saying anything.'
'Does it follow then that, as you are saying so much, you're not thinking at all?' said Curdie."

*The Princess and Curdie,* by George MacDonald

**Talk, talk, talk!** Babble, babble, babble!

People who talk a lot often get themselves into trouble.

Have you ever had someone just butt into a conversation, blurting out whatever pops into their head? That is called a transgression. We transgress, for example, when we shove over the top of someone else. It is easy to do, especially when we are excited. But if we do not check ourselves, it can become a habit. It is not respecting the order of things. It is important to ask ourselves: "Is someone else speaking?" "Is what I have to say true?" "Is it kind?" "Am I exaggerating?" People who do or say whatever they want often hurt other people.

The Bible says it is wise to *restrain*. That means: hold back—like holding back a horse that wants to run crazy! Someone who thinks before they speak, restrains. They wait for the right time, the right place…the right heart. They are mindful that they need the Lord's wisdom to speak wisely. Wisdom builds. Wisdom and thinking are friends. Listening and thinking are friends. And listening and wisdom will make you a wonderful friend.

*Blythe Followwill*
*For Ethan*

Where there are many words, transgression is unavoidable, But he who restrains his lips is wise.
**Proverbs 10:19**

# January 24

**When I was** a child, I remember my parents taking me to Sunday school. I would listen to Bible stories, color pictures, and sing songs about how Jesus loves little children. After listening to all the stories and sweet songs, and breaking more than a few crayons while coloring Bible scenes, I knew Jesus in my *head*, but I didn't know Him in my *heart*. Then, one day, I went with my parents to the main church service. The pastor preached on sin and how we should repent and give our hearts to God.

I felt something I had never felt before, and that day asked my mother to tell me more. I then asked Jesus to come into my heart as I repented of my sins. You see, Jesus will come to you with open arms. It does not matter if you are an adult, a teenager, or a child. In fact, Jesus said, "Assuredly, I say to you, unless you are converted and become as little children, you will by no means enter the kingdom of heaven." *Matthew 18:3* (NKJV)

He also told his disciples, "Let the little children come to Me, and do not forbid them; for of such is the kingdom of heaven." *Matthew 19:14* (NKJV)

When you repent of your sins, the angels in heaven begin rejoicing! How wonderful to know that God cares about each one of us. Every soul is precious to Him. You are never too young to begin serving the Lord.

*Deborah Williams-Smith*

Likewise, I say to you, there is joy in the presence of the angels of God over one sinner who repents.
**Luke 15:10 (NKJV)**

# January 25

> For I am not ashamed of the gospel, for it is the power of God for salvation to everyone who believes, to the Jew first and also to the Greek. For in it the righteousness of God is revealed from faith for faith, as it is written, "The righteous shall live by faith."
> **Romans 1:16-17 (ESV)**

**In the last** line of the verse above, the apostle Paul is quoting the prophet Habakkuk. God told Habakkuk that a nation that worshipped power would bring violence and death to Habakkuk's people. Habakkuk asked God, "How is it fair that the wicked men destroy the righteous?" God answers that the wicked will be punished, but the just will live by faith.

When Paul started following Jesus, not many people worshipped God like Paul did. Many people worshipped idols or demons. Some people worshipped God like Moses and Aaron had. Hardly any people knew about Jesus.

God's power does not depend on how many people agree with you or me or Paul. God's power does not depend on you and me at all. We can ask a lot of questions, like Habakkuk did, because God can handle that.

Because God is real, you can count on an answer if you are serious about your question. One of the ways God answers questions is by helping us understand the Bible. "From faith for faith" means we can grow in faith, just like a child grows into an adult. Jesus, help us today to grow in You and in our faith.

*Patrecia Jacobson*

# January 26

"In His deepest slumber, the soul of the king lay open to the voice of his child, and that voice had power either to change the aspect of his visions, or, which was better still, to breathe hope into his heart, and courage to endure them."
*The Princess and Curdie,* by George MacDonald

**A king is** a great and powerful man, but even kings have trouble. Who can comfort the heart of a king when everywhere around him are traitors and treachery? In the story *The Princess and Curdie,* the good king is in trouble. So the great, big grandmother, who acts very much like God in the story, sends her little granddaughter to go and be near to the girl's father, the king, in his time of trouble. It is the gentle, good, and kind voice of his daughter, Irene, speaking words of truth, and the wonderful, noble presence of Curdie, the little miner boy, that give the king comfort and courage. The words of kindness spoken by a child to a man of greatness can be more powerful than you know! Words like these, at a time like this, are as the utterances of God.

Children are small, but if the words they speak are from God, they bring hope and give courage to those who have troubles.

*Blythe Followwill*
*For Svendsgaard & Willa*

"Behold, I do not know how to speak, because I am a youth." But the Lord said to me, "Do not say, 'I am a youth,' Because everywhere I send you, you shall go, and all that I command you, you shall speak."
**Jeremiah 1:6b-7 (NASB)**

# January 27

**When Dawtie had** grown from a gentle child who loved Jesus into a gentle, faithful young woman, she went to work for a wealthy gentleman and his daughter. Over time, Mr. Fordyce came to trust her more than any other servant to handle and care for his collection of valuable objects.

Although the treasures were locked away in secret cabinets and unknown to his neighbors, Mr. Fordyce shared knowledge of them with George Crawford, a relative of the family. After Mr. Crawford suffered severe financial losses, he began to scheme how he might inherit the older man's property.

Mr. Fordyce, when he felt that death was near, called for George to bring his dearest treasure to him, and insisted on keeping it with him for his remaining hours. Upon his passing, however, George could not find the object he himself so desired. Knowing that Dawtie had been nursing the old man in his last minutes, he accused her of stealing it, and she was taken to jail to await trial.

Dawtie's friend Andrew had always been her great comfort and guide in learning to know God, but he was unable to visit her in jail. Her mistress, Alexa, did visit her, though, and brought Andrew the message that "Dawtie said she would trust God to the last, but confessed herself assailed by doubts." (from *The Landlady's Master*, by George MacDonald)

Some people think believing in God means that we aren't ever supposed to be afraid. But even the great shepherd-king David admitted fear, while still trusting in the Lord.

*Rebekah Choat*

When I am afraid, I will trust in you.
**Psalm 56:3 (NIV)**

# January 28

For you have not received a spirit of slavery leading to fear again, but you have received a spirit of adoption as sons by which we cry out, "Abba! Father!"
**Romans 8:15 (NASB)**

**There once was** a boy who wasn't happy. He was doing everything right; still deep down he was afraid to be himself. So, out of this deep unhappiness, he started to do the opposite: he started doing everything wrong. Everyone wondered what had happened to the outstanding student, friend, and son he had once been.

Do you want to know what made him so unhappy?

He didn't know who his father was. He didn't know to whom he belonged. He felt abandoned down to his soul. No matter what he did every day, whether it was good or bad, he prayed every night for the father he missed.

One night as he prayed, he realized that the God he loved and prayed to every night had always been with him, that God loved him when he was good and when he was bad. God saw it all and loved him anyway. God was his Father. He didn't have to be afraid. He had always been loved. No matter what.

*Karen Thornton*

# January 29

**What a wonderful** thing it is to hold something that is new! Maybe it is a new toy, or a new book, or a new shirt. As people we love new things, and so does God. This is a new year, and it is a good time for new dreams. What is something you are dreaming about for this year?

As George MacDonald so beautifully says, "If a dream reveals a principle, that principle is a revelation, and the dream is neither more NOR LESS valuable than a waking thought that does the same." God is doing new things all the time, and he wants to use us to accomplish His ends. Maybe there is a new kid at school who has no friends, and you can be a dream come true for them! You can be like a stream that gives cool water on a hot day to someone. Nobody is ever too young to be used by God, so look for chances to be like Jesus to everyone around you. People will see a difference in you, and want that same wonderful difference for themselves!

*Matthew Nash*

> See, I am doing a new thing! Now it springs up; do you perceive it? I am making a way in the wilderness and streams in the wasteland.
> **Isaiah 43:19 (NIV)**

# January 30

## Prayer

**Gavin sat on** his bike looking at the home-made ramp some of the guys had built. It was much higher than the last one. It would take them higher than any of them had flown before. His hands were sweating as he circled the ramp. The deep ditch at the end of it made the jump even more daring, more enticing.

He remembered only too well the words his parents had said as they left to go shopping. "Gavin, keep an ear out for your Grandpa and stay off that bike until your safety helmet arrives." Words from the Bible echoed in his head,

> Call unto me, and I will answer thee, and shew thee great and mighty things, which thou knowest not.
> **Jeremiah 33:3 (KJV)**

Temptation to disobey came harder as he repeated the verse over and over. He knew God heard him, why wasn't He answering him now? Then he knew that if he made the right choice, God would give him the strength to persevere.

As his parents drove into the yard, they were pleased to find Gavin sitting with Grandpa on the porch. Dad took a box from the trunk and handed it to Gavin. "We are giving you an early birthday gift because you obeyed us." What a great-looking safety helmet it was! Gavin told his parents how remembering God's Word had helped him. He knew God would always hear and help him to be obedient.

Sometimes making the right choice is hard to do, and might seem to be be less fun, but to obey is always the best way.

*Dottie Thornton*

# January 31

> But you, take courage! Do not let your hands be weak, for your work shall be rewarded.
> **2 Chronicles 15:7** (ESV)

**Once, long after** King David died, a king named Asa came into power. This king wanted to truly follow God and make Him happy. There had been many kings in Israel who did not follow God, and their whole country suffered as a result. Asa could have easily decided to just enjoy his power and majesty like the others, but he chose to do the tough work of getting rid of all the idols and anything else in the country that went against God. He commanded that everyone worship the one true God, and things went well for everyone: no wars, no fighting,—the whole country was at peace.

You might be an older brother or sister, or the leader of your school friends, and be a little like King Asa. The temptation to just enjoy your power or leadership to satisfy yourself will be like a lion roaring in your heart, but remember King Asa and God's words to him. He told Asa to have courage, to lead people well, to be kind, and to stand up for what is right, and he would be rewarded. You will, too, if you choose this leadership path! It might not be tomorrow or the next day, but the King of Glory is watching, and remembers everything that we do in following Him!

*Holly Van Shouwen*

# February 1

When a child's heart is all right, it is not likely he will want to keep anything from his parents.
*The Princess and Curdie,* by George MacDonald

"For everyone who does evil hates the Light, and does not come to the Light for fear that his deeds will be exposed. But he who practices the truth comes to the Light, so that his deeds may be manifested as having been wrought in God."
**John 3:20-21** (NAS)

**Once there were** two families, each with five children. One evening the parents were going out for dinner; each gave instructions to their eldest child, and times for bed, with a kiss on the head.

In the first house there was yelling and slamming of doors. At dinner, peas were thrown and naughty telephone calls made. When the parents returned home they found unclean clothes and dishes littered everywhere. No child was yet in bed.

The parents of the second home drove up and saw the porch light was on. They were greeted by a happy pup with a wagging tail. All the house was quiet. The children were sleeping and well fed. A cheery little note was left propped up for them to see—it read:

*I hope you had a wonderful time! Everyone ate their dinner and helped with evening chores. Ethan lost another tooth—I put it in a cup on the counter.*

The parents saw the cup, which was by a spotless sink. Then they peeked in at each of the sleeping children and kissed them on their cheeks.

The next morning which eldest daughter do you think was eager to see her parents and was full of happy chatter?

*Blythe Followwill*
*For Kennedy*

# February 2

So God created the human in his own image,in the image of God he created them; male and female he created them.
**Genesis 1:27 (Author's Translation)**

**In creating people** male and female, God created beings who were both the same and different, men and women who could love each other. This "otherness" marks not just our romantic relationships, but *all* of our relationships. If other people were exactly the same as us, we would love them automatically. But because they are different from us, loving them is a choice.

Although they are different, we share our humanity (we are both Adam, the being made from the earth—*adamah*) and we are both made in the image of God. Men and women reflect the image of God in both similar and different ways. We love other people because of what we share with them and because of how they are different from us. Can you think of an example from your own life of someone whose differences you love?

This Bible verse is also incredibly important as a reminder to us that all people, without exception—even those we dislike, even those who scare us, even those who are lost or poor or sick, and even those who do bad things!—are made in the image of God and carry that image inside of them.

*Matthew Levi*

# February 3

> The LORD said to Abraham, "Why did Sarah laugh and say, 'Shall I indeed bear a child, now that I am old?' Is anything too hard for the LORD? At the appointed time I will return to you, about this time next year, and Sarah shall have a son." But Sarah denied it, saying, "I did not laugh," for she was afraid. He said, "No, but you did laugh."
>
> **Genesis 18:13-15** (ESV)

**What do you** think you might serve to God if He came to have lunch with you tomorrow? Maybe spaghetti, or your favorite pizza, or a huge Thanksgiving-type feast, but would you "serve up" laughter at God?

Many years ago, God did come for lunch to speak with Abraham, and give him a wonderful promise. It was a miracle promise! Sarah was the age of your grandma, and God said she would have a child that year. But instead of being thankful or jumping for joy, Sarah laughed right at God as He was sitting there in their dining tent, right as they were probably having dessert!

But God's promises are no laughing matter, not at all. When you bring your needs or your heart's desire to God, however impossible your situation might seem, remember that God can do *anything*. He made the whole universe and even aardvarks, horseshoe crabs, and platypuses (which look pretty impossible)! Never doubt God's ability, or His caring about you personally, and never doubt that His promises and His answers to prayers are very real.

*Holly Van Shouwen*

# February 4

"Here I should like to remark, for the sake of princes and princesses in general, that it is a low and contemptible thing to refuse to confess a fault, or even an error. If a true princess has done wrong, she is always uneasy until she has had an opportunity of throwing the wrongness away from her by saying: 'I did it; and I wish I had not; and I am sorry for having done it."

*The Princess and the Goblin,* by George MacDonald

> But if we confess our sins to him, he is faithful and just to forgive us our sins and to cleanse us from all wickedness.
> **1 John 1:9 (NLT)**

**When you think** about it, isn't it silly for people *not* to say, "I did it," when they did it? Why don't they?

Are they afraid of not having an excuse? Afraid of being punished? Afraid of being ridiculed? Afraid of being ashamed? Afraid they won't be liked unless they seem perfect?

What's that one word in all those questions? I'll help you out: it's *afraid.*

Fear can really make you squirm! One writer says the letters in "fear" stand for "False Evidence Appearing Real." The fact is that, in real life, getting past your fear and telling the truth (especially *right away*) usually doesn't cost you friends. Most people admire the brave souls who admit when they're wrong. Yes, there may be a consequence, but you and Christ can handle it. He lived, died, and rose again for your wrongness! He's not shocked! He knows you mess up and He has promised to stand by you, because you're His.

*Mary Lichlyter*

# February 5

**Gibbie, the wonderful** boy in George MacDonald's book *Sir Gibbie*, had a dog named Oscar who loved to help him shepherd the sheep on the mountainside. "The mountain was Gibbie's very home; yet to see him far up on it, in the red glow of the setting sun, with his dog, as obedient as himself, handing upon his every signal, one could have fancied him a shepherd boy come down from the plains of heaven to look after a lost lamb."

My dog, Dawson, was a lot like Gibbie's dog, Oscar. He was a beautiful, smoky-gray Miniature Schnauzer. Dawson was my constant companion and the best dog I've ever had. Wherever I went I had to be careful not to stumble over Dawson, because he stayed as close to me as he could, and if I wasn't watching for him I could easily trip or bump into him. Not only did Dawson follow me wherever I went, but he also obeyed my every command. You see, Dawson trusted me completely. He knew that I would never command him to go anywhere or to do anything that would hurt him or others. I think it is because he knew that I loved him and would always take care of him.

We all need to be more like Dawson, Oscar, and Gibbie: obedient to our Shepherd, Jesus. We need to listen to His every word and then trust and obey Him, without delay, because Jesus commands us to do only what is best and good.

*Jolyn Canty*

Whatever he says to you, do it.
**John 2:5** (NASV)

# February 6

"There is a time when things must be
done and questions left till afterwards."
*The Princess and the Goblin,* by George MacDonald,

Why do you call me "Lord, Lord," and not do what I tell you?
**Luke 6:46 (ESV)**

**"Because I said so!"**

Is this what you hear when you reply, "Why?" to someone's direction?

Knowing why is great for learning: "You put your bicycle in the garage so it will be safe and out of the weather." "Saying please and thank you to Grandpa lets him know you value him as a person." "Look both ways before crossing—it's easier for you to see the car than for the car driver to see you."

But sometimes protesting, "Why?" means, "I don't want to!" or, "I might do it if you give me a good enough reason." Then you hear, "Because I said so!" and you pout.

People in emergency, military, and law enforcement jobs learn to obey right away, because they often have only seconds to react. They don't stop for the *why* because they can't—and they have learned to trust their commanding officers.

You don't have any such job. But you have "commanding officers" —parents, teachers, coaches, and others. If they are trustworthy, you need to do what they want without stalling or questioning. It's all right to question later, when the need is over.

Just about any country kid knows that when somebody says, sharply, "Stop where you are. Step backwards, *very* quietly, until you're here with me," you don't ask why. That person might be saving you from being attacked by a snake. Enough said?

*Mary Lichlyter*

# February 7

St. Caedmon's Day

He is the Maker of heaven and earth, the sea, and everything in them—he remains faithful forever.
**Psalm 146:6 (NIV)**

**I wish I** could sing. I can't. How about you? There once was a poor herdsman that could not sing. His name was Caedmon. In fact, Caedmon sang so badly that when the people around began to take turns singing, he ran away and hid in the stables. One day, a voice asked, "Why are you hiding?" Caedmon replied, "I am embarrassed. I can't sing." "Sure you can," the voice said, "Sing about what you know. Sing about me." And sure enough, Caedmon started singing! He sang about animals, about trees, about flowers, and about Bible stories too. His songs painted pictures about the fields around him, the animals he tended, the stars in the sky, and the God he loved. The God who made everything—the trees, the animals, the fish, and bugs, too.

When you are embarrassed, God is there, just as God was with Caedmon. No matter what goes wrong, God is there. Listen; you can hear God saying, "I'm here. Look around, see Me. Sing about Me and my creation."

I know I am sure glad that God is with me when I am embarrassed!

Tonight when you say your prayers, make up a song to sing to God about what you see around you—whatever it is, good and bad, and how God is right there in the middle of it.

*Frank Mills*

# February 8

**When Andrew and** Sandy Ingram were young boys, they were interrupted in the middle of a fight by a stranger, whom they came to believe was the Lord himself. The encounter started them on a course of learning all they could about Jesus by reading the Gospels. After a time, they came to Jesus' own words,

Why do you call me, 'Lord, Lord,' and do not do what I say?
**Luke 6:46** (NIV)

"(Andrew) read the words over a second time, then a third, and sank deep in thought…He read all the chapter again and found it full of *tellings*. When he read it before, he had not thought of actually doing a single one of the things Jesus said. He had not seen himself as involved in any of the matters at hand.

"'I see!' he exclaimed. 'We must begin at once to *do* what he tells us, not just read about it!'

*The Landlady's Master*, by George MacDonald

The Ingram boys and their friend, Dawtie, with whom they shared their discovery, were only children, but they read and understood God's Word more clearly than some grown-ups. Nor did they outgrow their simple faith and obedience as they got older.

You may feel sometimes that you don't understand what you read in the Bible. Perhaps the best thing you could do would be just what these young people did—act on what you do understand, and ask Jesus to help you know Him better.

*Rebekah Choat*

Do not merely listen to the word, and
so deceive yourselves. Do what it says.
**James 1:22** (NIV)

# February 9

**Josh sat in** the hallway with his legs swinging back and forth. This was a sure sign of his stressful state. Several guys had been guilty of thumping paper wads at the new kid, simply because he was new and different. Josh had thumped a few in his direction, not to hit him, but just to make the guys think he was cool. It was at the very last thump that the teacher walked in and clearly saw Josh.

There was no reason to dislike the new boy. In fact, Josh had never spoken to him. The principal was shocked at Josh. He was a good student, went to church, and had never been in trouble. Josh had plenty of time to think of the verse he had memorized in Sunday School:

Be ye strong therefore, and let not your hands be weak: for your work shall be rewarded.
**2 Chronicles 15:7 (KJV)**

Josh admitted to the bad deed, but never expected this! For the next six weeks Josh had to be a buddy to the new guy. At first it was tough, but as Josh came to know Chuck, it was an easy job. Chuck had been all over the world and had some neat stuff.

Josh and Chuck were together so much they didn't notice that six weeks had passed. Their friendship had grown and now they were almost inseparable. In Sunday School they got excited to hear about Joshua and Caleb. They could be conquerors like them! Friends because of a paper wad. With so many plans ahead of them, it looked to be a very adventurous summer.

*Dottie Thornton*

# February 10

Anyone who loves their brother and sister lives in the light, and there is nothing in them to make them stumble.
**1 John 2:10 (NIV)**

## Loving And Living In Light

**Do you love** your brothers and sisters? Maybe sometimes it's hard to like them, but deep down, you still love them, right? Do you ever argue with your siblings and wish they would just go away? Then, after a while, do you feel a little sad inside? Do you want to just forget about arguing and love again? The person who wrote this Bible verse thought that loving your brothers and sisters gives you so much light to live by that nothing could make you stumble!

Perhaps you don't have a brother or a sister to love. Does that mean that you can't live in God's light? Who *is* your brother? Who is your sister? Is it possible to have brothers and sisters all over the world? Suppose everyone is related to each other in one big, family of God! That's so many brothers and sisters we wouldn't be able to count them all. Living in one big family of God would mean loving brothers and sisters who don't look like us, who speak other languages, wear different clothes, eat unusual food, worship in various ways, sing unknown songs, play unfamiliar games, and live in a myriad of different cultures.

Can you imagine loving people who live all around the world? If so, that's great news because people need our love. More than that, living in God's light will be our reward and we will never stumble!

*Carol Wimmer*

# February 11

Tu B'Shevat | Jewish New Year of the Trees

> ...The trees are bearing their fruit; the fig tree and the vine yield their riches.
> **Joel 2:22 (NIV)**

**I like trees!** Don't you? I like how the Beech tree in George MacDonald's novel *Phantastes* comforts and protects his hero, Anodos, from the evil Alder and Ash trees. In J.R.R. Tolkien's trilogy, *The Lord of the Rings*, I like the way the usually patient Ents get angry at Saruman's army who are killing the trees. I like how in C.S. Lewis' *The Magician's Nephew*, Digory's apple tree becomes the wardrobe in *The Lion, the Witch and the Wardrobe*. I wish trees could really talk. Think of the stories they could tell us!

Trees are pretty special. There are actually several holidays in their honor: Arbor Day, when we plant trees; Rogation Sunday, when we bless trees; even their own New Year's Day—*Tu B'Shevat*—a Jewish holiday celebrating the budding of blossoms. Can't you just imagine the trees celebrating—their branches clapping, their leaves rustling? Maybe we can even hear them sing if we listen closely.

In the old days, it was thought that it took four months for the water to reach the roots and eventually create blossoms. Deuteronomy 20:19 reminds us that we, like trees, need to be rooted to take up water and bear fruit. Our roots are our love of God; our fruits are showing love and being honest, kind, and helpful to others.

We can celebrate with the trees by remembering when we eat fruit to thank God both for the fruit and for helping us to live bearing fruit.

*Frank Mills*

# February 12

**What's your favorite** kind of flower? The word is filled with beautiful flowers: daffodils, roses, daisies, violets, tulips, sunflowers, chrysanthemums…God takes good care of His creation, from the tallest tree to the smallest flower, from big elephants to tiny hummingbirds. But there is one part of His creation He cares about more than any other—His children, including you!

Jesus tells us,

> Look at the birds of the air; they do not sow or reap or store away in barns, and yet your heavenly Father feeds them. Are you not much more valuable than they?… See how the flowers of the field grow. They do not labor or spin. If that is how God clothes the grass of the field, which is here today and tomorrow is thrown into the fire, will he not much more clothe you?
>
> **Matthew 6:26, 28-30 (NIV)**

Think about having a beautiful bouquet of colorful flowers on your kitchen table. You can enjoy them for several days, but eventually, what happens? The flowers wilt and turn brown, and it's time to throw them away. Like Jesus says, flowers are here one day and gone the next. If God cares about flowers, He is certainly taking care of us!

When you are worried about a big test at school, troubles with a friend, or any other challenges, you can always trust that God will take care of you as you face the day ahead.

*Bethany Wagner*
*Dedicated to Joyce McCormick*

# February 13

"I don't try to consciously remember Him every moment. For He is in everything, whether I am thinking of it or not. When I go fishing, I go to catch God's fish. When I take Kelpie out, I am teaching one of God's wild creatures. When I read the Bible or Shakespeare, I am listening to the word of God, uttered in each after its own kind. When the wind blows on my face, it is God's wind."

*The Marquis' Secret,* by George MacDonald

**Every day is** a gift from God to you! As you go through your day, take time to see God and feel His presence. God doesn't hide from us—He wants to be known! Look for Him in nature, and in your family and friends.

May you sense God's presence as you watch a snowflake drifting through the air. May you sense His presence as you play with your friends, and laugh and explore the outdoors. May you feel God near when you look into the night sky and see stars twinkling and planets glowing. May you feel God's love like a warm hug when you talk with Him throughout your day.

Before you go to sleep, take time to thank God for the ways you saw Him and felt His presence today.

*Rennie Marie Sneed*

The heavens declare the glory of God;
the skies proclaim the work of his hands.
**Psalm 19:1** (NIV)

# February 14

> Love is patient, love is kind. It does not envy, it does not boast, it is not proud. It does not dishonor others, it is not self-seeking, it is not easily angered, it keeps no record of wrongs. Love does not delight in evil but rejoices with the truth. It always protects, always trusts, always hopes, always perseveres.
>
> **1 Corinthians 13:4-7** (NIV)

***In The Princess and Curdie*** by George MacDonald, the young boy Curdie sits with his mother, taking her hands in his. Her hands are rough and worn from years of hard work on their farm, but Curdie thinks they are as beautiful as any princess' hands—because her hard work was always to lovingly take care of him and his father. She says she would be ashamed to show her hands to anyone, except to someone like Curdie who loves her. "Love makes all safe—doesn't it, Curdie?" she says.

And it is the same between us and God! When we come to God to praise him, ask for forgiveness, or simply talk to him, we don't need to be afraid, because he loves us. In 1 John 4:6, John writes, "There is no fear in love. But perfect love drives out fear."

*Bethany Wagner*
*Dedicated to Betty and Charles Wagner*

# February 15

**Do you have** lots of things, or just a few? It honestly doesn't matter! What matters is what's in our heart. We need to have what the verse calls "the fear of the Lord." This isn't the same kind of fear like meeting a mama bear in the woods, or a shark in the ocean; this kind of "fear" is great love and respect. This is how some people feel towards meeting a King or a Queen, or the President. It's kind of like "fear" we have of for our parents; we aren't afraid of them, but we want to do good so we don't disappoint them.

George MacDonald teaches us about this through *Sir Gibbie*. Little Gibbie was an orphan in the street, and he had nothing to call his own. However, this didn't stop him from being kind and helpful and making friends everywhere he went. A shepherd and his wife took him in and taught him about the love of God and how to be a good shepherd. They didn't have very much, but they were very happy.

Whether you have one dollar or a million, having the "the fear of the Lord" is better than *anything* else.

*Annie Mae Platter*

Better is a little with the fear of the Lord
Than great treasure and turmoil with it.
**Proverbs 15:16 (NASB)**

# February 16

For I know the plans I have for you," declares the LORD, "plans to prosper you and not to harm you, plans to give you hope and a future. Then you will call on me and come and pray to me, and I will listen to you. You will seek me and find me when you seek me with all your heart. I will be found by you," declares the LORD, "and will bring you back from captivity. I will gather you from all the nations and places where I have banished you," declares the LORD, "and will bring you back to the place from which I carried you into exile.

**Jeremiah 29:11-14** (NIV)

**The words of God** to the prophet Jeremiah can bring us great comfort, or great conviction. How do you react when things do not go your way? Even common things; for example, when your time on the television, computer, or game box ends and your mom asks you to stop, or your dad interrupts your favorite song to ask you to help with a chore.

Do you explode in anger and take out your frustration on those around you? We all respond poorly sometimes. What else can we do?

One thing we can see from this passage is who is in charge of our lives. God, through His prophet, says to His people who have lost a war and been taken into captivity, that His plans for them are for prosperity, well-being, future, and hope. Do we believe that God can be trusted with our lives? He was faithful to Israel. He will be faithful to us.

*Amy Farley*

# February 17

**How big is** God's love? How far does it reach? How long will it last?

On July 20, 1969, something amazing happened. It was hot down here on Earth, but in space it was cold. Everybody was nervous. Your grandparents were probably watching the TV. Astronauts Buzz Aldrin (the guy they named Buzz Lightyear after) and Neil Armstrong had just landed their spaceship on the moon. They were taking a two-hour break before climbing down the ladder to walk on the moon for the first time.

There was a constant stream of radio talk going, with beeps and flight checks and such: *"Houston–Eagle: The gimbal manifold transcepter booster is functioning satisfactorily"* and *"Eagle–Houston: That's good to hear. We need you to run a test on the LM ascent engine by switching the..."*

As soon as Buzz caught a slight break he asked for a few moments of "radio silence." He got out a piece of bread and a cup of juice his pastor had given him and took communion.

How cool is that?! Communion is about remembering how much God loves us, by remembering that He died for us on the cross. And Buzz took time to remember that while he was on the moon! So when you lie down at night and look up into the sky, you can know that God's love has already reached to the moon.

And it won't stop there. It goes everywhere, and it will never end.

*Eric McCarty*

Give thanks to the God of heaven,
for his steadfast love endures forever.
**Psalm 136:26 (ESV)**

# February 18

**Once, there lived** a little boy named Levi, who loved God more than he loved playing. Often his mother would find him talking to God. One day she asked, "Levi, what are you talking to God about today?" Levi responded, "About the water—you know how God loves the water, because His water takes our thirst away and makes us clean, Mommy!"

Smiling sadly, she patted his head and said, "Yes, I know all about God's water: His name is Jesus, our Fountain of Living Water, our Wellspring of Life." He said, "Let's go right now to the stream, Mommy, to play and celebrate Jesus!"

Levi's mother sighed, "Levi, I've got too much work to do; I can't just take off and go play in the water." The sadness in her voice concerned Levi, so badly that he went straight to God and prayed, "God, You and I have always been friends, and always will be. I need Your help. See, my mom is really sad, and kind of mad, too, I think, since her heart got broken. Can you please fix it, God? I want Mommy to go with me to the water and let You wash all her brokenness away."

His mother heard that prayer, and she picked Levi up and hugged and kissed him. She said, "Levi, let's go on down to the stream and play; and we'll pray there, too, for Jesus to take all our hurt away!"

And that's just what they did.

*Lisa Blair*

The Lord spoke to Moses face to face, as one speaks to a friend...
**Exodus 33:11 (NIV)**

# February 19

In your anger do not sin. Do not let the sun go down while you are still angry.
**Ephesians 4:26 (NIV)**

**Have you ever** looked in a mirror when you are angry? It's not a pretty sight. Your face turns red, your muscles tense up, your breathing gets faster. You might look a lot like a balloon ready to pop. And yet, everyone gets angry sometimes. The sin is hanging on to anger and letting it take control of you.

Paul gives us good advice in Ephesians: "Don't let the sun go down while you are still angry." So how can we let go of anger? The first thing you can do is pray and ask God to help you be slow to anger. But sometimes you might still find anger creeping in.

One trick is to use that anger for something good. Go for a long walk or a run until you feel the anger melting away. Clean your room or scrub a bathtub. Try to do some physical activity that will release all of that anger from your body.

Another trick is to surround yourself with joyful friends and positive people. Find an adult that will let you come and talk about angry feelings. Talking with an adult may help you see how much anger hurts both you and others.

Don't let anger weigh you down. Once you notice how bad anger makes you feel, you will find yourself wanting to let it go so you can enjoy peace and joy.

*Phyllis Hostmeyer*

# February 20

**In George MacDonald's** story *At the Back of the North Wind,* a young boy named Diamond meets the beautiful, mysterious North Wind. She takes him on a whirlwind adventure and shows him wondrous sights. Even when they travel far away to strange lands, Diamond feels safe with the North Wind always beside him.

But at one point in the story, Diamond finds himself in a church, alone. "The church grew very lonely about [Diamond], and he began to feel like a child whose mother has forsaken it. Only he knew that to be left alone is not always to be forsaken." That last line is important. Even though Diamond couldn't see or feel the North Wind there protecting him, he knew he had not been abandoned for good. He knew she was still looking after him.

Jesus reassures us of the same thing! As the verse above shows, before He went back into heaven, He reminded His disciples, "And surely I am with you always, to the very end of the age." Even in those moments when we feel lonely or scared—when life seems dark and we feel abandoned—we know that Jesus is with us. He is always protecting us and is there to talk with us, even when we feel alone.

*Bethany Wagner*
*Dedicated to Roland McCormick*

And surely I am with you always, to the very end of the age.
**Matthew 28:20b (NIV)**

# February 21

How can a young man keep his way pure?
By guarding it according to your word.
**Psalm 119:9 (ESV)**

**Don't you feel** awful when you have done something wrong and are unable to fix it? I know I do. It is right that we should feel this way, but we should not spend too much time dwelling on it. Instead, the bad feeling should help us to consider how to do better in the future. And this is just what young Curdie begins to learn in the book *The Princess and Curdie,* by George MacDonald.

> "Remember, then, that whoever does not mean good is always in danger of harm...Therefore I say for you that when you shot that arrow you did not know what a pigeon is. Now that you do know, you are sorry. It is very dangerous to do things you don't know about."
>
> "But, please, ma'am—I don't mean to be rude or to contradict you," said Curdie, "but if a body was never to do anything but what he knew to be good, he would have to live half his time doing nothing."
>
> "There you are much mistaken," said the old quavering voice. "How little you must have thought! Why, you don't seem even to know the good of the things you are constantly doing. Now don't mistake me. I don't mean you are good for doing them. It is a good thing to eat your breakfast, but you don't fancy it's very good of you to do it. The thing is good, not you."

*Steve Fronk*
*For Samuel Jacob*

# February 22

## Fellowship

> But if we walk in the light, as He is in the light,
> we have fellowship one with another…
> **1 John 1:7a (KJV)**

"**Tell me what** 'fellowship' means next week," the teacher instructed after reading this verse to the class. Talon knew that 'to walk in the light' was to follow Jesus in His way, but he wasn't too sure about the 'fellowship' part.

This was Talon's first time on a bus, and his first time going to Five-Day Camp. He had never been away from home for more than three nights. He noticed another boy about his own age sitting alone on the bus. Before long, the ride ended as the bus pulled into camp, the boys piled out of the bus, and chaos broke out.

Sometime later, Talon and Jacob, the boy from the bus, sat together on the steps of their cabin. The empty feeling of loneliness went away as they laughed and talked; a new adventure was about to begin.

Talon and Jacob were partners in everything at camp—hiking, games, swimming, boating, crafts, and learning verses. The week went by too quickly. But on the ride home, Talon discovered that Jacob lived near him, and they would be attending the same school.

Talon learned that 'fellowship' is spending time with a friend who enjoys many of the same things you do. You may not always agree about everything, but that's ok—it's a normal part of growing up. Jesus is the bond that holds Christians together in fellowship.

*Dottie Thornton*

# February 23

I urge, then, first of all, that petitions, prayers, intercession and thanksgiving be made for all people... This is good, and pleases God our Savior, who wants all people to be saved and to come to a knowledge of the truth.
**1 Timothy 2:1, 3-4 (NIV)**

**If you are** reading this, you probably have someone who loves and cares for you and has taught you how to pray. You probably pray for your family and friends and others who you know need your prayers. Wonderful—don't stop!

Do you, however, also pray for the many people who do not have others to care for them and pray for them? Do you pray for all people? Perhaps praying for all people seems like too big a prayer, or not specific enough; but we know that God, the Father of all, is pleased when we pray for all.

I would like to share some suggestions on how to pray some bigger, but more specific prayers. Certainly you will come up with others! Pray for:

- All people to have a nice home, good food, and someone who loves them
- All people to come to know, love, and serve God
- All leaders to do what is good and just for all
- All who are sick and dying and need God's mercy

God has created every person. All are His children. To pray for the children of God, your brothers and sisters whom you do not even know, expresses love most pleasing to our Father.

*Sharon Edel*

Do we not all have one Father? Did not one God create us?
**Malachi 2:10 (NIV)**

# February 24

After six days Jesus took Peter, James and John with him and led them up a high mountain, where they were all alone. There he was transfigured before them. His clothes became dazzling white, whiter than anyone in the world could bleach them.
**Mark 9:2-3 (NIV)**

### What Could Be Whiter than White?

**When something is** transfigured, a *change* occurs. When Jesus was transfigured, his clothes became whiter than anyone in the world could bleach them. What caused Jesus' clothes to become so white? Was it the light within Jesus' heart, radiating outward, that caused Jesus' clothing to change? If so, what is the difference between white clothing and white light?

Raw cotton, wool, or fibers are sometimes bleached to remove any color that might be in the fiber. So, white cloth contains *no* color. By contrast, white light contains *all* colors. If one color is missing, white light will not be created. When all colors are present, they cancel each other out and white light is created!

The change in Jesus' clothing caused Peter, James, and John to see God's divine light within Jesus' heart. All colors were present, creating a bright, white light! To this day, the light of the whole world continues to be held in the heart of the risen Christ! Everyone's light is included, because a love for all people creates the white light of Christ. Your light is loved. My light is loved. No one's light is excluded.

Can you imagine a light that is whiter than the color white? What is the secret to creating white light? Would you want a heart full of white light?

*Carol Wimmer*

# February 25

This is the confidence we have in approaching God: that if we asking anything according to His will, He hears us.
**1 John 5:14**

## Praying Is Two Way

**When we first** learn to pray, we are usually thinking of all the things we want to tell God. It's an amazing thing that God has time to listen to us, and is extremely interested in us. He wants to hear from us at any time!

> "'Listen!' said the raven…I listened, and heard—was it the sighing of a far-off musical wind—… 'Some people are always at their prayers.— Look! look! There goes one!' He pointed right up into the air. A snow-white pigeon was mounting. 'I see a prayer on its way.— I wonder now what heart is that dove's mother!' There is one heart all whose thoughts are strong, happy creatures, and whose very dreams are lives."
> *Lilith*, by George MacDonald

The Lord is listening to you, and may be waiting for you to listen for Him!

*Marion T. Redding*

# February 26

Jesus answered, "I am the way, the truth and the life, no one comes to the Father except through me."
**John 14:6 (NIV)**

**In the well-loved book** *The Golden Key,* Tangle and Mossy set off to find a particular keyhole, and in their travels, Tangle learns that she must throw herself in a hole within a cave in order to go further and meet the Old Man of the Fire to carry on. "There is no other way," she is told. Jesus told us exactly the same thing when it comes to having a relationship with God today.

In our world, we are presented with many different paths which people tell us will lead to God. We need to be very careful when we are told or learn about other ways that are supposed to lead us to our God in Heaven. The Bible has been given to us as our guidebook and has very important truths and instructions that we need to follow in our everyday lives. As all of us who have ever lived have fallen short by sin in our lives; a sacrifice needed to be made and Jesus was the only one who could do this for us—and he did! All He asks is that we recognize our sin and ask for forgiveness and for Him to live in our hearts and in our lives always. No other way will do. Guard your hearts and remember that only Jesus is the keyhole to eternity and a life and heart filled with God's love and protection.

*Holly Van Shouwen*

# February 27

For I am convinced that neither death, nor life, neither Angels, nor demons, neither the present, nor the future, nor any powers, neither height, nor depth, nor anything else, in all creation, will be able to separate us from the love of God, that is in Christ Jesus, our Lord.
**Romans 8:37-39 (NIV)**

**Do you wish** you had super powers to fight off the bad stuff in your life—like when your mom and dad are fighting, or when that kid in gym won't let up on how you run? With super powers, you could make everything right!

There once was a man named Saul. He was a bully, and he cheered his friends on to beat up Jesus' friends. But one day, Saul had a sort of super power given to him: the power of God's love and forgiveness to change his heart. His name was changed to Paul, and he wrote a lot of encouraging letters to Jesus' friends. You may have read one of them in your Bible.

St. Paul tells us that *nothing* can come between Jesus and us. Do you believe that? You will always have Jesus to help you. That is a *promise!*

Can you ask Jesus to give you strength when you need it? Yes. You might have days when things don't work out the way you would like, but you will always have a way to Jesus.

Will you need super powers after all? Can you be empowered by Jesus in your life?

*Amy Adams*

# February 28

**God established** commandments to help us know right from wrong and to help us make good choices. But God knew that we would sometimes struggle with the rules and fail to follow them. If God chose only to judge on rules and inflict punishments, we would be without hope.

Thankfully, God chooses to be Father rather than Judge. He treats us as sons and daughters and will help us to grow and learn to do what is right.

In forgiving, God does not pretend that sin does not matter. In fact, it matters so much that without forgiveness, sin would lead to eternal death! We need forgiveness!

Because sin is so harmful, we need to acknowledge our sins and be truly sorry. We might even have to accept some consequences as a result of our sins. We need to make up our minds to try to avoid future sin. This is the only way that God's forgiveness can be effective in us and can help us to be better.

You know that Jesus did no wrong, but was crucified anyway. He asked His Father to forgive those who had crucified Him. In this, Jesus showed the full extent of God's mercy. God would forgive even those who crucified His Son! Therefore, you need never question or fear the great mercy of God. Fear only the ensnarement of sin that would keep you from His Mercy!

*Sharon Edel*

He forgave us all our sins, having canceled the charge of our legal indebtedness, which stood against us and condemned us; he has taken it away, nailing it to the cross.
**Colossians 2:13-14** (NIV)

# February 29

**President Ronald Reagan** once said, "Within the covers of the Bible are the answers for all the problems men face." It makes me wonder why we don't pay more attention to it. Many smart, famous people who have done great things in America and all over the world feel the same way about the Bible's wisdom.

The Bible is the only book that claims to be written by God about Himself. Shouldn't it be important enough to read, study, and memorize so it can guide our lives? And "don't just listen to God's word. You must do what it says. Otherwise, you are only fooling yourselves." James 1:22 (NLT)

What did Jesus say was the most important commandment? "Love the Lord your God with all your heart and with all your soul and with all your mind. And the second is like it: Love your neighbor as yourself." Matthew 22:37-38 (NIV) If each of us would do this in our own little part of the world, what would change? By putting God's word to work in our lives, we can be part of changing the world!

*Dear Jesus, thank you that we can read about what You did and said when You were on earth. This helps us know You and what you want us to do. Please help me to become more like You every day.*

*Vicki Ryder*

All Scripture is inspired by God and is useful to teach us what is true and to make us realize what is wrong in our lives. It corrects us when we are wrong and teaches us to do what is right.
**2 Timothy 3:16 (NLT)**

# March 1

"Her face was fair and pretty, with eyes like two bits of night-sky, each with a star dissolved in blue. Those eyes you would have thought must have known they came from there, so often were they turned up in that direction."

*The Princess and the Goblin,* by George MacDonald

## Where O Where Have I Come From? I Have Only to Look to Thee!

**We have come** from God. God is in heaven, a place we cannot see. Yet God wants all people to know Him, so He did a wonderful thing! He created us and tucked the knowledge of Him into our hearts, so that we would turn our eyes up, in that direction, to look for Him.

God wonderfully knit you together in a secret place inside your mother. You are exactly who He had in mind! He designed you, and God loves the one He designed! In some things you resemble your parents on earth; in some things you are like your Father in heaven! Your skin is beautiful; so are your dazzling eyes! You've got those crazy legs and elbows and toes!

But you also have love, joy, and peace. These qualities are like your Father in heaven! It's easy to draw eyes, but it is harder to draw peace. God shows others what He is like when they look at you! How wonderful! Lord, thank you.

*Blythe Followwill*
*For Kaete*

For you formed my inward parts; you wove me in my mother's womb. I will give thanks to You, for I am fearfully and wonderfully made; Wonderful are your works, and my soul knows it very well.

**Psalm 139:13-14 (NAS)**

# March 2

A gentle answer turns away wrath,
but a harsh word stirs up anger.
**Proverbs 15:1 (NIV)**

**In your world today**, much of your communication and discussion takes place online, through a smart phone, or while playing video games. Whether you are a boy or a girl, friends and enemies seem to be made without even seeing the other person. You know how awful it feels to have someone say something hurtful about you: about the way you look or dress, your family, or even about something as silly as the lunch you bring to school. It seems like a single comment can spread like a forest wildfire and make you a king or queen on the playground one day and an outcast the next.

Never forget that you are children of the ultimate King; God your Father has placed a special crown on your head that already sets you apart as His princes and princesses. Because of Jesus' sacrifice for you, you have a seat at the biggest celebration the world will ever see, and it will go on forever! Remember who you are in Christ in your lives right now, and listen to the words that were put down in the Bible to help you grow into the royalty that God has called you to be. Think before you say or type something unkind, even if you are just trying to be funny and get a laugh. Be kind in every interaction, online or in person, because that is what you are called to do. Words can hurt, but you can use words to heal, just as Jesus did.

*Holly Van Shouwen*

# March 3

"**We must not** choose our neighbors," wrote George Macdonald, "We must take the neighbour that God sends." This is one of the messages of Jesus' tale of the "good Samaritan." The Samaritan does not decide some people are deserving of his mercy and others not; he responds to the person before him, even when it is a Judean Israelite, an enemy of his people.

The amount of human evil which comes of deciding that some people are our neighbors and thus worthy of our mercy and help, and others are not, is incalculable. God does not give us the choice of selective love. The love we are to show is only dependent on God's *you shall.* You shall love your neighbor. Not if, or when—no, you shall. One might think that this unconditional love is only commanded to neighbors, but to guard against that, God says, "You shall love the stranger." (Lev 19:34) As Jesus would later explain, the command of love excludes no one.

*Matthew Levi*

"You shall not take vengeance, nor bear any grudge against the children of your people, but you shall love your neighbor as yourself: I am the Lord."
**Leviticus 19:18 (NKJV)**

# March 4

"Faith never knows where it is being led,
but it loves and knows the One who is leading."
Oswald Chambers

And we know that in all things God works for the good of those who love him, who have been called according to his purpose.
**Romans 8:28 (NIV)**

**Have you ever** thought about this verse in Romans? Let's look at it carefully. First, it says we *know!* We don't believe, think, or imagine…we *know* that *all things* (that means everything that happens to us) are working together for our good, if we love God and are called according to His plan for our lives. Does that mean you? Of course, because God is calling everyone to love and serve Him and to choose to live the way He leads us.

Some things that happen in our lives may not seem good. Someone may die, or we may get sick. Someone may even hurt us. However, if we believe and trust in God, He will take that bad thing and use it to make us stronger, or better, or more thankful for the goodness of God. Many stories in the Bible show this is true.

The story I often think of is of Joseph, whose brothers sold him as a slave into Egypt. He was even thrown into prison, but in the end, God used all those trials to keep Joseph, his brothers, and all of his family alive. That is turning the bad to good, don't you think? Joseph even told his brothers, "What you intended to destroy me, God has used to save all of our family." (Genesis 50:20)

*Linda S. Storm*

# March 5

Put on the full armor of God, so that you can take your stand against the devil's schemes.
**Ephesians 6:11** (NIV)

**I imagine that** many of you play video games. My grandchildren sure do! They tell me about some of them—how their character has to earn weapons and special powers to fight off their enemies.

Did you know that every day we fight a real enemy, not just a video game creation? He is called the enemy of our souls. His goal is to steal, kill and destroy. He is a liar, too. It is a real battle, not one we can turn off with our video controller. But just like in the game, we must be fully armed and ready for battle.

The later verses of Ephesians 6 talk about the full armor of God. There is the belt of truth, the breastplate of righteousness, shoes ready with the gospel of peace, a shield of faith, the helmet of salvation, and the sword of the Spirit, which is the word of God. Each piece of armor has its purpose. Each one helps us to stand our ground, to stand firm.

Sometimes in video games, the warrior only has part of his tools, special powers, or armor to protect him. But we can have all of our armor at once! We don't have to earn points to get it; God gives it to us to use. So, whenever you face a battle against lies, hurt feelings, temptations to steal or destroy, or even to give up, remember you have your armor. Use it! Stand firm!

*Patricia S. Becker*

# March 6

**"Mine, mine, mine!"** cries the angry child as he grabs his toy. Children learn this sense of possession very early; but if they do not outgrow their selfishness, they will become greedy, unpleasant adults! As children grow older and become teenagers and young adults, this sense of possession often goes beyond material things and extends to one's own life. "It's MY life," cries the angry teenager trying to justify his poor choices and disobedience.

The error lies in believing that one's life is one's own. For God has created each of us, and we belong to Him. *"Everyone belongs to me,"* God reminds us through the prophet Ezekiel. The same chapter in Ezekiel goes on to stress personal responsibility and consequences for one's actions.

People often confuse the following two truths:

1. My choices belong to me.
2. My life belongs to God.

If you memorize these two statements and repeat them often to yourself, you will learn to make the right choices, the kind of choices that one who recognizes that he is a child of God and belongs to God will want to make.

*Sharon Edel*

Everyone belongs to me...
**Ezekiel 18:4** (NIV)

# March 7

The Lord watches over you—
the Lord is your shade at your right hand;
**Psalm 121:5 (NIV)**

**Most people, when** they are put in distressing or scary situations, pray—even people who say they don't believe in God. Why? Because by praying we are saying that we no longer have control, that we can't do it alone. We need help!

Have you ever struggled with a problem, tried for a long time to handle it yourself, and then finally asked for help? Do you remember the relief and regret you felt for not having asked for help sooner? We all do this sometimes. We struggle when we don't have to.

We have rest. We have peace. We have a place to run to when the world around us is coming apart. Just be still. Wait. Listen for the beating of your heart. Then pray from that place, knowing that the God that created your heart and knows you better than you know yourself will take your cares, worries, and problems on Himself.

He died for you and He loves you. It is a simple truth and a simple faith that lead to a solid life. Finding peace through prayer will see you through your storms and calm your seas. Just ask for help.

*Karen Thornton*

# March 8

> In the days of Herod, king of Judea, there was a priest named Zechariah, of the division of Abijah. And he had a wife from the daughters of Aaron, and her name was Elizabeth. And they were both righteous before God, walking blamelessly in all the commandments and statutes of the Lord. But they had no child because Elizabeth was barren, and both were advanced in years.
>
> **Luke 1:5-7** (ESV)

**Zechariah and Elizabeth** were advanced in years—they were *old!* "Barren" means Elizabeth hadn't and couldn't have children. Had they done something wrong to deserve a punishment? No, the Bible says they were both righteous before God.

You may want to read on and find out how an angel came to Zechariah and brought him very good news. Zechariah and Elizabeth had been praying for children for many, many years, and kept praying out of habit even though they may have given up hoping God would answer their prayers. Did Zechariah believe the angel? Not at first. It seemed too good to be true. Some of the people in the Bible had a hard time believing miracles, just like I do. But God's word came true, and baby John—who became John the Baptist—was born even though Elizabeth was too old for her body to have a baby.

Please remember this story when you are discouraged and feel like giving up on saying prayers. God's abilities are so much bigger and more wonderful than ours! Even if the only prayer you can say is "Jesus, help," say it. Jesus is real. Jesus is alive right now!

*Patrecia Jacobson*

# March 9

## Sacrifice

**As Amber glanced** around the shop, she saw the most beautiful sweater in a perfectly pink shade. It was so soft and cuddly. She wondered how to approach her parents about an early birthday gift. The weather was still cool even though Easter was late. The sweater would be perfect!

Amber stood looking at the calendar them read the scripture verse at the bottom.

"But to do good and to communicate forget not:
for with such sacrifices God is well pleased."
**Hebrew 13:16 (KJV)**

Amber sighed, "I am trying to communicate how much I need that sweater."

Days flew by and Amber found herself helping to bake Easter cookies for Church parties, family gatherings, and shut-ins. The elderly neighbor opened the door to receive Amber and some homemade cookies. Amber had not noticed how tiny Mrs. Johnson was or how poorly she was dressed in old slippers and holes in her sleeves. But she was so thankful for the cookies and Amber's company.

Days later, Amber was eagerly opening her gifts for her birthday. The last box held the much desired soft, perfectly pink sweater. As Amber touched it, all the excitement left and remorse took its place. Amber grabbed the gift box, the sweater, and some tape as she went to her room. In a moment Amber was gone.

Mrs. Johnson was pleased to see Amber so soon. The old sweater with holes in the sleeves lay discarded on the floor as she modeled her new soft, perfectly pink sweater. And Amber thought, it did feel much better to give than to receive, and thus to please God!

*Dottie Thornton*

# March 10

**"I give up!** I quit!" Have you ever been so frustrated that you felt like giving up? Maybe you just couldn't understand your math homework; or maybe your team was so far behind that it seemed hopeless. Parents, teachers, or coaches will tell you that you have to keep trying. You might not be the best at math, or your team might not win; but you will not learn or become a better player if you give up.

Following Jesus leads to joy, but perfect joy will only be attained at the end of the race! Jesus often reminds us that it won't be easy, and He encourages us to endure. You may struggle; you may have setbacks. What matters is that you don't give up – that you fix your eyes on Jesus and continue the race.

In all things that God puts before you to do, practice perseverance. Whether it is your math homework, playing a game, reaching for a personal goal, or trying to be kind to someone who is unkind – each is an opportunity to grow. You will experience both struggle and joy now; but you will receive the promise of perfect joy when the race is done!

May God grant you a willing and steadfast spirit!

*Sharon Edel*

Let us throw off everything that hinders and the sin that so easily entangles. And let us run with perseverance the race marked out for us, fixing our eyes on Jesus, the pioneer and perfecter of faith.
**Hebrews 12: 1-2** (NIV)

The one who endures to the end will be saved.
**Matthew 10:22** (NIV)

# March 11

**Angus MacPholp**, Mr. Thomas Galbraith's gamekeeper, did not hesitate to follow his master's orders to beat the child who had been caught in the act of secretly doing other folks' work. Over a year later, Angus sought Gibbie out and shot him in the leg.

Rob and Janet Grant, who had taken the orphan in, laid hold of MacPholp with the intent of seeing justice done. But Gibbie, taking matters into his own hands, forgave and released the gamekeeper before the constable could be brought.

Not long after, Mr. MacPholp was again in a tight spot, being stranded in a tree during a severe flood, and once again, Gibbie rescued the man from his trouble. (Scenes from *The Baronet's Song*, by George MacDonald)

When someone hurts us, especially on purpose, we are more likely to want to hurt them back than to forgive them and do good to them. But the Bible teaches us that young Sir Gibbie did what was right in God's eyes. Perhaps remembering his story will help us to do right as well.

*Rebekah Choat*

Do not repay evil for evil. Be careful to do
what is right in the eyes of everybody.
**Romans 12:17** (NIV)

# March 12

**Today is a special celebration** among the Jewish people. The Feast of Purim celebrates their freedom from almost being wiped out from the face of the earth by a man with an evil plot. Esther can teach all of us that there will be times in our lives when we must speak the truth and trust God to make the outcome all right.

I remember when I was younger we had a Sunday School teacher who was wonderful. He was a colored man who spoke our kid language and understood everything we were facing in our little lives. About a month after he came, my classmates were not treating him nicely at all. They would make fun of him and make racial comments right to his face. One Sunday, when we got to class he was sitting there waiting for us to sit down. In a calm voice he said, "Tell me what you guys think about my class." One by one, my "friends" tore him apart with words and I watched as tears streamed down his face. He turned to me and said "Holly, what do you have to say?" I said a quick prayer for help and began to speak. I told everyone that they would never find a better teacher and that they were like the people who stoned Stephen in the Bible for teaching about Jesus. I lost friends that day, but had peace in my heart for having the courage to tell the truth when one of God's people was hurting.

*Holly Van Shouwen*

Then the king extended the gold scepter to Esther and she arose and stood before him.
**Esther 8:4 (NIV)**

# March 13

## Pressing Toward a Goal

**Winning prizes!** It's so much fun! Have you ever been to an amusement park, a carnival, or a fun house that gives prizes for playing games? This Bible verse talks about moving toward a goal in order to win a prize. In this case, the prize isn't given for playing a game. It's given for completing God's goal for us. The goal is a heavenward journey in Christ Jesus. Have you ever thought of taking a life-long trip with Jesus as your companion? That's the goal.

When great athletes train for their games or prepare for the Olympics, they often face difficult days, sore muscles, tired bodies, and even injuries. After a time of healing, they put their difficulties in the past and press toward the future. They keep on training in order to meet their goals.

As followers of Jesus, we are disciples in training. We, too, can face set-backs, become tired of the challenge, or get hurt as we try to be the best followers we can be. We are to stay focused on this type of heavenward goal, leave the difficulties behind us, and press forward to move ahead. One thing we can count on: Jesus will not abandon us along the way.

In what way is our friendship with Jesus like running a race? In what way is traveling with Jesus like moving toward a prize?

*Carol Wimmer*

Forgetting what is behind and straining toward what is ahead, I press on toward the goal to win the prize for which God has called me heavenward in Christ Jesus.
**Philippians 3:13b-14** (NIV)

# March 14

**We live in** God's world, filled with wonders and beauty. We also live in a world into which sin has entered. Our loving Father has sent His Son to pay for our sin, yet we still experience some of its effects, like sickness and weakness. It can be scary to be sick or injured, and it can feel like it will never end. God promises that one day there will be no more sickness or sadness. While we wait for that day, He has given us something to remember:

> My flesh and my heart may fail, but God is the strength of my heart and my portion forever.
> **Psalm 73:26 (NIV)**

The hardest time to remember God and His goodness is when we are hurting—especially when we don't understand why we are suffering! It can make our heart feel weak. It can help a lot to know what to do.

In a story about a girl named Annie, we are told that when she was feeling bad,

> "Annie said her prayers, read her Bible, and tried not to forget God. Ah! could she only have known that God never forgot her, whether she forgot him or not..."
>
> *Alec Forbes of Howglen,* by George MacDonald

Remember that God is our portion, which means He is always with us, even when we forget He's there.

*Ginger Akers*

# March 15

"God is love. Therefore love. Without distinction,
without calculation, without procrastination, love."
Henry Drummond

**Paul had many** dear friends in Colossae and wrote a letter to the Colossian church, advising them how they should live now that they knew Jesus as Savior. In Colossians, Paul tells his friends some things they should not do: get angry, hold grudges, curse and use bad language, lie, or want anything that God had not permitted as good and holy.

Next, Paul told them some good things which they *should* do: They should be like Christ. They should be merciful, kind, and humble; they should be patient and forgiving since Jesus had forgiven them. They were also to be holy; that is, they were to be separate or different from the world. Paul wrote this advice for us, too. The world is not the standard for our behavior; Jesus is. If you want to know more about Him, please read the book of John. In it, you will see that Jesus was kind, merciful, humble, and patient. He was holy and forgiving. And as the Son of God, Jesus is LOVE! He loved us enough to give His life for us, that we might someday live forever with Him.

All these good characteristics can be summed up in that one word, *love!* For God is love, and wants us to be loving. If we love others as we love ourselves, we will naturally be kind, forgiving, and patient. We will not even have to think about it!

*Linda S. Storm*

And over all these virtues put on love, which
binds them all together in perfect unity.
**Colossians 3:14 (NIV)**

# March 16

## Caring

**As soon as** school was out, Corey began his walk home. Drawing near, his eyes were on the big yellow house next door. He had seen a boy his age being carried into the house, but he had not seen him since.

One day Corey noticed the boy in a small bed by the large windows. Corey had heard the boy was sick and was having some kind of treatments. "I sure wish a guy I could play with had moved in," he thought. It was easy for Corey to feel sorry for himself. "Maybe that boy could also use a friend," his Mom said; she looked at things differently.

With fresh-baked cookies in hand, Corey went to the big yellow house. An hour quickly passed as Corey and Mark talked about stuff they liked to do, and then Mark told him about the lump on his leg and his treatments.

Corey came daily even when Mark was weak; sharing his books and games helped them both, and sharing Sunday School lessons was best. The Bible says,

> He that hath a bountiful eye shall be blessed;
> for he giveth his bread to the poor.
> **Proverbs 22:9 (KJV)**

Mark asked Corey if God blessed him for sharing his books and games, and if that was the same as sharing bread. God blessed both boys in ways only God can. Corey learned how to help someone by being a true friend. God helped Mark through his illness.

A year later, Mark and Corey were still best friends, walking home after school, planning a camp-out on Friday night, and since Mark had received Christ too, Sundays were always the best of all!

*Dottie Thornton*

# March 17

**Have you ever wanted** to help someone but found that you couldn't? Maybe they were too far away, or you didn't know just what was needed. Did it make you want to cry? It's quite all right if you did cry. But maybe we are not so helpless as we seem.

In his story called *A Rough Shaking*, George MacDonald writes about a boy named Clare Skymer who finds himself in just this situation. After spending his days helping those he loved, he found he was no longer able to be there to help them. Here is how Mr. MacDonald describes it.

"Fears and anxieties, such as he had never known before, began to crowd upon him—not for himself; he was not made to think of himself, either first or second. Something dreadful might be going on that he could not prevent! He had never been so miserable. It was high time to do something—to ask the great one somewhere, he did not know where, who could somehow, he did not know how, hear the thoughts that were not words, to do what ought to be done for little Ann, and Abdiel, and Pummy! He prayed in his heart, lay still, and fell fast asleep."

Perhaps you have heard of the woman who used to say, "When I go to bed at night, I just turn the universe over to God since He's going to be awake anyway." A Father who is always awake and alert to every need of his children is a comfort indeed.

*Steve Fronk*
*In memory of Josie Nina*

Behold, he who keeps Israel will neither slumber nor sleep.
**Psalm 121:4**

# March 18

**Gibbie, in his** sheepskin coat and deerhide leggings, with a great crown of reddish-gold hair, had come to be known as the wild beast-boy who haunted the mountain. Ginevra was even more frightened of him than she was of being lost in unknown country. He had no wish to startle her, but could not sit still when she began to run right into danger. Unable to escape Gibbie's care, she threw herself on the ground in despair.

"When finally she raised her head, Ginevra was looking into two eyes of heaven's own blue, and through the eyes looked out something that dwells behind the sky...she was now certain he would not hurt her."
*The Baronet's Song*, by George MacDonald

He looked wild and perhaps even dangerous, but Gibbie was good right through, and learning to love Jesus more each day. True to his nature, he protected and helped the lost girl, even though she was fearful of him.

It is important for us to remember that someone's appearance may not show the truth of what he is like.

*Rebekah Choat*

The Lord does not look at the things man looks at. Man looks at the outward appearance, but the Lord looks at the heart.
**1 Samuel 16:7 (NIV)**

# March 19

**I was staying at** Grandma's for the weekend, and after I finished my Religion homework, I asked her who Joseph was. She picked up my book and read,

> Seek good, not evil, that you may live. Then the Lord, God Almighty will be with you, just as you say He is. Hate evil, love good; maintain justice in the courts. Perhaps the Lord God Almighty will have mercy on the remnant of Joseph.
> **Amos 5:14-15 (NIV)**

I heard her exclaim, "Joseph!" Then, Grandma found a video about Joseph and his coat of many colors for us to watch.

Who was this Joseph? From Grandma's smile, I could tell he was a good kid. He was his father's favorite over all of his brothers, and his father gave him a coat with all these cool colors, just like Grandma's quilt on the couch.

Joseph had hard times, but he always tried to do good. God saw this, protected him, and brought him back to his family after he was taken away to a far country. Joseph forgave those who had hurt him. He even got his coat back!

After the movie, Grandma explained what a remnant was. Like the left-over fabric on her quilt, she didn't throw it out; she used it to make something beautiful. She said that is what Amos meant by "the remnant of Joseph." We can be like Joseph, a piece of goodness in God's beautiful family!

God urges me to stay close to the good even when I think about doing something bad.

Can I say "no" to doing bad?

Can I stay close to the good?

*Amy Adams*

# March 20

"'Now, Curdie!' she cried, 'won't you believe what I told you about my grandmother and her thread?' For she had felt all the time that Curdie was not believing what she told him. 'There! - don't you see it shining on before us?' she added. 'I don't see anything,' persisted Curdie. 'Then you must believe without seeing,' said the princess...'"

*The Princess and Curdie,* by George MacDonald

**In the story** *The Princess and Curdie*, Irene is a princess who has a wonderful grandmother. She is neither young nor old, frail nor strong, but she is always good. She and Irene share the same name. She is also of the royal family. This great grandmother has given Irene a special ring; from it, a marvellous thread comes out whenever there is danger, and it leads Irene to safety. Though the way it leads may "seem a very round about way," she must not doubt. The princess must follow and trust. Because Irene believes, she can see the thread; but there are those who will not believe, and they see nothing! How bewildering to see the effects of something but not see the thing itself! Curdie was just such a lad; he did not believe, therefore he did not see the thread . . . at least, not yet!

Faith is like that. We who have come to believe in Jesus Christ find His truth everywhere! He is like the wind: we don't see the wind, but we see its effects! Some do not see the Lord. Perhaps they do not believe, just yet; but perhaps one day they will!

*Blythe Followwill*
*For Jackson & ♥*

Now faith is the assurance of things hoped for, the conviction of things not seen.
**Hebrews 11:1** (ESV)

# March 21

**Today is officially** the first day of Spring. Spring is a time for new life to come up from the ground, and it can be a time of Jesus doing something new in your life as well. We are only a short time away from Easter, and on that Resurrection Sunday, Jesus defeated death—the Holy Spirit's power brought Jesus back from death itself.

The reason the book of Proverbs is so good for us to read is that the writers paint pictures for our mind that help us think about the things of God. Imagine you live in a country with a king. He is coming through your town, and you run out to see him. He comes over to you and picks you up and spins you around, laughing. You can see the light in his face and you feel his love for you and the people. When the writer says, "his favor is like a rain cloud in spring," it means joy and life are present.

Sometimes it seems like God does things slowly, but there is joy in the waiting. This is what living in tune with Jesus is like. Today, make a list of some new things that God has been doing in your life, and thank God for each of those.

Jesus loves you. Jesus is FOR you. There is nothing you can do that would make God love you any more or less than He does right now.

*Matthew Nash*

When a king's face brightens, it means life;
his favor is like a rain cloud in spring.
**Proverbs 16:15** (NIV)

# March 22

## Comfort

**Gabriel saw the** paper announcing baseball tryouts tacked on the bulletin board. Excited, he imagined himself in uniform playing his first real game. He spent a lot of time playing with the guys in the neighborhood, and they had all told him he was a good pitcher. He believed them! He was *always* the pitcher. As he shared the news, several guys decided to try out, too.

Practice was the goal for the week on the empty lot, each working to be ready for Saturday. Gabriel was confident waiting for the tryouts. He knew practice was important and he knew the blue and white uniforms would look great.

Finally the big day came. Excitement filled the air as the boys gave everything they had to impress, even cheering for each other. Then tryouts were over and the waiting began.

With a look of complete disbelief, Gabriel ran his finger down the list and found his name near the bottom. His position was outfield, not pitcher or catcher. It hurt even more when his friend Jamie was chosen as pitcher. A few months before he would have been angry, but since he was saved he wanted to please the Lord Jesus. He did a lot of thinking about obeying and listening to God's Word.

> In the multitude of my thoughts within
> me thy comforts delight my soul.
> **Psalm 94:19 (KJV)**

This verse gave him comfort. If Jesus wanted him to play outfield he would do his best and be happy for Jamie, too!

*Dottie Thornton*

# March 23

**In his amazing** tale *The Lost Princess*, George MacDonald writes about a girl who is a princess, but doesn't act like one. After being snatched from the palace where her every desire is granted, Princess Rosamund learns many lessons about self-control from the Wise Woman.

At one point, the Wise Woman tells Rosamund, "Nobody can be a real princess until she is princess over herself."

All of us have to learn self-control. We have to learn how to say "yes" to right things, and "no" to wrong things. How did Rosamund learn to do that? By learning to think differently.

Our thoughts lead to actions, so it's important that we learn whether our thoughts line up with God's truth in the Bible. If they do, that's great! If they don't, we need to take action and deal with our wrong thoughts.

How do we do that?

We take them captive! We mentally "tie up" those thoughts and bring them to Jesus in prayer. It's not enough to identify the bad thought; we have to replace it with something else. So, we tell Jesus we know the thought is bad, and ask Him to help us think of something good and true instead.

Taking our thoughts prisoner to Jesus helps us to have the self-control we need. He helps us learn to control our thoughts, and our actions, as we make a habit of dealing with wrong thoughts.

*Dawn Morris*
*In memory of Lindsey Kathryn Morris*

We demolish arguments and every pretension that sets itself up against the knowledge of God, and we take captive every thought to make it obedient to Christ.
**2 Corinthians 10:5** (NIV)

# March 24

## "Corage, God mends all"

**George MacDonald once** took the letters from his name and transformed them into his own personal motto. He even used a really old way of spelling "courage" to help him write a saying that summarized what he believed about life: "Corage, God mends all." He believed with all his heart that no matter what happens in life, God will take care of you, so no one ever needs to fear or worry.

He must have read the story about Joseph in the Bible. The book of Genesis talks about him and the bad times he faced. First, Joseph was thrown into a pit by his brothers because they were jealous of him. Then he was taken away into slavery. Then, as if things weren't already bad enough, he was thrown in jail for something he didn't do.

Yet in the midst of all these terrible things that happened to him, the Bible says:

> But the Lord was with Joseph
> and showed him steadfast love...
> **Genesis 39:21 (ESV)**

God was with him; He was working *in* him, and *through* the bad things that were happening. Joseph soon was able to become a very important man, helping thousands of people make it through hard times. If Joseph had a message to give to you today, I think it would be the same as George MacDonald's motto. When things go bad and your life is hard, remember: "Corage, God mends all."

*Darren Hotmire*

# March 25

## A Good Story

They celebrate Your abundant goodness
and joyfully sing of Your righteousness.
**Psalm 145:7 (NIV)**

**It is so** fun to get caught up in a good story! Stories are powerful! They shape us, and their messages influence the way we think. That's why it's important that we chose to read and watch only the best kinds of stories. But what are the best kinds of stories? The best stories are those whose message is in line with God's character and that celebrate the things that are like Him. Those kinds of stories are true and reliable, helping us to be able to think more clearly.

But there are other kinds of stories. Isaiah 5:20 warns us not to paint a rosy picture of things that are evil or to make terrible things seem sweet. Unfortunately, some stories do this and yet are highly praised. These kinds of stories make the truth harder to see. So, God wants us to choose to focus our minds on stories that point toward truth and agree with His ways.

Over the next three days, the devotional thought will come from George MacDonald's fairytale *The Day Boy and the Night Girl,* a very good story. Find this story and read it over the next few days. (Because MacDonald's works are in the public domain, you can get this story free by searching for it on the internet!) Just like it says in today's Bible verse, all of MacDonald's wonderful stories faithfully "celebrate God's abundant goodness and joyfully tell of God's righteousness!" MacDonald's are the kind of "good stories" that make us better for reading them.

*Renita Koehn*

# March 26

## Watho's Folly

*The Day Boy and the Night Girl*, by George MacDonald

**Watho, the witch**, thought a lot. She would sit and think and suppose things, like what would happen if she did things that were bad. One day she got the nasty idea in her mind to steal two children from their mothers and raise them herself as an experiment to feed her wolf-like appetite for knowledge.

Watho did not care that other people were hurt by what she did. The wolf in her mind made her want things so badly that she became very cruel. Watho started out tall and graceful, straight and strong, but she kept feeding the hungry wolf in her mind until she became bent and ugly. In fact, she became more and more wild until finally her experiment ended in her own destruction.

Sometimes a "wolf" may get into our minds and try to get us to do something we should not do or something that would hurt others. But if we feed the wolf by doing what it wants, it gets hungrier and meaner, and we, like Watho, become ugly and selfish.

The Bible says that

> Your enemy the devil prowls around like a
> roaring lion looking for someone to devour.
> **1 Peter 5:8** (NIV)

just like the wolf consumed Watho. But the Bible also tells us,

> Submit yourselves, then, to God.
> Resist the devil and he will flee from you.
> **James 4:7** (NIV)

So watch out for the hungry wolf and don't give him a bite!

*Renita Koehn*

# March 27

## Differing Perspectives

**In Chapter 8** of George MacDonald's *The Day Boy and the Night Girl,* the boy, Photogen, who has only known the blaze of daylight, and the girl, Nycteris, who has only known the darkness of night, meet unexpectedly one night in the garden near the castle. When their two worlds collide, they experience the night around them in completely different ways. Photogen is weak with fear. Nycteris is delighting in a moth's flight. He hears the wind and river as a treacherous roar, but Nycteris speaks of them lovingly and cannot understand Photogen's fear. The more they talk, the more each of them finds the other has a completely different and odd understanding of things. While each of them grasps noble insights, each of their views is quite incomplete as well, and neither can understand the other.

Sometimes we meet people we don't understand, people who seem to experience things entirely differently from us, just like Nycteris thought Photogen "did not know what he was saying." But it is good to be kind even when we don't understand someone. Even though Photogen was very mistaken in the reasons for his fear and Nycteris couldn't understand why he was afraid, she could see that he really was scared, and she helped him endure the terror by staying with him. That's what compassion is: to feel along with another. She was compassionate to him that night in the garden.

God's word says,

> ...clothe yourselves with compassion...
> **Colossian 3:12 (NIV)**

Today, ask God how you can be compassionate and kind to people who have a different perspective from you.

*Renita Koehn*

# March 28

## Selfishness Turned to Love

**As George MacDonald's** story *The Day Boy and the Night Girl* concludes, we see that the Night Girl, Nycteris, grew to love the day best because it was "the clothing and crown of Photogen," the Day Boy. Likewise, Photogen came to love the night best because it was the "mother and home of Nycteris." They genuinely began to look to the interests of the other rather than their own interests. They began to truly love and care for one another.

Earlier in the story we see how selfish Photogen had been toward Nycteris. After she sat with him through his night of fear, he arrogantly ran off at daybreak leaving her helpless and terrified. Later, he was conscience-stricken, ashamed of how he had behaved toward her. When he at last saw her again, he was able to express the compassion that he failed to show the first time.

Jesus wants to teach us how to stop being selfish – thinking that our concerns are the only things that matter – and to begin to see and help the needs of others. When Photogen learned of his selfishness, he was sorry and learned to care for Nycteris. God will help us, too, so that we may learn to care about the needs of others.

*Dear Jesus, sometimes I'm selfish like Photogen was! Teach me humility so I may see and value the needs of others. Amen.*

*Renita Koehn*

They celebrate Your abundant goodness and joyfully sing of Your righteousness.
**Psalm 145:7 (NIV)**

# March 29

## Loving God, Loving Others

"And you must love the lord your God with all your heart, all your soul, all your mind, and all your strength. The second is equally important: Love your neighbor as yourself. No other commandment is greater than these."
**Mark 12:30-31** (NIV)

**I wonder what** it looks like to love like *that?*

Lottie Moon loved God so much that she left her home and went to China as a missionary in the 1800's. She loved others so much that, during a famine, she gave her food to the starving people around her, eventually causing her own death.

There are many other who have left their homes and jobs, for however long, to preach the gospel. They love victims of floods, hurricanes, and earthquakes; they love sick, injured, and poor people so much they often pay their own travel expenses and give their time to do strenuous work to help them.

The apostle Paul wrote much of the New Testament, guided by the Holy Spirit. He preached the gospel of Jesus and helped people all over his world. He was beaten, rejected, put in prison, went hungry and thirsty, and finally died for the gospel.

Many others remain at home, living faithfully. God knows who they are.

It appears that the people we admire most are the ones who have these two commands engraved on their hearts. It starts with loving God extravagantly. We demonstrate it by loving others the way God loves all of us.

*Dear Jesus, Thank you for being our example of loving God so completely it overflows to others. Help me to practice loving God and loving others every day.*

*Vicki Ryder*

# March 30

> If we are thrown into the blazing furnace, the God we serve is able to deliver us from it, and he will deliver us from Your Majesty's hand. But even if he does not, we want you to know, Your Majesty, that we will not serve your gods or worship the image of gold you have set up.
> **Daniel 3:17-18** (NIV)

**If you have not** yet had the opportunity to experience the exciting story of Shadrach, Meschach, and Abednego which is related in the third chapter of Daniel, don't wait! This is one of my favorites, and the words quoted above give me goosebumps! These men are about to be thrown into the fire for refusing to obey the king who has ordered his people to worship a golden statue as a god.

Clearly Shadrach, Meschach, and Abednego have the faith to believe that God can deliver them from the king's punishment; but what thrills me are the words: "BUT EVEN IF HE DOES NOT!" The boldness and bravery of Shadrach, Meschach, and Abednego, who would rather die than disobey God, whose trust in God will stand even if He *does not* save them from this horror, exhibits a courage worthy of imitation! Oh, if only all Christians could be so stubborn for the sake of God's Kingdom!

Sometimes Christians are disappointed when God does not answer their prayers to take away a great difficulty—perhaps a friend or relative's illness or impending death, or perhaps one's own struggles with school or friends or siblings.

Because this kind of crisis is so threatening to faith, we will discuss it a little more in tomorrow's devotion.

*Sharon Edel*

# March 31

He humbled himself, becoming obedient
to death, even death on a cross.
**Philippians 2:8 (NIV)**

**Yesterday we discussed** keeping faith even if God doesn't give us what we ask. Today's scripture reminds us that even the Son of God, who prayed that the trial might be taken away, submitted to His Father's plan.

You might think to yourself: "Well, even Jesus didn't get what He wanted!" But it might surprise you if I tell you that Jesus DID get what He wanted. How is that, you ask? Because what Jesus wanted more than any other desire was to do the will of His Father!

In fact, if your greatest desire is to do the Will of God and to be made like Jesus, God will grant you that desire. I do not say that this is an easy desire to have. Rather, I can assure you that other desires will constantly compete, and you will likely struggle and fall many times. But take courage! God is with you!

Let me share a word and a challenge. The word: Perseverance. It means to keep going no matter what. It means faithfulness, strength when you feel weak, and bravery when you feel afraid.

The challenge: When you read or listen to the words of the New Testament, especially the letters and the Book of Revelation, look for either the word or the idea of perseverance. You will be amazed and encouraged!

*Sharon Edel*

Do not be afraid of what you are about to suffer…Be faithful, even to the point of death, and I will give you life as your victor's crown.
**Revelation 2:10 (NIV)**

# April 1

"You can't live on amusement.
It is the froth on water — an inch deep and then the mud."
*Mary Marston*, by George MacDonald

I said to myself, "Come on, let's try pleasure. Let's look for the 'good things' in life." But I found that this, too, was meaningless.
**Ecclesiastes 2:1** (NLT)

**Ever try to** eat bubbles? It can't be done. They're pretty, yes, and you might catch a few in your mouth, but then you find yourself with…NOTHING!

Some kinds of fun (that's another word for amusement) are more like bubbles than anything else. Cotton candy is sweet, but it disappears in a second. Can you imagine running a big race when all you've eaten is cotton candy? For that matter, can you imagine taking a math test when all that's in your head is the video game you were playing that morning?

Fun and junk food simply don't meet all your needs.

Your body needs real food, not just treats. Your mind needs real study and thinking to get strong. Your soul needs nourishment, too. That's why you're told over and over to learn God's Word, pay attention as much as you can in church, ask questions, and get answers. Give your soul good stuff, not just the froth on water. That way you won't get stuck in the mud.

*Mary Lichlyter*

# April 2

**We can imagine** our lives as a journey; a big adventure as we walk on a long road. Along the way, we will meet many joys and challenges, but one thing always stays the same: God walks right alongside us!

The prophet Isaiah tells the nation of Israel that God will be with them wherever they go. He says,

> And your ears shall hear a word behind you, saying, "This is the way, walk in it," when you turn to the right or when you turn to the left.
> **Isaiah 30:21** (ESV)

The same can be said for us! Jesus says in Matthew 28:20, "And surely I am with you always, to the very end of the age." As we wake up in the morning, eat breakfast, head to school, talk with our friends, and go about our days, we know that Jesus is walking with us every step of the way. When we choose to trust in Him and listen for His voice, He helps guide our steps.

There is an old hymn called "In the Garden" that talks about walking with God. Imagine going on a walk through a beautiful garden alone with God as you read the chorus:

And he walks with me, and he talks with me,
And he tells me I am his own;
And the joy we share as we tarry there,
None other has ever known.

*Bethany Wagner*
*In memory of Charles Wagner*

# April 3

## Seeing God's Light

**The story of** Creation begins in utter darkness as God's Spirit moved about over the waters of the earth. Then God said, "Let there be light," and God's light was revealed in Creation! Imagine if *you* could bring light into existence. How would *you* color the world? Would you create a green sky? Red plants? Blue animals? No?

The story of Creation begins at the darkest end of the spectrum as God separated dark from light on the first day of Creation. Then, God created a beautiful *blue* sky, lush *green* plants, and a bright *yellow* sun, moon and stars. Next, God filled the living creatures of sea, sky, and land with deep *orange* and *red* lifeblood. Six days. Six colors. Violet, blue, green, yellow, orange, and red.

The story ends with purple light—a holy light for God's Sabbath Day of Rest. Purple is an extra-spectral color that appears when the blue and red ends of the spectrum form a circle of light. The ancient storytellers didn't mention any color by name, but they used the color order of the rainbow to tell their story. The colors are silently present in the story if we have the eyes to see them.

Do you like the way God colored your world? It's quite beautiful, isn't it?

*Carol Wimmer*

And God said, "Let there be light," and there was light. God saw that the light was good, and he separated the light from the darkness. God called the light "day," and the darkness he called "night." And there was evening, and there was morning—the first day.
**Genesis 1:3-5 (NIV)**

# April 4

...Jonathan became one in spirit with David, and he loved him as himself...Jonathan made a covenant with David because he loved him as himself. Jonathan took off the robe he was wearing and gave it to David, along with his tunic, and even his sword, his bow and his belt.
**1 Samuel 18:1, 3-4 (NIV)**

**Once, there were** two Native American boys named Jonathan Mighty Spirit and David Who Loves His Song, who were best friends. They were always together, swimming, hunting, riding horses, and tracking buffalo upon the great prairie. They were such good friends that they wanted to be united as brothers, their spirits eternally one.

Becoming "brothers" was a serious matter, so the boys went into the great tipi, where they fasted and prayed, seeking God's wisdom and guidance regarding the bonded covenant they were about to enter into. Afterwards, they entered the sacred circle where they kindled a fire in its center. Standing face to face, Jonathan presented David with gifts. First, he gave him his shirt, sword, bow and belt. His final gift was a buffalo robe which he wrapped around him speaking, "Forever, David Who Loves His Song and I, Jonathan Mighty Spirit are brothers in the circle of life, where the fire of our covenant will never die. We shall be bound one to the other by thc Lord, into the everlasting fellowship, our hearts and spirits now bound as one!" David Who Loves His Song was moved by his new brother's generosity. He spoke, "All I have to give to you, my new brother, is my heart and a song; hear our heartbeat as I drum and sing the sacred song of our unified brotherhood!"

*Lisa Blair*

# April 5

> But Gideon told them, "I will not rule over your, nor will my son rule over you. The Lord will rule over you."
> **Judges 8:23 (NIV)**

**Why do you** think that Gideon didn't want to be a ruler? Don't we all like to be in charge? Doesn't it make one feel important to rule over people or things? Who doesn't want to be the boss, especially when you're young? It makes you feel like a grown up.

Many times, we forget that the Lord is our ruler. Yes, it's true that there are people whom we need to obey; there are people above us; and there are laws for us to follow. But ultimately, we are to obey our Lord, as He is our ultimate ruler. The Lord will judge us and hold us accountable. Gideon knew that, and because he obeyed and trusted the Lord, he was humble enough to remind the people that the Lord is the one who rules.

As you go on with your day, remember that there are people and laws that society has made for the safety of everyone. You must trust the Lord and obey Him. If you do that, the Lord will bless you and you will see great things happening to you. Always remember, you serve the Lord.

*Laura Bennin*

# April 6

> And he said, "The Lord is my rock,
> and my fortress, and my deliverer."
> **2 Samuel 22:2 (KJV)**

### Worry

**As Troy opened** the door to the market, he was met by two guys on the run. The manager had seen them stealing but couldn't stop them. Troy gave descriptions to the police but said nothing about seeing them before. As the boys continued the stealing, people grew more concerned. Troy kept silent because he was afraid of them. What if they followed him home from school? What could he do?

Troy's lesson in Sunday School was about young David facing the giant Goliath. His teacher said the people were afraid because of Goliath's size, but David simply saw Goliath as an enemy that needed to be stopped. The teacher said we will face giants in life that we need to overcome, but we shouldn't let fear and worry overcome us. God gives His promise that He will be with us to help fight our battles. He will help us know the right thing to do.

Troy knew the lesson was for him. It would take courage, but Troy knew what he must do. He put a rock in his pocket to remind him that God was with him just as God was with David the young shepherd boy.

After Troy talked to his parents and the police, the two boys were arrested. Both admitted their guilt and never knew how they were found out. Troy was so relieved—he thought he must feel like David did after he brought the giant down!

*Dottie Thornton*

# April 7

"A torrent of water struck Annie and tumbled into the boat as if it would beat the bottom out of it. Annie was tossed about in fierce waters and ceased to know anything.

When she came to herself she was in an unknown bed, with Mrs. Forbes bending anxiously over her."

*The Maiden's Bequest,* by George MacDonald

**Have you ever** been at the beach, playing in the ocean, when a wave came up behind and washed over you, knocking you down completely under water? It's a frightening experience, and a large part of the fright is that it is unexpected.

Sometimes things happen in our lives that feel a bit like that surprise wave crashing into us—sudden, dangerous, frightening things. Maybe we have to move to a faraway place, or we get hurt badly while playing baseball, or we're in a car wreck, or someone we love dies. It's normal to feel scared and to have trouble understanding what is going on.

Annie's friend Alec, a good, strong young man, rescued her when their boat was suddenly filled with raging water. Someone far better and stronger even than Alec Forbes has promised to guard and protect us.

*Rebekah Choat*

When you pass through the waters, I will be with you; and when you pass through the rivers, they will not sweep over you. When you walk through the fire, you will not be burned; the flames will not set you ablaze. For I am the Lord, your God, the Holy One of Israel, your Savior.
**Isaiah 43:2-3 (NIV)**

# April 8

## Strength

**Growing up was** not simple anymore. Ryan had a best friend, but he was changing. The boys had been friends since they started school. They spent so much time together that most people thought they might be brothers. They were still friends, but seemed to be going in different directions.

Ryan decided that asking Jesus to save him was the most important thing he had ever done. The next thing for him was going to Church, especially Sunday School. Learning about God's creation and His great power over all things was awesome. Ryan tried to tell Brad about some of the Bible stories and that the Bible even talks about dragons, but he wouldn't listen.

One day when they were together, Brad asked Ryan to go with him to a house in a bad neighborhood. Ryan wanted to spend time with his friend, but he felt this would not be a good choice. The Bible says,

> Finally my brethren, be strong in The Lord, and in the power of His might.
> **Ephesians 6:10 (KJV)**

Ryan knew God promised to be with him and help him make right choices. "How can I help Brad if he won't listen to me?" Ryan went to his teacher with this question. Mr. Turner told Ryan he must pray for Brad and be faithful to the Lord.

Brad started getting into trouble. His new friends were leading him deeper into bad choices. Each time Ryan listened to his troubles, Ryan always tried to tell him how much God loves him.

Ryan would keep on praying, and maybe one day his prayers would be answered and Brad would come to know Jesus, too.

*Dottie Thornton*

# April 9

...your kingdom come, your will be done, on earth as it is in heaven.
**Matthew 6:10** (NIV)

**Who doesn't like** to have his own way? I know I do! But sometimes you have to submit and go along with what someone else wants. Many of us, when we do give in, do so begrudgingly.

Often when we pray "Thy will be done," we have that same uncomfortable feeling that we don't like it, but we'll go ahead and let God be in charge. How silly we are to think that our Father does not have the absolute best thing in mind for us!

In a letter to his son, author George MacDonald tells him: "Let Him do with you, my beloved son, as He wills. Be hearty with His will. Submission is not the right feeling when we say 'Thy will be done.' This will is the only good..."

Let us try to have greater faith in our Father and not simply submit, but *lovingly and cheerfully* submit to His good and perfect will. And if we want to go even further, why not practice being cheerful when allowing others to have their way! Such goodness will please others and our Father as well!

*Sharon Edel*

# April 10

**What do you** know about Jesus? Why should we obey Him?

You may be familiar with many of the stories about Jesus, but today I would like to share with you some of the basic things that Christians believe about Jesus.* This is important because sometimes people are confused about who He is and why we should obey Him.

- Jesus was truly human.
- Jesus was truly the Son of God, and therefore God.
- But He was not half human and half God. He was human in every way we are (except without sin); and He was God in every way.
- Jesus really did suffer and die.
- Jesus really did rise from the dead. His human body rose from the dead. He didn't turn into an angel or dispose of his human body. (By the way, when people die they do not become angels either. Like Jesus, we will get our bodies back!)

We love and obey Jesus because He is truly God! We know that He loved us so very much that He was willing to become human like us, even to the point of suffering and dying!

**If some of these ideas are new or confusing to you, your parents, pastor, or another adult Christian may be able to explain more.*

*Sharon Edel*

For this reason he had to be made like them, fully human in every way, in order that he might become a merciful and faithful high priest in service to God, and that he might make atonement for the sins of the people.
**Hebrews 2:17 (NIV)**

# April 11

**When the women** went to the tomb to help with the burial process of Jesus, they wondered who would help them to roll the stone away. I'm sure they must have been sad and filled with grief, and the great boulder in front of the tomb which held their Savior was a large and looming obstacle. When they reached the Garden of Gethsemane and the tomb where they had placed our Savior's body, the boulder had been rolled away, and an angel of the Lord was sitting on the right side. The obstacle was moved, and the greatest news of all was told to them. Their Savior had risen from the dead and death had been conquered!

Have you ever had to do something, or needed something done, that was much too big for you to do all by yourself?

Whatever we may think our difficulty is—something we do not know how to do, or something we are struggling about in our hearts—if we ask God for help, we shall see it rolled away, and more than that, we shall see Him turn it into some unexpected good.

*Jolyn Canty*

> And they were saying to one another, "Who will roll away the stone for us from the entrance of the tomb?" And looking up, they saw that the stone had been rolled away, although it was extremely large. And entering the tomb, they saw a young man sitting at the right, wearing a white robe; and they were amazed. And he said to them, "Do not be amazed; you are looking for Jesus the Nazarene, who has been crucified. He has risen; He is not here; behold, here is the place where they laid Him."
> **Mark 16:3-4 (NASV)**

# April 12

**There is a** story in the Bible of the disciples of Jesus arguing about who was the best. "I am the greatest!" said Peter. "No, I am!" said John. Sound familiar? Often we get caught up with the idea of being better than others. To stop the disciples from arguing, and to teach them an important lesson, Jesus brought a little child to sit on his lap. He said,

"Truly, I say to you, unless you turn and become like children, you will never enter the kingdom of heaven. Whoever humbles himself like this child is the greatest in the kingdom of heaven."
**Matthew 18:3-4** (ESV)

Can you imagine the silence in the room? I'm sure the disciples were shocked. Isn't greatness measured by a man's strength and stature? Surely, an adult would be considered greater than a child. It made no sense. But Jesus knew that the nature of God was far closer to that of the little child's than it was to that of an adult man; for God is whole-hearted in all He does. Think of a baby—a child cares nothing for what the world says, it simply and whole-heartedly loves. Jesus was saying that to truly be of the kingdom of heaven, we must see the childlikeness of God Himself and return again to the simplicity of whole-hearted affection. Put aside the arguing and fighting, for God is whole-heartedly for you, as your father, your mother, and your more-than-friend.

> "In this, then, is God like the child: that he is simply and altogether our friend, our father—our more than friend, father, and mother—our infinite love-perfect God."
> *The Child in the Midst, Unspoken Sermon,* by George MacDonald

*Heidi Livingston*

# April 13

*"Our walk counts far more than our talk, always!"*
George Muller, Christian Evangelist

**Anybody can talk.** Most everybody does. Don't think that what comes out of your mouth doesn't matter!

God tells us to keep our talk clean, keep it true, and say what builds other people up (or defends them if they need defending). That honors Him. God isn't snarky, crude, abusive, or super-critical. He doesn't want us to be.

But words alone aren't enough. We have to put "feet" on them.

What can you do for your neighbor in the hospital? With your parents, can you take food to the family, or mow the grass for them? What can you do for the kid at school who has no friends? Can you stop in the hall to say hello every time you see him (not just when your buddies aren't around)? What can you do for the grouchy teacher? Can you say something good to her every time you go in to her classroom, no matter how sour she is?

Words are important (say the good ones out loud!) – but, unhappily, we're good at saying one thing and then doing something else. When, instead, you back up your words with your actions, people notice. They start to think, "That's one of the folks who really mean what they say."

By the way, don't do this to be impressive. Do it to be expressive – of your love for Jesus. After all, this is His world.

*Mary Lichlyter*

Whoever says he abides in [Jesus] ought to walk in the same way in which He walked.
**1 John 2:6 (ESV)**

# April 14

**As a boy,** I discovered that adults love children to memorize Bible verses. So naturally, I memorized many verses to please my parents. Then one day I decided to play a joke: I discovered a "silly" verse, and with all seriousness I quoted it:

> Whether a tree falls north or south, it stays where it falls.
> **Ecclesiastes 11:3** (NLT)

I tried my best to hide my smirk,
But who wouldn't rather laugh than work?

My pious airs increased the jest,
And with pompous pride, I puffed out my chest.

The joke worked so well I repeated it often,
Though I knew it's not right, my heart did not soften.

No longer serious, a joker I'd be,
Less rules to follow, I'd be much more free!

Then the Lord God, so infinite wise,
He set me straight and opened my eyes.

Reading Psalm One put and end to my fun,
I suddenly knew that the tree was me!

From my old joke I wanted to run,
Else, when I fell, forever a joker I'd be!

Now, I wasn't worried,
The Lord God is so fair,

He let me off easy,
Just tussled my hair.

I think I made God laugh, you see—all along my joke was on me!

"The Lord of gladness delights in the laughter of a merry heart."
*The Marquis of Lossie,* by George McDonald

*Michael Gailey*

# April 15

Charm is deceptive, and beauty is fleeting; but a woman who fears the Lord is to be praised. Honor her for all that her hands have done, and let her works bring her praise at the city gate.
**Proverbs 31:30-31 (NIV)**

**What are you** thankful for? I know that normally that question isn't asked until November during Thanksgiving, but I think it is good for us to do it more than once a year. Today is my wife's birthday and I am thankful for her. She is a godly woman who is changing the lives of thousands of women in the world, giving them dignity and helping them realize their value to Jesus. Be thankful for the life you have been given, and find ways to thank others for the things their hands have done.

Did you know that Jesus values you? He does! He has created you in His very image. That means that you can imagine a better world, you can cry and laugh about things around you, and you have a will to make decisions about what kind of person you want to be.

When Jesus was on Earth, he blessed so many people! I have a friend named Aaron who always says this great phrase that I have adopted for my life: Jesus, may I bless the person I meet next.

You have been loved by God, to bring love. You have been blessed to be a blessing. Be thankful for the life God has given you, and for the people in your life. They will appreciate hearing how you feel about them today!

*Matthew Nash*

# April 16

"...She hoped as much as she could, and when she could no longer hope she did not stand still, but walked on in the darkness. I think, when the sun rises upon them, some people will be astonished to find out just how far they have got on in the darkness."

*Paul Faber, Surgeon,* by George MacDonald

**I can't think** of a Christian who *never* walked in the darkness—who never wondered, sometimes, if everything he or she believed was really true.

Mother Teresa wondered, and Martin Luther, and John Calvin, who wrote that we should *expect* such times. Being tempted to give up on the Truth is part of living in the war zone that this world is.

It's easy to be "redirected" by friends, activities, the loud voices of unbelievers—not to mention disappointing and disastrous events—and start wondering if the Bible isn't just a lot of make-believe.

But God didn't make us with only feelings. He made us able to think, to reason. Brains and hearts are made to help one another. Sometimes Christianity *can* seem unlikely to be true—as many Christians will tell you. Others, who do not honor Christ, may say they sometimes feel as if Christianity might indeed be true—though they don't want it to be!

So what should you do? Don't let your moods boss you around. Hold to what you know is true. God will help you with your emotions. Just ask Him!

*Mary Lichlyter*

I had said in my alarm, "I am cut off from your sight." But you heard the voice of my pleas for mercy when I cried to you for help.

**Psalm 31:22 (ESV)**

# April 17

**Did you know** that there are 195 countries in the world? They are usually ruled by kings, queens, or presidents. If you have a passport, you can travel to see fascinating places. People speak foreign languages, they eat interesting foods, and the clothes they wear might look very different from yours.

Interestingly, the Bible says that there are only two kingdoms in the world: the kingdom of God and the kingdom of darkness. These kingdoms are not visible, but they are in our hearts. In God's kingdom, He is the Father and we are His children. His children want to follow His example. In the kingdom of darkness, the ruler is rebelling against God. People in that kingdom are the enemy's slaves.

God loves all people, including the slaves in the kingdom of darkness. He made a plan to rescue them. He sent Jesus, who chose to live in the enemy land and invite the slaves into His Father's kingdom, where there is peace, joy, and a loving Father. Jesus told the slaves they can be forgiven.

You don't need to travel far to get to God's kingdom. You just tell Him that you want to be His child, and He will accept you. You don't need to have a passport to enter: Jesus has paid the price with His blood when He died on the cross for you. You can be free and live with God in the kingdom of light as one of His children.

*Henna-Marie Tucker*

For he has rescued us from the dominion of darkness and brought us into the kingdom of the Son he loves, in whom we have redemption, the forgiveness of sins.
**Colossians 1:13-14 (NIV)**

# April 18

> "Yet I will not totally destroy the descendants of Jacob," declares the Lord. "For I will give the command, and I will shake the people of Israel among all the nations as grain is shaken in a sieve, and not a pebble will reach the ground."
> **Amos 9:8b-9 (NIV)**

**When I got** home from school today, I threw my backpack on the floor with a loud thud.

Mom was upstairs, but she heard it, so she called, "Margaret, what was that?" I told her it was me.

Mom came downstairs and found me in the kitchen munching some cookies she had made. Mom sat down beside me, and took a cookie for herself.

I looked at Mom and said, "The whole class is being punished because Stephanie and Jean wrecked the girls' bathroom during recess, and it's not fair!"

Mom took my hands and said, "No, it isn't fair, but I know who is: God. God loves His children when they live the truth. When He sees His children doing good and telling the truth, He remembers them. He will not forget you, even when you don't know what to do. And even if you stray from God, and come back to Him, He will forgive you, too."

After talking with Mom I felt better, not only for the great cookies, but for telling me what is important: God loves me! His love stands taller than having to stay after school!

Can you count on God when things don't work out?

How do you know you can?

*Amy Adams*

# April 19

## Divine Time and Temporal Time

When you were born, your parents probably thought *you* hung the sun, the moon, and stars. The entire galaxy revolves around newborn babies. Time seems to stand still when a baby is born. Then, something happens. Babies cry during the night. Tired parents begin to think, "Maybe my baby didn't hang the sun, the moon, and stars! After all—time isn't *really* standing still, and we need our sleep."

You see, babies live in *divine time*, but their parents live in *temporal time*. Babies don't know the difference between day and night. This is something they must learn. The difference between divine time and temporal time is basically this: human beings slice divine time into little chunks which are then measured and counted. Silly, really. Yet, our observance of the sun, moon, and stars make this possible. So, grown-ups have this 24-hour clock in their heads that ticks out chunks of time, rings alarms, and establishes calendars, etc. Little kids don't know anything about clocks.

By the time children enter kindergarten, they've probably figured out that the clock is an important thing that all adults obey. Once kids learn to obey the clock, grown-ups are usually thankful. Yet, obeying the clock is a little sad because children lose the freedom they had without the clock. Want to know a secret? As people grow old, they wish they could get rid of the clock. Old people look forward to living in divine time!

*Carol Wimmer*

God made two great lights—the greater light to govern the day and the lesser light to govern the night. He also made the stars.
**Genesis 1:16 (NIV)**

# April 20

> He has shown you, O mortal, what is good. And what does the LORD require of you? To act justly and to love mercy and to walk humbly with your God.
> **Micah 6:8 (NIV)**

**When I was young,** I enjoyed reading stories about great men and women of God. Oh, if only God would show ME His will so that I could follow it and be counted as one of the saints of God!

We may think that God hides from us and wish that we could hear the mighty thunder of His voice! But I assure you that God is much closer to you than you realize, and that His will for you is not hidden. God does indeed hide knowledge of the future from us, because we have no need of it. All we need is to know what to do here and now!

Here is a basic checklist based on Scripture to help you know if you are on the right path:

- ✔ Love Goodness and Mercy and Act Accordingly
- ✔ The Ten Commandments
- ✔ Obey parents and all in authority
- ✔ Beatitude (Sermon on the Mount)
- ✔ Pray Always

If you are like most honest people, you will humbly realize that God has given you more than enough to know and follow His will, and that you have plenty to do just for today!

I pray "that the God of our Lord Jesus Christ, the glorious Father, may give you the Spirit of wisdom and revelation, so that you may know him better. I pray that the eyes of your heart may be enlightened in order that you may know the hope to which he has called you…" Ephesians 1:17-18 (NIV)

*Sharon Edel*

# April 21

> Though the mountains be shaken and the hills be removed, yet my unfailing love for you will not be shaken nor my covenant of peace be removed," says the Lord who has compassion on you.
> **Isaiah 54:10** (NIV)

**Have you ever** had a really bad day? Maybe it's your first day of fifth grade, and your best friend isn't in your class; or you drop your binder on the sidewalk, and all the papers fall out.

Well, let me tell you about John's bad day. His dad had been gone all summer looking for a new job, and when he came home, his mom told John that they were moving to a far-away state.

His world has turned upside down, like the shaking mountains he'd read about in the Bible! Then, just like the crumbling hills in that story, his mom said that his dog, Denny, couldn't go because the new place didn't allow pets.

At the end of this bad day, John's mom found him in his room, crying. "How about we pray?" she said. "Let's give this one to God, and see what He can do for us."

So John stopped crying, and he and his mom got quiet, and then he said, "Dear God, please hear me. I need you to help me with this problem. I have Mom and Dad, and they are great. I'm going to be ok, but Denny needs a good home. You know what I mean, Lord—can you find him a good home? Amen."

Can you write an ending for John's story?

Do you believe in God's love to carry you through bad days?

*Amy Adams*

# April 22

"I find that doing the will of God leaves me
no time for disputing about His plans."
*George MacDonald*

**Peter and his brother** Andrew were fishermen; so were their friends, John and James. Fishing was how they fed their families. Some of the fish caught were for eating at the family table and some were sold to buy other necessities. Their families needed those fish. But one day, they met Jesus. Jesus said, "Come and follow me." And the Bible says that all four of those young men *immediately* left their boats and fishing nets and followed the Lord. They had no idea what they would be asked to do, or where they would go, but each of them knew this was what God was telling them to do.

Have you ever felt as if God was telling you to do something, right at that moment? Maybe you had hurt someone's feelings and needed to say you were sorry, or perhaps you felt that you should share something you'd been given with someone less fortunate. Many times, if we listen, God will speak to our hearts and tell us to do a thing—right then! No waiting around!

When God speaks to our hearts as Jesus spoke to the disciples, we should say, "Yes, Lord," and obey quickly. We should also be quick to obey our parents and teachers. When we obey quickly, without questioning or hesitation, God will direct our lives in the way we should go, and we will be happy because we obeyed.

*Linda S. Storm*

And they immediately left the ship
and their father, and followed him.
**Matthew 4:22 (KJV)**

# April 23

The LORD is with me; I am not afraid;
what can mortals do against me?
**Psalm 118:6**

**Christians often share** their favorite Bible verses with friends. I am sharing what I used to consider my *least* favorite Bible verse! I would often read this verse from Psalms, get to the part "What can mortals do against me?" and grimly answer to myself, "A lot!"

I must be honest. Sometimes being a Christian is hard. People can be mean and hurtful even though you are trying to do what is right. But I have discovered a secret: NOTHING makes you more like Jesus than to suffer for doing good!

The perfect, most loving, and most compassionate Son of God was tortured and crucified despite doing only good. Yes, this kind of suffering Jesus understands more than anyone. When He sees you hurting for righteousness' sake, His gentle heart is filled with such deep love and approval that even though you may not feel it yet, you will one day know that His love infinitely outweighed any evil that mortals did or could have done to you.

Of course most of us would prefer not to be hurt, and we know that God can and often does protect us from harm. But if we do suffer for doing God's will, faith assures us that we are walking more closely with Jesus and becoming more like Him.

May God grant us the joy of becoming conformed to the image of His Son, and the faith, the hope, and courage to sing: *"The LORD is with me; I am not afraid; what can mortals do against me?"*

*Sharon Edel*

# April 24

"The more we know of God, the happier we are."
*A Narrative of Some of the Lord's Dealings with George Mueller*,
by George Mueller

**It would seem** just the opposite. People lose their friends, their families, and their jobs for being followers of Jesus. They have bad things said about them—or to them. They may be arrested and even sent to prison. Sometimes they die because they belong to Jesus; at one point Christians were the main course for lions' lunches!

But the quote above doesn't say, "The more we know of God, the easier we have it." Life is hard for everyone, full of little problems and big ones. Even the people who *seem* to have easy lives carry burdens we can't see.

So how can we be happy? Wouldn't you be happy if you knew—*really* knew—someone who loves you, is always there for you, who is with you in all your troubles, who will take care of you when you can't take care of yourself, who will take charge of you and tell you where to go so you'll know what is good? I think so.

This isn't the temporary "happy" feeling you get winning a soccer game or getting a birthday present. It's much deeper, and much longer-lasting. Another word for it is *joy*.

*Mary Lichlyter*

For in the day of trouble he will
keep me safe in his dwelling…
**Psalm 27:5** (NIV)

# April 25

"'But, as I told you, it is not everybody can see it.'
'How is it that I can, then? I'm sure I don't know.'
'It is a gift born with you. And one day I hope everybody will have it.'"
*The Princess and the Goblin,* by George MacDonald

Jesus replied, "Very truly I tell you, no one can see the kingdom of God unless they are born again."
**John 3:3**

**Eyes are meant** to see.

African lions see eight times more than you can see at night! They have some special cells in their eyes that are particularly sensitive to light. Under their eyes is a white line of fur which also works to reflect light into their eyes. Lions are made for night! For them it is clear—for us it is dark. It takes time for our eyes to adjust!

Our eyes are to see in this world—but there are other eyes that help us see things of Spirit.

These are spiritual eyes. They come from God and you must be born again in your spirit to have spiritual eyes. The spiritual eyes that the Lord God gives us enables us to see things that are of Him; it is like having the light turned on and everything becoming clear to us. This is a gift! To be born again is a gift from God! If in your heart you are calling out—wanting God—it is because God is calling out, wanting you! It is He who wants to be your life. He wants to give you His spiritual eyes! He wants that for everyone! I wonder what will be your answer when He calls?

*Blythe Followwill*
*For Charles*

# April 26

> The LORD is gracious and compassionate, slow to anger and rich in love. The LORD is good to all; he has compassion on all he has made.
> **Psalm 145:8-9**

**How would someone** describe you? Could anyone describe you as gracious and compassionate, slow to anger, rich in love, good to all? To be like God must be our goal!

Your personality is not determined at birth; other people or events are not responsible for the kind of person you will become. You may be born with a certain temperament; and other people and events will certainly influence you. But only you can decide how you will respond to life, and how you will shape your own character.

Maybe you think that unfairness or cruelty in life keeps you from being good. It need not be so. Years ago, I was badly hurt by someone. I was angry and bitter. Yet I knew that I did not want to be an angry, bitter person! I prayed every day for God to help me. I had to fight the ugly thoughts that were in my mind and heart. It took time and effort and the grace of God to help me to overcome influences which might have allowed me to become a very sad person. I continue to strive to grow into a more loving, compassionate person.

Praise be to God who is truly gracious and compassionate; slow to anger and rich in love; good to all and compassionate to all His children! Praise be to Him who chooses and calls us and who helps us with grace to become as He is!

*Sharon Edel*

# April 27

So, because you are lukewarm—neither hot nor cold—I am about to spit you out of my mouth.
**Revelation 3:16**

**Do you drink** your lemonade warm, or do you like your French fries cold? Favorite foods can taste unsavory if they aren't at the right temperature! Love, like some foods, disappoints if it is merely lukewarm.

God uses this funny analogy for a serious message. God, who is absolutely passionate in loving His children, is insulted if we treat Him casually, indifferently.

A young George MacDonald once wrote these words to his father: *"Pray that I may not be that hateful thing, a lukewarm Christian."* As a young man who would go on to become a powerful preacher and writer, MacDonald understood that Christianity is not simply being a member of a church or calling oneself part of a particular group. MacDonald said that *"indifference itself is an injustice"* and insisted that we must become true sons of the Father, striving to be made into the image of Christ, the perfect Son, obedient and humble. The child of God learns to obey and to strive for goodness, not for fear of punishment; but for fear of offending the Father he loves.

Can you strive to make this glorious exclamation of George MacDonald your own?

"He is my life, my joy, my lord, my owner, the perfecter of my being by the perfection of his own. I dare not say with Paul that I am the slave of Christ; but my highest aspiration and desire is to be the slave of Christ."
*Unspoken Sermons,* by George MacDonald

*Sharon Edel*

# April 28

**When you are** hungry, you go to the refrigerator or the cupboards and find something to eat. If you're thirsty, you can turn on the faucet and fill up a glass with water. Thanks to your parents, you don't have to worry about being hungry, because they have filled the cupboards with groceries, even your favorite foods.

In Bible times, it was a shepherd's responsibility to watch over his flock of sheep, just like your parents care for you. The shepherd would look for a pasture of grass where the sheep could eat, and also a stream of water when they were thirsty. He also watched out for danger, so the sheep always knew they were safe under his care.

Jesus is our Shepherd. He watches over us to supply our needs and keep us safe. When we pray, we thank Him for the blessings we have received, and we ask Him for the things we need. Is God like a vending machine, giving us anything we ask for? No. Elisabeth Elliot said, "God has promised to supply all our needs. What we don't have now, we don't need now." Isn't it good to know that we have a heavenly Father who supplies not our every want, but our every need?

*Thank you, Jesus for keeping me safe. I lack nothing that I need. Amen.*

*Barbara Hollace*

The Lord is my Shepherd, I lack nothing.
**Psalm 23:1** (NIV)

# April 29

**I admit it.** Cheerfulness is not my natural disposition. And even those who *are* by nature cheerful will have bad moments or days! Most Christians are nowhere near perfect, but each is struggling in his or her own way to better follow Jesus.

Some days the Golden Rule of treating others the way I want to be treated may seem like more than I can muster! Sometimes I just can't seem to smile and think of happy things to say. I may not be the first to volunteer to help my neighbor or to offer sparkling conversation. On those days, I try to fall back on what is known as the "Silver Rule," which is "do no harm." I try to do the next best thing, which may mean not saying the unhappy thoughts I am thinking; not refusing to help if asked; not deliberately offending my neighbor simply because I am not in a joyful mood! Sometimes love for God is shown by what you *don't* do, as much as what you do!

If we were perfect, we would always go beyond the minimum; but sometimes even the minimum may greatly please God! Simply to keep oneself from acting unpleasantly may be real and significant progress in following Jesus!

*Sharon Edel*

Love does no harm to a neighbor.
Therefore love is the fulfillment of the law.
**Romans 3:10**

# April 30

"'I am weak,' says the true soul, 'but not so weak that I would not be strong; not so sleepy that I would not see the sun rise; not so lame but that I would walk! Thanks be to him who perfects strength in weakness, and gives to his beloved while they sleep!'"

*Unspoken Sermons, Third Series,* by George MacDonald

**Have you ever** felt frustrated when you're working really hard to understand a new subject in school and you just don't get it? Do you sometimes forget to clean your room—or just don't want to clean it—and your mom or dad takes privileges away from you? Have you struggled to get up early to catch the bus or be ready on time for an event? The simple fact of life is that we all struggle at times. It could be anything from the little daily challenges, or things like sickness and even diseases like cancer.

Your Heavenly Father understands your struggles. When you are weak in yourself, then you are strong in God's grace. It isn't something we can easily understand with our minds. It's a mystery. But, God says you can brag about your weaknesses and know that God's power will rest on you. Isn't that amazing!? He says to us in His word,

"My grace is sufficient for you, for my power is made perfect in weakness." Therefore I will boast all the more gladly about my weaknesses, so that Christ's power may rest on me.

**2 Corinthians 12:9 (NIV)**

It is important to realize our need for God's help, and then allow Him to show us that His power is like a shelter and a protection for us.

*Rennie Marie Sneed*

# May 1

**In George MacDonald's book** *Sir Gibbie,* when the child Gibbie was no longer an orphan but was welcomed into the Grant family, his new mother, Janet, would read to him and teach him about what she knew best: her Savior, Jesus.

"So teaching him only that which she loved, not that which she had been taught, Janet read to Gibbie of Jesus, and talked to him of Jesus, until at length his whole soul was full of the Man, of His doings, of His words, of His thoughts, of His life. Almost before he knew, he was trying to fashion his life after that of the Master."

Isn't that wonderful? No matter how young we are, or where we are, or what mistakes or poor choices we have made, as we learn about Jesus and try to fashion our lives after His, grace and wisdom will grow in us. Even though we may be young, each day we can grow in wisdom and the grace of God. Bit by bit, little by little, if we decide to learn about Him and try to follow His example, we will grow wiser. We will learn and grow into the man or woman God wants us to be one day.

*Jolyn Canty*

And the Child continued to grow and become strong, increasing in wisdom; and the grace of God was upon Him.
**Luke 2:40** (NASV)

# May 2

> By day The LORD went ahead of them in pillar of cloud to guide them on their way and by night in a pillar of fire to give them light...
> **Exodus 13:21 (NIV)**

**Ayden loved nothing** more than fishing with his dad, stealing away at any chance together, just to get a hook wet. These were special times between father and son. They wore identical baseball caps to keep the sun out of their eyes. Breezes were always a welcomed comfort, cooling off their sweaty brows. Patient delight came, as Ayden reeled in those fish foolish enough to take his bait.

Cloud formations upon the blue canopied sky fascinated Ayden; he always pointing out the unusual ones to his Dad, who eagerly observed all his son shared.

"Once," his father said, "God used a cloud to lead the Israelites through the desert on their journey from Egypt to the Promised Land. As the cloud moved, they moved; whenever it rested, they rested. Also, God gave them a pillar of fire at night, His light of assurance that He was protecting and watching over them. The Israelites followed the cloud and the pillar of fire, learning to trust God's steadfast love.

"Trust is powerful, built between two people who love each other—kind of like the relationship between a father and a son! God's a promise keeper; always has been, always will be. His greatest promises—Jesus Christ, and The Holy Spirit—remind us of this. I'm a promise keeper too, but I'm human, and sometimes I fail. But God will never fail you, never!"

The sun was starting to set low in the sky, and Ayden knew it was time to reel the lines in and head home.

*Lisa Blair*

# May 3

**Imagine for a** moment that God is coming to your house for a visit tonight! How would that make you feel?

Your Father God longs to be invited into your life. He wants to move in and stay! Your heart is such an important part of your body, kind of like the kitchen or the living room is the heart of a home, a place where love is shared and your family gathers. Everything you do flows from your heart, so protect it.

In the Bible, in the Old Testament, God lived in a temple, a really fancy building. Today God lives in the hearts of people who invite Him to make Himself at home in them.

We have to make choices daily. Jesus helps us make *good* choices. As our love for Jesus grows, it's easier to do the right thing. Do you know when you obey your mom and dad, you are also obeying and pleasing God? When we obey Him, Jesus feels at home in us and we bring a smile to His face!

*Rennie Marie Sneed*

Jesus replied, "Anyone who loves me will obey my teaching. My Father will love them, and we will come to them and make our home with them."
**John 14:23** (NIV)

And in Him you too are being built together to become a dwelling in which God lives...
**Ephesians 2:22** (NIV)

# May 4

> Keep this Book of the Law always on your lips; meditate on it day and night, so that you may be careful to do everything written in it. Then you will be prosperous and successful.
> **Joshua 1:8 (NIV)**

**The captain of** your school team will not be able to lead the team for the competition this time. The principal comes to you and says, "We need you to be the lead for this game. You've been on the team for a little while, and we need you to step up and lead."

How do you feel?

That is probably how Joshua felt when Moses, the great leader of Israel, had died and God asked him to lead the Israelites into the land that He had promised to give them.

What? How? Where do I start?

God told him exactly what and how to do this enormous job in our verse today. He told Joshua that he would be successful as long as he studied and thought deeply about God's Law. That would tell him all he needed about how to act and what to do.

He also told him to be "strong and courageous," because it would be a tough job, but God Himself would be with Him.

What scary situation are you facing today? God tells you, like Joshua, to study His Word and think about it deeply so you can understand Him and do things His way. He will give you the strength and the courage you need to do even the scariest jobs!

*Alba Rice*

# May 5

> Trust in the Lord, and do good; dwell in the land and befriend faithfulness. Delight yourself in the Lord and he will give you the desires of your heart.
> **Psalm 37:3-4 (ESV)**

**Have you ever** found yourself upset or worried because someone got away with being naughty? It happens all the time, and it can be very frustrating. But Psalm 37:1 tells us to, "Fret not because of wrongdoing," and to not be jealous of those who get away with bad behavior "...for they will soon fade like the grass." In other words, there are many evils in this world, and we cannot stop them all from happening. Instead of worrying about them, God tells us to trust Him and focus on His presence, which is a delightful thing.

In *Phantastes*, a fairy-tale by George MacDonald, a man discovers a way into Fairy Land. While he is there he finds himself followed by a dark shadow which represents his evil, or sinful, side. Yet when he visits the Fairy Queen's palace, his shadow disappears because evil cannot abide in the presence of Good. So it is with God. Focus on the goodness and faithfulness of God. Delight yourself in His presence, which is as vast and beautiful as Fairy Land itself. And one day He will make all the wrong things right in the world and He will give you the pure desires of your heart.

*Heidi Livingston*

# May 6

**We people like** tangible things—things that we can see and feel. We think that we can relate to a person or understand a person because we can physically see them and the things they have. What if the Lord looked at us the same way that we look at others? Worse, what if He judged us in the same way that we judge others? How would it feel to know that in order to receive grace and forgiveness, we had to be exactly as the Loard intended us to be?

It is comforting to know that our Lord doesn't care what we look like or what tangible items we may have. Our Lord is more concerned with our heart. Our heart gives so much life to us. We need to share that same thing with others. Being kind, helpful, and loving are attributes that come from our heart. It isn't hard to extend a helping hand or give a compliment by being nice to another person.

Today, walk in the way of the Lord. Practice being kind and helpful to someone. Do not look at the outward appearance of a person, but look into their heart.

*Laura Bennin*

But the Lord said to Samuel, "Do not consider his appearance or his height, for I have rejected him. The Lord does not look at the things people look at. People look at the outward appearance, but the Lord looks at the heart."

**Samuel 16:7 (NIV)**

# May 7

She opens her mouth with wisdom; and
on her tongue is the law of kindness.
**Proverbs 31:26 (NIV)**

**Princess Olivia played** beneath an ancient Shemesh tree, as her guardian Gigi, a tiger, faithfully watched over her. Zayith, her Kingdom, was situated on the north side of the everlasting star, just a little west of the great Milky Way. Olivia was a beautiful little princess, with white shining hair, illuminated by the sun's rays. Her eyes were big, blue, soft vessels of God's peaceful love. She was a gentle soul, and was called "The Little Princess of Peace."

Her precious hands dripped with glowing oil that compassionately brought healing to everyone she touched or hugged with tight arms, never turning away anyone in need, even the outcast. Sick people from near and far came to receive healing from the little princess.

Gigi guarded Princess Olivia closely. One day, a gravely ill old woman was brought for healing beneath the ancient Shemesh Tree. Without hesitating, Princess Olivia wrapped her arms around the sickly old woman. Princess Olivia began to cry, as the old woman was very ill. Gigi, fearing for the little princess, tried to stop her, but the little princess would have none of it, shouting, "Gigi, leave me alone, I must help her, I must!" Obediently, Gigi backed away. Suddenly the old woman began to cry loudly, miraculously changing into an angel, rising instantly off her sick bed. She spoke to the princess, "Little princess, your unchained compassion to heal the very sick and unwanted has been seen in heaven above; truly you have the wisdom of the ages, and from your mouth come rivers of kindness!"

*Lisa Blair*

# May 8

**I slipped in** the mud today!

Walking with a friend, I incautiously stepped on a slick, steep spot of ground and almost immediately found myself sitting in the grass! I wasn't hurt, but I was very dirty. Mud covered my shoes, my arms, my trousers. I washed off the most obvious mud, but I missed a few spots, later discovering a smear along my lower leg. It was impossible to get completely clean!

Being muddy reminds me of what being a sinner is like. Sometimes we do things that make us feel dirty inside. Sometimes we just *think* something, and we feel dirty inside! And no matter how hard we try to wash ourselves inside, no matter how hard we try to do what is right, it's impossible to altogether stop doing the things that make us feel dirty.

Yet even though we can't make ourselves clean, God can. The apostle John writes,

> If we confess our sins, he is faithful and just and will forgive us our sins and purify us from all unrighteousness.
> **1 John 1:9 (NIV)**

To "purify" something means to clean it up, to get rid of the things that do not belong there. When God purifies us, He scrubs off all the dirt that does not belong on us, so that we become again as He wants us to be: clean, holy, beautiful.

Do not give up on yourself, nor think you are ever too dirty for God. He loves you deeply, and through His Son Jesus Christ, He will wash all the dirt away till you are shining white again!

*Megan Von Bergen*

# May 9

Children, obey your parents in the Lord, for this is right.
**Ephesians 6:1 (NIV)**

**"Make your bed."** "Drink your milk." "Do your homework." "Brush your teeth." "Stop hitting your brother." "Pick up your toys." "Feed the dog."

Parents spend a lot of time giving orders. It is hard to do everything they expect. Sometimes, it just seems parents are being mean with all their endless commands.

The Bible says children are to obey their parents. But, that just takes all the fun out of life, right? Why are they always ordering their kids around?

A missionary came to our church. The missionary had a wife and two children. They lived in remote area of the world. Just outside their yard was a dense jungle. The jungle held many fascinations and great beauty, but also many dangers. One day the missionary's two children were heading in to the jungle on an adventure along a path. The missionary watched from the porch for moment, then called to his children to walk calmly and immediately back to the house. The children had learned to obey their parents, so did as their dad asked without arguing or questioning. When they got back to the house, their dad turned them around to look toward the jungle where they had just been. From one of the trees, a deadly snake was dangling just over the path they had taken.

Because these children had learned the importance of obeying their parents without question, their lives were saved.

Why obey parents? They are on this earth to teach, to train, and to protect.

Thank you, Lord, for parents.

*Sharon Kadlub*

# May 10

## Humility

**The weather was** frightening with close lightning flashes and thunder that shook the ground. Bailee Nicole felt safe as she leaned against the warm bricks of the fireplace. It was not only comforting, but gave light to the dark house.

A knock at the door broke the silence within. A woman with two wet, frightened little girls was invited in; with their car broken down and no way to call for help they had walked through the rain.

Bailee Nicole watched as her mom brought them near the fire. With Bailee's help they were given towels to dry with and blankets for warmth. Hot cocoa and donuts were served and enjoyed. Bailee thought, it's almost a party. The Bible says,

> For I say, through grace given unto me, to every man that is among you, not to think of himself more highly than he ought to think…
> **Romans 12:3a (KJV)**

Bailee's Pastor said we were not to think of ourselves as better, but we are to humbly serve others in need.

Her mom had given the strangers warmth, shelter, and food. Off Bailee went with the flashlight to her bedroom. Grabbing two of her cherished stuffed animals, she gave them to the little girls. The girls were thrilled with their gifts and said, "Thank you" with shy smiles.

Bailee's unselfishness certainly was a way of serving the Lord. As the lights came back on, the storm moved on and help was on the way. It certainly did seem like a party. There are times when we must be Jesus's Hands, to bring others joy in the darkness.

*Dottie Thornton*

# May 11

> Be strong and courageous. Do not be afraid or terrified because of them, for the LORD your God goes with you; he will never leave you nor forsake you.
> **Deuteronomy 31:6 (NIV)**

**Have you ever** wondered how the men and women of old were able to accomplish such extraordinary deeds—how they shut the mouths of lions, or became powerful in battle, where they got the strength and courage to do what needed to be done? In his story *At the Back of the North Wind,* George MacDonald tells of a little boy named Diamond who must learn to overcome his fear. Let's listen in as he and North Wind talk about this.

> "But I wasn't brave of myself," said Diamond. "It was the wind that blew in my face that made me brave. Wasn't it now, North Wind?"
>
> "Yes: I know that. You had to be taught what courage was. And you couldn't know what it was without feeling it: therefore it was given you. But don't you feel as if you would try to be brave yourself next time?"
>
> "Yes, I do. But trying is not much."
>
> "Yes, it is—a very great deal, for it is a beginning. And a beginning is the greatest thing of all. To try to be brave is to be brave. The coward who tries to be brave is before the man who is brave because he is made so, and never had to try."

*Steve Fronk*
*For Calli Rae and all who have to try to be brave*

# May 12

**When I was** a child, my mother would read to me from a large Bible story book. I would sit next to her and see beautiful drawings of the Garden of Eden, Noah and the Ark, and many more, accompanied by a lovely story from the Bible. But there was one that was different. It was a drawing of a man whose hair was untidy, his eyes like nothing I had ever seen, and barely any clothes covering him. Who was this man? Why was the story called "Legion?"

The book of Mark gives the most detail (Mark 5: 1-20) about a man who was demon-possessed and healed by Jesus. Jesus was traveling by boat to the country of Gadarenes, when he encountered a man living in a cemetery, cutting himself with stones. When the man saw Jesus, he cried out, "What have I to do with You, Jesus, Son of the Most High God? I implore You by God that You do not torment me." Even the demons knew that Jesus is the Son of God!

Jesus addressed the demons, asking their name. The reply? "My name is Legion; for we are many." Jesus cast the demons into pigs, and the pigs threw themselves off a cliff. The man was healed! He asked to go with Jesus, but Jesus told him to stay and tell his friends how he was delivered.

Jesus will hear everyone who cries out to Him for help.

*Deborah Williams-Smith*

> Go home to your friends, and tell them what great things the Lord has done for you, and how He has had compassion on you.
> **Mark 5:19 (NKJV)**

# May 13

**Imagine a father** who is watching his son take his first steps. He is pleased and full of joy, because the boy is starting to grow. But the father does not wish him to remain that way; he wants his child to grow to be a man.

A great Christian writer, George MacDonald, once said, "God is easy to please and hard to satisfy." MacDonald meant that at each step of our lives, God is pleased with us. He gives us life, and watches us grow in our relationship with Him and others. At the same time, God will not be satisfied until we are perfect and that will only happen when we enter into his eternal kingdom, the new Heaven and the new Earth.

Please do not think that I am saying that you must work hard for the pleasure of Jesus. He is pleased with you just the way you are, but he is not content to leave you that way. How we use our words, how we spend our money and our time, and how we treat others—these are the ways we live the Kingdom of Heaven every day.

When Jesus taught his disciples to pray, he said, "on Earth as it is in Heaven."

Think about the love and faithfulness of Jesus in your life. It is not about *our* name being great, but the name of Jesus. Each step we take, God is pleased. He is helping us to grow up fully, and that takes a lifetime.

*Matthew Nash*

Not to us, Lord, not to us but to your name be the glory, because of your love and faithfulness.
**Psalm 115:1 (NIV)**

# May 14

> For the Spirit God gave us does not make us timid, but gives us power, love and self-discipline.
> **2 Timothy 1:7** (NIV)

**There once was** a girl that was very fearful and unsure of herself. She even found it hard to talk! People had a hard time understanding her, and kids at school made fun of her, which didn't help her self-esteem.

But she had a friend. She had always known that God loved her. He was always by her side. He stood with her when everyone else made fun of her. He knew her loneliness. He knew her strength. He knew her heart. And most of all, He knew her fear.

Her greatest fear (and the one that paralyzed her constantly) was that her father would, one day, never again come home. But he always did! No matter how big the fear, God always brought her father home.

So, in time, she realized that God could conquer all her fears. She knew who she was, and that no matter what life handed her, she was never alone. She began to speak more clearly. She was not afraid. She was strong.

*Karen Thornton*

# May 15

**There is an** amazing book called *The Princess and Curdie,* written by George McDonald, that tells of a miner boy who must go on a sacred and sometimes scary quest. In order to make him ready, an old princess "cleansed" him by burning his hands with a special fire that allowed him to see what was in a person's heart.

When we give our hearts and lives to Jesus and choose to live for Him, He purifies us by testing our faith and giving us opportunities to trust Him in every area of our lives. This refiner's fire is something that, over the course of our lives, makes us into the people God has called us to be, living for His glory and honor as our King. But don't be scared away, thinking that your life is going to be full of hills that you can't climb, temptations that are just too much for you (like playing that video game for two days straight, or gossiping about the new girl in class), or things that are too hard even to think about. Yes, life will have its tests, and not everyday can be a trip to the local fair. Remember that it is our God and Saviour Jesus that will walk hand in hand with us through the difficult parts; we just have to grasp the hand that is waiting to show us the way!

*Holly Van Shouwen*

These have come so that the proven genuineness of your faith—of greater worth than gold, which perishes even though refined by fire—may result in praise, glory and honor when Jesus Christ is revealed.
**1 Peter 1:7 (NIV)**

# May 16

Cast all your anxiety on Him because He cares for you.
**1 Peter 5:7 (NIV)**

**Have you ever** worried about what is going to happen to you? How your school year will go? Who will come to your birthday party? Whether it will it rain on the day you want to go to the beach? Why someone in your house is yelling? Why there is so much fighting in the world? These are legitimate things to be concerned about.

But what happens when concern turns to constant worry? That is some of what anxiety means. Who do you talk to when you are worried? Mom and Dad? Grandma and Grandpa? Your pastor, priest, or a good friend?

What about God? Do you tell Him your worries?

In the Bible, the Apostle Paul says we should pray without ceasing. How can we do that? And why? Doesn't God already know what we are going to say? Yes, He does. Yet, He asks us to be in contact with Him as much as we can. And Peter tells us why: "…because He cares for you." God wants you to understand how much He cares. He cares enough to listen when you pray. He cares enough to help you when you ask. He cares enough to send Jesus to become a baby, to live a perfect life, to die a terrible death, to rise again to life, and to return home to heaven. What wonderful care!

God will take your anxiety, and allow you to live freely and confidently in the love that He has shown you, so that you can show love and care to those around you.

*Amy Farley*

# May 17

> David said to the Philistine, "You come against me with sword and spear and javelin, but I come against you in the name of the LORD Almighty, the God of the armies of Israel, whom you have defied."
> **1 Samuel 17:45** (NIV)

**This verse is** in part of the Bible that tells about David meeting Goliath. David was a young shepherd boy in Israel; Goliath was a giant and one of the mighty warriors of the Philistines, who hated the Israelites. The giant stood in a valley, cursed against God, and dared the Israelite army to send someone to fight him. When young David came down the hill, Goliath made fun of him and promised to defeat him. However, unlike the giant's proud boast in his own strength and skill, David announced his reliance on the Lord.

Well, things did not turn out the way the giant expected them to. David was a young man, perhaps only a few years older than you are; however, as it says in today's verse, he did not depend on his own strength. Instead, David trusted in God and beat Goliath in a surprise victory.

People your age have an advantage over grown-ups. Some people might not think about trusting God fully until they are adults; by then, they already have doubts and fears that are hard to overcome. I challenge you to be like David, starting right now while you are young. Do not be conceited like Goliath, but do not be afraid. Stand for God, and trust Him to lead you in the way that honors Him.

*William F. Powers and Jerian Powers*

# May 18

## Commitment

**Brandi thought of** the verse and the challenge in Sunday School. "What can I commit to for the Lord; I'm just a kid!"

Several days went by and Brandi still did not have a plan. She sat on the porch, rocking and thinking. Brandi heard her neighbor pushing a wheelchair out of the home next door. Beth's mom was blind, so being outside was a treat. "It's me, Brandi, Mrs. Carter. Would you like some company?" Brandi loved to visit with her. They talked, and the visit was good. Brandi listened as her elderly friend talked about the things she used to do; reading, writing letters, even sketching… all in the past.

That night, Brandi sat up in bed, unable to sleep. "Why didn't I think of this sooner? It's so simple." She realized how hard it must be not to read her books, not to see, to write, or to draw. The next day she committed herself to spend Saturday afternoons with Mrs. Carter. She would read and write letters for her; this would take a burden off of Beth, too. Brandi was excited about her commitment, but she knew she would have to trust the Lord to help her.

The Lord kept His word, and Brandi grew in her faith as she committed to helping others.

*Dottie Thornton*

Commit thy way unto the Lord; trust also in him, and he shall bring it to pass.
**Psalm 37:5** (KJV)

# May 19

They show that the requirements of the law are written on their hearts, their consciences also bearing witness, and their thoughts sometimes accusing them and at other times even defending them.
**Romans 2:15 (NIV)**

***The Shadows* is** a fascinating tale written by George McDonald. In it, some very bizarre shadows spend their entire lives casting black images of the wrongs that people have done, in the hope that they will see what they have done and repent. Imagine if every sin that we committed was shown to us in such a public and scary way: that time that you cheated on a math test but were sure no one saw it; or that movie that you should not have watched even though your friends told you it was okay, but then you found yourself thinking about situations that were very violent and cruel.

God has built into the heart of every human being, even children, a conscience that tells us when we shouldn't be doing something, or when we have done something to hurt someone or disobey God's commandments. Our conscience is a very private thing and we should be grateful for this. As we grow in our relationship with Jesus and God our Father, our conscience, which is the Holy Spirit, grows stronger and we can feel Him guide our lives and direct the paths we are taking. Your path in school, at home, or at play can be firm and your feet will go exactly where God wants you if only you listen and trust what He is saying to you.

*Holly Van Shouwen*

# May 20

> I will give thanks to You, for I am fearfully and wonderfully made; wonderful are Your works, and my soul knows it very well.
> **Psalm 139:14 (NASB)**

**Life is a** miracle. God made you as a unique and amazing individual. *You* are a miracle. Have you ever thought about that? No one in the world can say that they have never seen or experienced a miracle, because they *are* one. There is no one exactly like you. You are "fearfully and wonderfully made."

Words we find in the Bible don't always have exactly the same meaning that they do now. The word "fearfully" does not mean to be afraid. Instead it means respect or reverence. The word "wonderfully' means to be set-apart, special and unique. God created you with an endless love and reverence to be set-apart and uniquely you.

Sometimes we worry and wonder, why am I here? What is my worth? There are millions of people on this earth, why was I created?

Think about this: God did not have to make you. There are lots of people in the world. But God *did* make you. He lovingly crafted you because He wanted you. He created you, and only one you. There will never be and has never been another like you. You are loved. You are special. You are enough. You have purpose.

Remember to take the time to thank and praise God for creating you. Treat His creation with care and respect. Honor the body and mind and soul with which God has blessed you.

*Kelly Schweiger*

# May 21

## Y.O.L.O.

People have to die once. After that, God will judge them.
**Hebrews 9:27 (NIRV)**

**You Only Live Once.** The popular term Y.O.L.O., meaning "You only live once," is frequently used as a license to party, splurge, and live for the moment, without considering the consequences. However, even though the phrase is accurate, it is incomplete. The Bible says in the book of Hebrews that after we die we face judgement. "We do live only once. The choices we make during our life determine our final destination. The Bible says in Joshua 24:15, "Choose ye this day whom you will serve, As for me and my house we will serve the Lord." Serving the Lord is not a difficult task: He is not a harsh taskmaster, requiring us to forsake everything we enjoy for a life of subjugation and boredom; He is a friend that sticks closer than a brother. In His presence is fullness of joy and at His right hand are pleasures forevermore. He cautions us against a lifestyle that leads to death, destruction, and eventually to eternal separation from God, simply because He loves us and wants to spend eternity with us. The Bible says, "Eye has not seen nor has it entered into the heart of man what God has prepared for those that love Him."

Again, as the Word says, "Choose life and you shall live." God has given us a choice to make regarding our final destination. Jesus said in John 14:6, "I am the way, the truth and the life. No one comes to the Father except through me." Choose wisely, for your choice is irrevocable after death.

*Prithika*

# May 22

"I could give you twenty names more to call me, Curdie, and not one of them would be a false one. What does it matter how many names if the person is one?"

"Ah! But it is not names only, ma'am. Look at what you were like last night, and what I see you now!"

"Shapes are only dresses, Curdie, and dresses are only names. That which is inside is the same all the time."

"But then how can all the shapes speak the truth?"

"It would want thousands more to speak the truth, Curdie; and then they could not."

*The Princess and Curdie,* by George MacDonald

**God has many** names, but HE never changes. He is the same yesterday, today, and forever!

If you turn back all the pages of time to the very, very beginning, you will see Him there as Creator, and if you go back further—before time began—He is still God Almighty! If you find the 'Year of our Lord', you will find that God became man, and after He left earth He sent Himself in Spirit! He may change His appearance—but *He* remains the same!

Water is like that: water can be solid when it is frozen, water can be fluid and pour, water can also be steam which evaporates into the atmosphere. Still, it is water! The body of it changes form, but what it is, the substance, remains the same.

God has many names, but there is only One God, One Lord, One Spirit, and they remain One.

*Blythe Followwill*
*For Paden*

"I AM the Alpha and Omega," says the LORD GOD, "Who is and Who was and Who is to come, the ALMIGHTY."
**Revelation 1:8 (NIV)**

# May 23

For we live by faith, not by sight.
**2 Corinthians 5:7 (NIV)**

**If you have** ever been high up in the air, in a plane or on top of a building, you may understand the fear some people have of heights. But imagine the feeling of having to step out onto what appears to be nothing. This is just where Curdie finds himself in George MacDonald's story *The Princess and Curdie*.

"'Come in,' said the voice of the princess.

Curdie opened the door—but, to his astonishment, saw no room there. Could he have opened a wrong door? There was the great sky, and the stars, and beneath he could see nothing, only darkness! But what was that in the sky, straight in front of him? A great wheel of fire, turning and turning, and flashing out blue lights!

'Come in, Curdie,' said the voice again.

'I would at once, ma'am,' said Curdie, 'if I were sure I was standing at your door.'

'Why should you doubt it, Curdie?'

'Because I see neither walls nor floor, only darkness and the great sky.' 'That is all right, Curdie. Come in.'

Curdie stepped forward at once. He was indeed, for the very crumb of a moment, tempted to feel before him with his foot; but he saw that would be to distrust the princess, and a greater rudeness he could not offer her. So he stepped straight in—I will not say without a little tremble at the thought of finding no floor beneath his foot. But that which had need of the floor found it, and his foot was satisfied."

*Steve Fronk*
*For Isaac Albert*

# May 24

**You have life** because God saw fit to give it to you. He knew everything that you would do, yet He still loves you. Not a single one of us is perfect, nor deserving of His awesome grace, yet there it is, a free gift from our living and loving Heavenly Father. Stop trying to do anything to earn His free gift of grace. Pray and ask God for His awesome strength, wisdom, guidance, and encouragement in all of your decisions, so that all that you think, do, and say are honoring to God. Recognize the fact that every one of us fails at trying to be exactly like Jesus, but that should not discourage us from serving others in His name. Learn from your mistakes and trust God to change you from the inside out. Grow a genuine relationship with Him and see how He transforms your life. He will never leave your side. He loves each of us perfectly, and way too much to leave us in our sinful lives. Repent and agree with God that we need Him every single hour of every single day.

*J. Richard Martinez*

O LORD, you hear the desire of the afflicted: you will strengthen their heart; you will incline your ear to do justice to the fatherless and the oppressed, so that man who is of the earth may strike terror no more.
**Psalm 10:17-18 (ESV)**

# May 25

He took the blind man by the hand and led him outside the village. When he had spit on the man's eyes and put his hands on him, Jesus asked, "Do you see anything?" He looked up and said, "I see people; they look like trees walking around." Once more Jesus put his hands on the man's eyes. Then his eyes were opened, his sight was restored, and he saw everything clearly.

**Mark 8:23-25** (NIV)

## People Who Look Like Trees

**When reading this** story, most kids don't like to think about Jesus spitting on someone's eyes. It's true! Kids say, "Yuck! That's gross!" But this is one of the best stories in the Bible—spit and all!

After Jesus placed His hands on the blind man's eyes, He asked, "Do you see anything?" The man replied, "I see people; *they look like trees* walking around." Trees! Do you realize how important this is? Jesus gave the man a chance to see people through God's eyes. He opened the man's spiritual eyes first. Then, He restored his physical eyesight. From that point forward, the man knew the difference between spiritual and physical eyesight.

People are like living, growing trees planted on the earth to produce seed and fruit for the world. This is our spiritual image! When we look at people through God's eyes, we too will be able to see them as trees walking around. What kind of tree are you? A tall oak tree with deep roots and acorns? An aspen with white bark and golden yellow leaves? A pear tree? A pine tree with long, slender needles? A willow with weeping branches swaying in the wind?

*Carol Wimmer*

# May 26

"I was doing the wrong of never wanting or trying to be better. And now I see that I have been letting things go as they would for a long time. Whatever came into my head I did, and whatever didn't come into my head I didn't do."
*The Princess and Curdie,* by George MacDonald

**Many of us** live with a very dangerous thought in our heads. We might not even be fully aware of the thought or the danger. The thought is: "I'm good enough." But why is this bad? "After all," you may think, "I really am not so bad!"

Firstly, it is clearly not what Jesus has in mind for us, as He tells us:

Be perfect, therefore, as your heavenly Father is perfect.
**Matthew 5:48** (NIV)

Secondly, the idea that I am good enough implies that I am better than others, an attitude of pride and self-righteousness. And finally, it suggests that I am not much in need of Jesus, who came to call sinners, rather than "good enough" people like me.

Do not be alarmed by the command to be perfect, a seemingly impossible command. Know that God has the power to perfect, and He will do so at the proper time. Until then, the command to be perfect reminds us that we are still in need of God's mercy; that we are indeed the sinners that He has come to call, and that we are ever being called to more goodness, more loveliness, more compassion.

Praise be to God who calls us upward in Christ Jesus!

*Sharon Edel*

# May 27

"Yes, Lord," she replied, "I believe that you are the Messiah, the Son of God, who is to come into the world."
**John 11:27 (NIV)**

**We usually think** of prayer to God as asking, thanking, or praising. Many Christians also include, whether in their public or private prayer, a statement of beliefs based on what has been revealed to us by God. This prayer is known as a creed from the Latin word "credo," meaning "I believe." Two often-recited creeds are the Apostles' Creed and the Nicene Creed.

It may seem odd that a statement of beliefs is considered prayer; but if prayer helps us to better know and understand God, as well as to proclaim Him, then this makes perfect sense. A creed summarizes and reminds us of what we believe; gives us words to express what we believe; and positively affirms our faith before God.

If you have heard or are familiar with one of the Christian creeds, you may at first think that it sounds a bit dull for a prayer. However, take as an example the words of Martha. Her brother had just died. Full of grief and disappointment, Martha yet proclaims: *"Yes, Lord, I believe that you are the Messiah, the Son of God, who is to come into the world."* Her faith triumphs in the face of despair!

Remember also that many Christians have been, and still are, martyred for these beliefs. Suddenly the words of the Creed take on crucial significance and are spoken in earnest. If you were threatened with martyrdom, could you faithfully and fearlessly proclaim the Creed?

*Sharon Edel*

# May 28

> "You have stood more than one trial already, and stood them well; now I am going to put you to a harder. Do you think you are prepared for it?"
>
> *The Princess and Curdie,* by George MacDonald

**This spring, we** raised a yellow and black striped Monarch caterpillar at our house. He hatched from his tiny egg, munched milkweed, and soon morphed into a jade green and gold chrysalis. While he was in the chrysalis, it would tremble and swing precariously. It soon turned dark, then black! During the darkest time, we wondered if our butterfly would make it. Soon, there was a rip, and out came a rumpled Monarch butterfly. Spreading his wings, he showed off his new-found flying skills. Though you may feel like you are cramped in a chrysalis, God is making something new in you. You may wonder if God is still working, even in the darkest times. Through the power of His Holy Spirit and the conviction of His Word, he will change you—and you, like the Monarch, will soar!

*Karise Gililland*

Therefore, if anyone is in Christ, he is a new creation.
**2 Corinthians 5:17** (ESV)

# May 29

## Gentleness

**Bailey sat on** the end of her bed, watching as her new friend played with one of her prized dolls. She had asked Caitlyn to be careful about bending the doll's arms and legs. Bailey's older sister, Alahna, had given her this doll. It was old and it was treasured. Finally, tired of the doll, Caitlyn tossed it onto the bed.

Bailey's mom walked in asking, "Why don't you two play under the water sprinkler?" It was a great idea, but Bailey was not sure she wanted Caitlyn to wear the new swimsuit she had just gotten for her birthday. But, seeing Caitlyn's excitement, she handed it to her. After two hours of hopping, squealing, and playing in the water, two tired little girls went into Bailey's room to change. Both girls, at the same time, fell on the bed. At the sound of a loud snap they jumped up, realizing the doll, now with one arm, had been under the towels. "I told you to be careful with my doll!" Bailey said angrily.

She was certain it was Caitlyn's fault, but Bailey could see she had hurt Caitlyn's feelings. She remembered a wonderful lesson she had heard in Sunday School about being kind. The Bible said:

…be ye kind one to another…
**Ephesians 4:32a (KJV)**

"It's okay, Caitlyn, I think I fell on the doll too. Anyway, my dad can fix anything. I'm sorry I yelled at you. You're still my best friend, aren't you?" Caitlyn giggled, "Yes, I'll be your best friend forever!"

The girls lapsed into squeals of giggles and laughter.

*Dottie Thornton*

# May 30

"And still as she told what Curdie had done, Sir Walter and others added to what she told, even Lootie joining in the praises of his courage and energy. Curdie held his peace, looking quietly up in the king's face. And his mother stood on the outskirts of the crowd listening with delight, for her son's deeds were pleasant in her ears…"

*The Princess and the Goblin,* by George MacDonald

**The greatest gift** a son or daughter can give a mother or father is a life full of good works that honor Jesus Christ, our King.

Everything you do reveals what is in your heart. What is in your heart reveals what you believe is true. Your mother and father love you. They want you to know and hold onto all that is true. They pray and think a lot about how they can teach you the right and pure way to go. They want you to grow strong and beautiful in your mind, heart, and body. When they see you choosing to do what is right, when they hear your behavior has been wise, it is like someone placing on their heads garlands of flowers with the sweetest fragrance! There is no greater gift you can give your parents than the praises of your right and wise behavior.

*Blythe Followwill*
*For Michael*

The father of the righteous will greatly rejoice And he who sires a wise son will be glad in him. Let your father and your mother be glad, And let her rejoice who gave birth to you.

**Proverbs 23:23-24** (NASB)

# May 31

"The phrase, 'the fear of God,' is used, especially in the Old Testament, for the whole of piety…The man who had the fear of God before his eyes was one who believed in God, worshiped God, loved God, was kept back from evil by the thought of God, and moved to good by the desire to please God…But this is our fear: the fear which a dear child has of a tender father. It is not afraid that its father will kill it, or cease to love it, or banish it, and turn it out of his house. It knows better; it trusts its father too well to indulge in such mischievous suspicions; but, because it loves him, it fears to offend him. This is the very atmosphere in which a Christian breathes."
C.H. Spurgeon

**Have you ever** wondered about that expression—"the fear of God?" Some people say God is mean to want people *afraid* of him!

But it's not that kind of fear. It's a really good healthy respect, plus awe and reverence—and trust! Could you trust anyone who frightens you? No way.

You can't fear the Lord but not care about Him. You can't fear Him but go your own way. If that's your attitude, you *might* be afraid of Him. But if you want to please Him because He's wonderful, you have godly fear, and you'll want more of it. Respect, awe, reverence, trust: Someone for whom you have those feelings is Someone to follow and obey.

*Mary Lichlyter*

The fear of the Lord is the beginning of wisdom…
**Proverbs 9:10** (NIV)

# June 1

If any of you lacks wisdom, you should ask God, who gives generously to all without finding fault, and it will be given to you.
**James 1:5 (NIV)**

**Willie was a** boy who found great happiness in being useful to others. George MacDonald wrote about him in the book *Gutta-Percha Willie.*

Willie learned that doing good for others is part of the "general business" of God's work in the Universe—and, "Isn't it a fine thing to have a hand in the general business?" If we try hard to act as God's hands, he will help us do His work.

When Willie was a boy, his mother had a baby girl named Agnes, who cried during the night for a bottle. Because of this his mother was not getting enough sleep and was therefore not very well. Willie "resolved within himself that he would try to get a share in the business of the night: why should his mother have too little sleep rather than himself? They might at least divide the too little between them!"

Willie tried for a few nights to wake up and take care of Agnes, but alas, he always slept too soundly and did not wake up to help so his mother could sleep. He tried very hard to find or think of a way to wake up (in Willie's days there were not alarm clocks or baby-monitors).

Finally, Willie said to himself: "I don't see what I am to do. I wonder if God would wake me if I were to ask Him?" Willie did pray for help, and in the middle of that night "he sat up in bed instantly."

*James House*

# June 2

**Have you ever** wondered what it would be like to talk to the Creator of the universe? Well, you can! Father God will listen to you and wants to have a close personal relationship with you. Sometimes you will hear Him speak to you in a still small voice, deep in your belly. God will give you something designed especially for you to do, and you can set your heart to follow His will.

Would you like to invite a neighbor boy or girl to a game of baseball, but you know they don't have a baseball glove? Maybe you could ask your older brother for that dusty glove in the basement, clean it up, and give it to them. What a smile you would receive for being so kind, and you might even gain a friend for life!

Over two thousand years ago, Jesus included the neighborhood children in his walks through the Galilean countryside. Children would sit on his knee as he talked to them about His Father, God.

> But as for me, I watch in hope for the LORD, I wait for God my Savior; my God will hear me.
> **Micah 7:7** (NIV)

*Father God, thank you for being Lord of my life, and that I have faith that you will help me to succeed day by day with my hand in Your hand. After all, You are Creator God and put a lot of details into making me!*

*Thank you, Jesus. When you and I walk together to accomplish your purposes, You are only a prayer away. Thank you that I am your handiwork!*

*Kathy Foottit*

# June 3

**Imagine with me** just for a moment, that the Creator of the Earth, the moon, the sky and the stars has written your name on the palm of His hand.

Wow! You are really special to Him and are so loved. That is why He wants to be so close to you. He knows your thoughts even before you do!

Sometimes we want to run and jump and play, and then we're so tired after a fun day that we forget to include God in our prayers at night. Even then, He is closer to you than your best buddy. Believe!

Father God wants you to enjoy the life that He has prepared for you, and He will show you the way in His word:

> This is what the Lord says: "Stand at the crossroads and look; ask for the ancient paths, ask where the good way is, and walk in it, and you will find rest for your souls."
> **Jeremiah 6:16 (NIV)**

Praise: Your Heavenly Father will give you sweet dreams filled with special messages and answers to help you to find your way in this wonderful life, because Father God has written your name on the palm of His hand. He is the creator of all that is good!

Psalm 19:1 says: The heavens are telling of the glory of God; and their expanse is declaring the work of His hands.

*Thank you, Father God: Thank you that I am important to you, that my name is always in front of you in giant letters!*

*Kathy Foottit*

# June 4

Be still before the Lord and wait patiently for him...
**Psalm 37:7 (NIV)**

**Waiting—even the** thought of it can make us impatient. Waiting in lines, waiting for birthdays, waiting for Christmas Day...

Life is made up of many times of waiting. Some of the greatest difficulties that we face require us to wait when we would choose to act, sometimes foolishly and outside of God's will. But then the Lord's Word reminds us to "Be still and know that I am God..." (Psalm 46:10). All through the Holy Bible are instances when the Lord required someone to wait in faith for His guidance or instructions on how to act. Look at the lives of Noah, Moses, King David, and our blessed Lord Jesus. God led them, and surely He will lead you if you seek Him with all of your heart.

*J.S. Donald*

Take delight in the Lord, and he will give you the desires of your heart.
**Psalm 37:4 (NIV)**

# June 5

> For God was pleased to have all His fullness dwell in Him (Christ Jesus), and through Him to reconcile to Himself all things, whether things on earth or things in Heaven, by making peace through His blood, shed on the cross.
> **Colossians 1:19-20** (NIV)

**Have you or** someone that you know recently had a beloved pet that died? Are you afraid that the cherished friend will never be seen again? Please know that when Christ Jesus died on the cross and arose again on the third day, He *redeemed* all of mankind that will come to Him by faith, as well as all of Creation.

When Adam and Eve sinned in the Garden of Eden, they and the natural world were put under the control of sin's power, and began to suffer from sickness, getting older, and death. God saw that all living things needed to be restored back to their original state. Because Jesus reconciled all things (made all things right) by dying on the cross, all of creation is saved, and all of mankind can be saved. The only ones who will not see Heaven are the people who say no to the gift of salvation. I have also heard several pastors say that God will do whatever it takes to make us happy in Heaven. What a wonderful thought!

Have you accepted God's free gift of salvation? If so, then you can be sure that you will see all your loved ones that are in Heaven again someday.

*J.S. Donald*

> Therefore, if anyone is in Christ, the new creation has come: The old has gone, the new is here!
> **2 Corinthians 5:17** (NIV)

# June 6

**Tonight the clouds** lay low on the ridge above my home, so that I could hardly see them, and the stars which usually shine brightly over our valley were completely covered. But as I watched, just when it seemed as though the ridge was quite lost in the mist, the highest peak poked through and the brightest stars shone through the misty cloud. It reminded me that even though the ridge, the trees, and the stars were completely covered, they were still standing steadfastly there, and the stars did not cease to shine even when I could not see them.

I find this very comforting. It is a simple truth: our feelings do not affect God's facts. I may feel alone, unloved, worthless, or forgotten, but those feelings are not truth. The truth is that I am never alone, because Jesus said that He will never leave me or forsake me. I am not unloved or worthless or forgotten, because He says that I am loved with an everlasting love, and underneath are the everlasting arms. So I must remember this when feelings cloud my heart. We may not actually see His shining promises, but they are still there, shining. The strength of the hills and mountains reflect His strength, despite my human weakness. Feelings may come and go like the winds and clouds, but the hills and the stars abide, and He will never leave us nor forsake us.

*Jolyn Canty*

...and they were afraid as they entered the cloud. And a voice came out of the cloud, saying, "This is My Son, My Chosen One; listen to Him."
**Luke 9:34-35** (NASV)

# June 7

A new command I give you: Love one another. As I have loved you, so you must love one another.
**John 13:34 (NIV)**

## What Does Love Look Like?

**How do we** obey God and love one another? He gave us a good example. God didn't just *tell* us He loved us, He *showed* us. God loved us by sending Jesus. Jesus helped people who were sick, taught people who wanted to learn, and fed people who were hungry. He gave people what they needed wherever He went.

It's easy to find ways to love one another. Just look around for people who need help. See someone who looks sad? Smile and say hi, or ask if they are ok. Share your lunch with a friend. Be a friend to someone who doesn't have any friends. Help your mom carry the groceries, or hold the door open for an elderly person. There are countless ways to show people love. You don't have to do them all, just remember to be kind to everyone, because kindness is what love looks like.

*Angela Harrison*

# June 8

"'Perhaps some people can see things other people can't see, Curdie,' said his mother..."
*The Princess and the Goblin,* by George MacDonald

**God reveals truth,** but not everyone can see it; God speaks, but not everyone can hear.

God's whole desire is that we know Him! And so He speaks. He speaks through creation, He spoke through His prophets long ago, and He still speaks through His written word today! In the Bible, Jesus often spoke in parables. Why? Parables are stories that tell a truth, though it's a little bit hidden. The truth is tucked away in the way gold is hidden in mountains. Why does God do that? Because only the earnest will find it. He does that to reveal what is in a person's heart. Those who really want to know God will find Him. This is the person who wants to know God so much they will search for Him like gold. What a joy this person is to the Lord! When that kind of person is looking to know and understand, God meets him with His Spirit and explains things. God enables him to see truths and unearth treasure more precious than silver and gold! So that which is hidden to others—they discover! Eureka! ('I find'!) Seeking the Lord is a daily adventure! But not everybody can see it. He gives eyes to those who want Him! And O, the treasures you will find!

*Blythe Followwill*
*For Dorman*

Therefore, I speak to them in parables; because while seeing they do not see, and while hearing they do not hear nor do they understand.
**Matthew 13:13** (NAS)

But blessed are your eyes, because they see; and your ears because they hear.
**Matthew 13:16** (NAS)

# June 9

> Did you not clothe me with skin and flesh and knit me together with bones and sinews.
> **Job 10:10-11 (NIV)**

**Think about how** complex our bodies are. Our wonderful Lord made each one of us specifically to His design and we are knitted the same way. Skin and flesh cover our bones, which are the strength of our body.

We all go through times that are hard and tough. We may think that our lives are falling apart, nothing is going well, and we desperately need strength. A good example is when things or people are taken away from us. This can be devastating! In such times, we need to turn to God and ask for strength and power. We need the Lord to knit us back together when we feel broken. Our bones will be our strength, and the sinews our power.

By calling upon God, our mind and body will be made whole again. The bones that make up our body may be our physical frame, and our sinews our strength, power, and resilience, but it is through our Lord that we receive *divine* strength and power.

Today, ask the Lord to renew your strength: not only your physical strength, but your mental strength as well. Renew your trust in the Lord and feel the presence of His love.

*Laura Bennin*

# June 10

**Beauty is all** around us, but often we are moving too fast to notice. We live in a world with almost eight billion people, and it is really important to take time to pause and spend time in silence and solitude.

Allow ourselves the space to let Jesus speak to us! So often we think that activity is the answer for intimacy, that if we are always busy, then God will be pleased with us.

There are some books that are so meaningful that they change the direction of a person's life! The book *Phantastes*, by George MacDonald, did that for C.S. Lewis, author of the *Narnia Chronicles*. Lewis read this book and said that it "baptized his imagination," and he was never the same.

This is what MacDonald says about the beauty of loving another person: "It is by loving, and not by being loved, that one can come nearest the soul of another; yea, that where two love, it is the loving of each other, that originates and perfects and assures their blessedness."

Wow, I had to read that again when I wrote this! Take a moment to read it again, and let it sink deep within you.

Jesus has made us not just for this life, but for the life to come. We only get one life, and how we live and, more importantly, how we love, makes all the difference in the world.

*Matthew Nash*

He has made everything beautiful in its time. He has also set eternity in the human heart; yet no one can fathom what God has done from beginning to end.
**Ecclesiastes 3:11 (NIV)**

# June 11

But I say to you, love your enemies, and pray for those who persecute you, that you may be children of your heavenly Father, for he makes his sun rise on the bad and the good, and causes rain to fall on the just and the unjust.
**Matthew 5:44-45 (NIV)**

**Imagine if everyone** you knew, in fact, if everyone in the whole world knew, loved, and served Jesus. What a different and lovely world this would be! But it isn't that way yet, and there may be people who have hurt you or whom you don't like very much. Imagine if these people began to love and serve Jesus so much that you could not help but like them! Could such a thing even happen? Yes! This is why Jesus tells us that we must pray for our enemies. Pray that they will come to know, love, and serve Jesus.

You are not expected to like the bad things that enemies do. You don't even have to like your enemies yet. But you can love them by praying for them and hoping that they will learn to love Jesus. You can love them by not wishing bad things for them. God our Father loves everyone He has created and wants all of us to be happy together in heaven. By loving Jesus and praying that others will love Him too, we are working for the goodness and happiness of all people.

*Sharon Edel*

# June 12

Jesus went to the Mount of Olives. Early in the morning he came again to the temple. All the people came to him, and he sat down and taught them. The scribes and the Pharisees brought a woman who had been caught in adultery, and placing her in the midst they said to him, "Teacher, this woman has been caught in the act of adultery. Now in the Law Moses commanded us to stone such women. So what do you say?" This they said to test him, that they might have some charge to bring against him. Jesus bent down and wrote with his finger on the ground. And as they continued to ask him, he stood up and said to them, "Let him who is without sin among you be the first to throw a stone at her." And once more he bent down and wrote on the ground. But when they heard it, they went away one by one, beginning with the older ones, and Jesus was left alone with the woman standing before him. Jesus stood up and said to her, "Woman, where are they? Has no one condemned you?" She said, "No one, Lord." And Jesus said,"Neither do I condemn you; go, and from now on sin no more."

**John 8:1-11 (NKJV)**

**I think that** this story was so shocking that some early manuscripts censored it and didn't include it, and only when the Christian message was more popularly understood was it restored to the text.

Adulterous women were hated and punished severely in the time of Jesus, as they sadly still are in some countries. Imagine someone who is hated and reviled in our time being brought before Jesus, and Jesus letting them go free, and saying, "Neither do I condemn you. Go and sin no more."

Sadly, most, if not all of, us have people we condemn in our hearts as beyond redemption, or as worthy of spite and dismissal. For Jesus, there are no such people, and even when He turns away His kinder face from some, it is only to bring them closer in repentance. Is there someone you have cast out, whom you need to let back into your heart?

*Matthew Levi*

# June 13

> In the beginning was the Word, and the Word was with God, and the Word was God. He was in the beginning with God. All things came into being through him, and without him, not one thing came into being. What has come into being. In him was life, and the life was the light of all people. The light shines in the darkness, and the darkness did not overcome it .
>
> **John 1:1-5 (NRSV)**

**People often say** that God created the universe *ex nihilo*, which is an old way of saying, "out of nothing." George MacDonald rebelled against this idea, and once wrote that he repented that he "had ever said that God made humans out of nothing; there is no nothing out of which to make anything; God is all in all, and Divinity made us out of Divinity." The verse in John above shows that he was right: God did not create out of nothing, but out of "the Word," which means out of Christ. God created everything through the Word; He created everything "in and for" Christ. Christ is what the world was created in, through, and for. Christ is the Word in which God sees Himself and then creates with the Spirit, which is love.

The being—the essence—of God is love, and therefore His essence is creation, says MacDonald.

If we want to know the ultimate purpose of life, the secret is in Christ. What do you think that secret is?

*Matthew Levi*

# June 14

**Do you have** a favorite example of the books you like to read, or the music you enjoy?

Did you know that the best example of how to live is God's Son, Jesus Christ? Not only did Jesus create us (so He knows who and what we are), but He came into our world as a human being, fulfilling God's plan to save us from our sins. His earthly life is now a perfect example for us of how to relate to God as our Father.

One day, when Jesus had to explain why He was doing things a particular way, He described it like this:

> "Very truly I tell you, the Son can do nothing by himself; he can do only what he sees his Father doing, because whatever the Father does the Son also does."
> **John 5:19 (NIV)**

Can you imagine having so much love for your parents that you would only do the things they did? Jesus said that everything we read about Him in the Bible are examples of how He always did the same things His Father was doing.

Later, Jesus told His disciples that they were to relate to Him in the same way. He said,

> "I am the vine; you are the branches. If you remain in me and I in you, you will bear much fruit; apart from me you can do nothing."
> **John 15:5 (NIV)**

This means that everyone who has faith in Jesus can do everything with Him, just as He does everything with His Father.

So, what do you think Jesus is doing in your life today?

*Monte Vigh*

# June 15

"Knowing that God is faithful, it really helps me to not be captivated by worry. But knowing that He will do what He has said, He will cause it to happen, whatever He has promised, and then it causes me to be less involved in worrying about a situation."

Josh McDowell

"Gather the riches of God's promises. Nobody can take away from you those texts from the Bible which you have learned by heart."

Corrie Ten Boom

"True faith means holding nothing back. It means putting every hope in God's fidelity to His Promises."

*Crazy Love: Overwhelmed by a Relentless God,* by Francis Chan

**Has anyone ever** made you a promise that they did not keep? The Bible is full of promises, and the ways God has kept those promises. Read and memorize the promises He has made, and rest in the assurance that God will do what He says.

*Laurel Shepherd*

He said: "LORD, the God of Israel, there is no God like you in heaven or on earth—you who keep your covenant of love with your servants who continue wholeheartedly in your way. You have kept your promise to your servant David my father; with your mouth you have promised and with your hand you have fulfilled it—as it is today."

**2 Chronicles 6:14-15** (NIV)

# June 16

## Honesty

**As Blaine watched** his neighbor washing his car, he decided to walk over and talk with him. His neighbor, Pete, sat down for a second. "Blaine, would you like a soda pop?" As Blaine waited, he saw Pete's keys and a shiny, silver whistle on the step. He wanted to blow it, just once. "It isn't stealing; I just want to borrow it." He slipped it in his pocket as Pete was coming back.

The whistle was forgotten for a few days, and anyway, he had not had a chance to blow it. Now as he sat on the steps alone, it was the perfect time. He blew with all his might, but there was no sound until dogs came from every direction, barking and pouncing on him. Blaine realized his sin had found him out. The shiny whistle was for dogs. After all, Pete was a trainer.

His Sunday School teacher had recently shared a Bible verse:

> Order my steps in thy word; and let not any iniquity have dominion over me.
> **Psalm 119:133 (KJV)**

Not being a Christian very long, Blaine still had some habits he needed to get rid of. There was something he had to do, and that was to ask for forgiveness from God and from Pete. He would give the whistle back and tell Pete he knew it was wrong to take it. He hoped this would not cause him to lose a very good friend.

Pete had steered him away from some guys who were always in trouble; now Blaine realized how important it is to read the Bible and trust God in situations where you may be tempted to do wrong.

*Dottie Thornton*

# June 17

**One of the** expressions God gives us to help us know how to talk to Him is this:

To you, O Lord, I lift up my soul.
**Psalm 25:1** (NIV)

Our soul is us; it is our life. When God invites us to lift up our souls to Him, He means that He cares for our inside lives, the people we really are, and everything to do with us. He wants us to lift up ourselves to Him.

Do you remember times when you were young, and you hurt yourself, and you would run to your parents, or a caregiver, and you would lift up your hands so they would pick you up? That is the idea of what this verse means. Someone was going through a difficult time, and their first thought was to lift up their life to their Father who is in heaven.

When we think of lifting up our souls to God, it is a way of saying that we trust God more than anyone else in the whole wide world. This is why it says, "*To you, O LORD…*" It is the LORD we come to because He alone can help us with whatever we are going through.

What is going on in your life today that makes you aware of your deep thoughts and feelings? God does not want you trying to figure out exactly what words to say. He wants you to lift up your soul to Him by talking to Him about everything in prayer. He will help you, even though you must wait patiently for His help to come.

*Monte Vigh*

# June 18

## The Gracious God for Lonely Hearts

**I can still** remember many times as a child when I was all alone. Whether playing by the seashore, or walking as far from home as I was allowed, often I simply enjoyed doing something by myself.

However, at other times I was lonely because no one wanted to be with me. Maybe someone was mean to me and never wanted to be my friend again.

What do children do when they are left all alone because someone very important to them is gone? Some children have parents who are separated; or someone they love has died, and they miss them like crazy.

Does God care when we have that kind of loneliness that hurts us more than we can bear? Yes, He does! In His Book, He even tells us how we can talk to Him about such things. Here is one example of how God wants us to pray to Him:

> Turn to me and be gracious to me, for I am lonely and afflicted.
> **Psalm 25:16** (NIV)

The man who wrote this was not enjoying a quiet walk along the seaside, or sitting alone to read a good book. He was alone because he was afflicted. This means that someone had done something mean to him. Someone had hurt him, and now he was feeling very lonely.

There will be times in life when we feel so lonely that we think that even God is far away from us. God gave us this prayer from His Book to show that He wants to help us in our brokenhearted loneliness. All we need to do is ask.

*Monte Vigh*

# June 19

The Passover of the Jews was near, and Jesus went up to Jerusalem. In the temple he found people selling cattle, sheep, and doves, and the money-changers seated at their tables. Making a whip of cords, he drove all of them out of the temple, both the sheep and the cattle. He also poured out the coins of the money changers and overturned their tables. He told those who were selling the doves, "Take these things out of here! Stop making my Father's house a marketplace!"
**John 2:13-16** (NRSV)

**This story shows** a fiercer image of Jesus than we usually see. What has made Him so fierce? The money changers and merchants in the Temple have taken over a sacred place and turned it into an opportunity to enrich their pockets. This is a deep insult to Jesus' Father, and Jesus reacts with righteous rage.

In our consumer society, there are many examples of people taking sacred things and turning them to personal profit. They may not be directly insulting God, but they surely insult his Creation, and often insult the human beings made in God's image. How do we drive these moneylenders and merchants from the Temple?

*Matthew Levi*

# June 20

> Taking the five loaves and the two fish and looking up to heaven, he gave thanks and broke the loaves. Then he gave them to his disciples to distribute to the people. He also divided the two fish among them all. They all ate and were satisfied
>
> **Mark 6:41-43a** (NIV)

## Division That Multiplies!

**If you had** five loaves of bread and, after giving thanks, you broke them in half, how many pieces of bread would you have? Ten? In this way, dividing five loaves into ten pieces actually multiplies the number of original pieces. The quantity of bread remains the same, but the number of pieces to be distributed becomes greater.

The story of the miracle feeding of five thousand is a lesson in division that multiplies in order to distribute food. Distribution is an act of sharing, circulating, or dividing. As the disciples distributed the ten broken loaves of bread, each piece was broken again and again, until everyone received their piece of bread. That's how division multiplies.

Jesus taught us to divide our food supply for distribution. But the world has been slow to learn this lesson of love. Many people in all parts of the world lack enough food to eat. During the last supper with His disciples, Jesus repeated the lesson by breaking bread once again and saying, "Do this in remembrance of Me." Do you think we should follow Jesus' way of breaking and passing bread?

Do you think all people would have enough food to eat if we trusted that division actually multiplies? Could a miracle of distribution help a hungry person in your neighborhood?

*Carol Wimmer*

# June 21

Consider it pure joy, my brothers and sisters, whenever you face trials of many kinds, because you know that the testing of your faith produces perseverance. Let perseverance finish its work so that you may be mature and complete, not lacking anything.
**James 1:2-4** (NIV)

**Remember the last** time you had one of those amazing mountain-top days, where the day was especially great, and the sky seemed extra blue, and things just kept going right? Ever wonder why every day can't be like that?

While those days are wonderful, our character is primarily developed in the midst of struggles.

Patience grows when we surrender to God's timing. Love grows when we pray for those who hurt or frustrate us. Joy grows when we thank God for our blessings in the midst of difficulties. Self-control grows when we stay strong in the midst of a temptation.

Peace grows when we set our eyes on Jesus in the midst of a storm. Kindness grows as we fight our selfish desires and think of others first. Faith grows when you trust that God is working in a situation, even when you don't yet see Him moving.

Enjoy and thank God for those amazing blue-sky, happy days. Be comforted, on the challenging days, that God is developing and strengthening your character.

*Kirstin Kasa*

# June 22

## Thirsty No More

But anyone who drinks the water I give them will never be thirsty. In fact, the water I give them will become a spring of water in them. It will flow up into eternal life.
**John 4:14** (NIRV)

**Is your soul** thirsting for a drink from the wells of heaven? Jesus said to a sinful woman drawing water from a well, "If you drink of the water that I give you, you will never thirst again." People look to different things to try and reach a higher high or to numb their senses.

My people have committed two sins: They have forsaken me, the spring of living water, and have dug their own cisterns, broken cisterns that cannot hold water.
**Jeremiah 2:13** (NIV)

If you are truly looking to satisfy your thirst, look to the Holy Spirit. It is written, "Be not drunk with wine but be filled with the Holy Spirit." There is no high like the Most High. Look up to Jesus and ask Him to fill you with the Holy Spirit. He promises "Joy unspeakable and full of glory." "In the presence of the Lord is fullness of joy and at His right hand are pleasures forevermore." The very first miracle of Jesus was to turn water into wine at the wedding in Cana. Once Jesus enters into your life, He will turn the waters of bitterness, worry, cares, and concerns into the wine of joy and gladness.

*Prithika*

# June 23

**The young miner,** Curdie, finds himself in a difficult situation in George MacDonald's exciting story *The Princess and Curdie.* A discussion is taking place among the miner-folk, and they have touched upon a subject which is very dear to Curdie, but he has been instructed to hold his tongue on this very subject. Now, if remaining silent during a discussion that interests you very much isn't hard enough, what do you do when you are pressed for your opinion? Let's see how Curdie handles this.

"'Come, young Curdie, what are you thinking of?'

'How do you know I'm thinking of anything?' asked Curdie.

'Because you're not saying anything.'

'Does it follow then that, as you are saying so much, you're not thinking at all?' said Curdie."

Finally, Curdie does have some things to say about how important it is to only speak about what you are certain is true, but with this result.

"Thus they all mocked and jeered at him, but he did his best to keep his temper and go quietly on with his work. He got as close to his father as he could, however, for that helped him to bear it. As soon as they were tired of laughing and mocking, Curdie was friendly with them, and long before their midday meal all between them was as it had been."

Others opinions of us will likely vary over the course of our relationships. But, like Curdie, we should never waver in truth and kindness.

*Steve Fronk*
*For Benjamin John*

Even fools are thought wise when they keep silent; with their mouths shut, they seem intelligent.
**Proverbs 17:28 (NLT)**

# June 24

Those who cling to worthless idols forfeit the mercy that could be theirs.
**Jonah 2:8 (NET)**

**Some of the** words seem big, but there is a lot of meaning here. Look closely. When we cling, it means we hold tightly to something. So it is saying that when we hold on tightly to one thing, clenching it in our hands, we are not free to receive something else. "Worthless idols" bring up pictures of horrible things—scary looking images of pretend gods—and yet *anything* that keeps us from God can become an idol.

An idol is something we make more important than anything else. It could be sports, friends, family, games, and even our looks. God wants to be first in our lives. He gives us grace, and if we are not paying attention to Him, we miss it. We miss all God's gifts for us when we put other things in His place. Think of it this way: imagine that you have an old toy, but it is broken and worthless. Then someone tells you that you can have a new one, a better one, you just have to give the old one up. Will you do it?

*Marjorie Strasner*

# June 25

"My friend never explained anything to me. He thought, perhaps, that I was like himself. But I, alas, do not know how to see sheep through the walls of boxes. Perhaps I am a little like the grown-ups. I have had to grow old."
*The Little Prince*, by Antoine de Saint-Exupéry

Jesus...asked his disciples, "Who do people say that the Son of Man is?" And they said, "Some say John the Baptist, but others Elijah, and still others Jeremiah or one of the prophets." He said to them, "But who do you say that I am?" Simon Peter answered, "You are the Messiah, the Son of the living God."
**Matthew 16:13-16 (NRSV)**

**Your grandma or** grandpa can tell you that when you get old, it becomes harder to see. Jesus taught this, too, but He did not mean we will need special glasses! He meant we forget to see things as they are, and instead see what others see, or only what we *expect* to see. Jesus said to "be like little children" (Matthew 18:3) and look with fresh eyes. This is very hard for a grown-up to do! Of all the Apostles, only Peter could do it and see that Jesus was God's Son.

One way to keep seeing clearly is to go into nature and sit with the things God has made. Listen to the sounds around you. Notice what you feel on your skin and what you smell. Finally, open your eyes and look without expecting anything. If you can do this, then even when you are a grown-up you will still see what God wants to show you: the beauty of the world, the value of yourself, the good in everyone, and Christ in all things.

*Race MoChridhe*

# June 26

And Mary said, "My soul glorifies the Lord and my spirit rejoices in God my Savior."
**Luke 1:46-47 (NIV)**

**Princess Madison had** just been born, and the whole kingdom celebrated her long-awaited birth. King Joshua and Queen Michelle soon presented the princess to her adoring subjects. She grew honoring the Lord, carrying with her the strength of her father and the kind grace of her mother. She masterfully used her grace, growing in strength and overcoming any challenge given her.

Princess Madison prayed in the castle's beautiful garden, called Gletheden. One day, an angel of the Lord appeared, saying, "Fear not, Princess Madison! God, the Ancient of Days, watches you, and you have found great favor with Him!" Princess Madison fell upon her face. The angel spoke once again, "You willingly walk in grace, which has become your greatest strength, always giving God honor and praise in all things. Therefore, the Most High is endowing you with His greatest gift of all, Virtuous Love, established by forgiveness, mercy, and grace, and confirmed in you through Jesus Messiah! Your crown forever will be proven by God Himself, and you will be remembered as Her Majesty, Madison, Princess of Virtuous Love. Clothed in the gold of Opher will you be all the days of your life. But know this Princess, Virtuous Love comes with great sacrifice. The strength you will need to bear your sorrow shall be found in the Lord Jesus Himself."

Princess Madison spoke, "My soul and spirit glorifies and rejoices in God my Savior. Be it unto me as God ordains!" With this, the angel was gone.

*Lisa Blair*

# June 27

"'I know that,' whispered Irene.
'But this is the way my thread goes, and I must follow it.'"
*The Princess and the Goblin,* by George MacDonald

**Truth is the** way things really are.

It is not something we make up; it is not something we wish or want to be true. Truth is what actually is…exactly.

When you have truth, it is like having a light inside! You can see! That keeps you out of trouble!

Jesus Christ says "I am the truth."

Jesus Christ sees everything, He knows everything! He hears every word, sees every action—He knows all because He made all. And because He made all, we just need *Him!*

Jesus Christ is pure Truth. He knows the way to live!

Have you asked Jesus to live inside you? If so, not only do you have a light that guides you but something more: you also have the power to live in a good and right way. A light is good, it shines and it reveals things; that helps. But the person of Jesus also gives us also His power to live and obey! When we have Jesus, we have the truth, and having Him means we have understanding, and in our understanding, we have His ability to do what is good. Living the right way keeps us from getting tangled and tied up in problems, hooked on ugly attitudes and habits. The truth is…Jesus! And He knows the way! When you know Him, you will live free! And that is the truth—exactly!

*Blythe Followwill*
*For* Αληθεια

Then you will know the truth, and the truth will make you free.
**John 8:32 (NIV)**

# June 28

**If school isn't** already out, it will be within a day or two. No more thinking about practicing writing, math equations, or how volcanic rock is formed, you are outta there! Maybe you have plans to go on a vacation with your family, or you have mapped out a summertime filled with pool trips, beachcombing, or days spent at your friend's house playing the latest video game or exploring a new part of town on your bikes. Or maybe you have no plans at all and are just happy to get to sleep in a little and go on a few trips to the mall for a new nail polish color with glitter in it.

I spent my summers during Grades 5-7 earning as much money as I could by taking on a paper route. I had big plans for all the money I would save and what it could buy me in the way of clothes and a trip to the local waterslide later in August. While my friends were out enjoying pool parties and biking around the town, I was going door to door with heavy flyers from every store around. I even took on a job to deliver notices from a real estate office once a week, and that took even more time. Today, as you look ahead to your summer plans, remember that you are only a child once and that God *wants* you to play. While it is good to learn about responsibilities, make plans to enjoy the world God created for you!

*Holly Van Shouwen*

The City streets will be filled with boys and girls playing there.
**Zechariah 8:5** (NIV)

# June 29

> Do to others whatever you would like them to do to you. This is the essence of all that is taught in the law and the prophets.
> **Matthew 7:12** (NLT)

**Have you ever** been the new kid at school or church? Whenever you are the newcomer who walks into a group of kids who are already friends, it can be a little frightening at first. The person who recognizes that, and treats the first-timer the way he or she would want to be treated, is doing what Jesus said to do.

Maybe you have been bullied by someone, and feel bad when you see it happening to someone else. That is feeling empathy, and will probably cause you to want to help the person being picked on. That is behaving as Jesus would.

Sometimes treating someone the way you want to be treated can take courage. Sometimes it is easy, sometimes hard, but it is always right. Selfishness is thinking only of ourselves, and is always wrong.

Does your little brother or sister hang around you all the time and want to play with you and your friends? What will you do to be obedient to what Jesus is saying in this verse? Thinking of ways to follow Him now will help you do the right thing when you have the chance.

*Dear Jesus, Sometimes I am afraid of standing up for someone who is being picked on. Sometimes I even join in, and I know that isn't what You want for me. Please forgive me for those times, and help me to have the courage that comes from You.*

*Vicki Ryder*

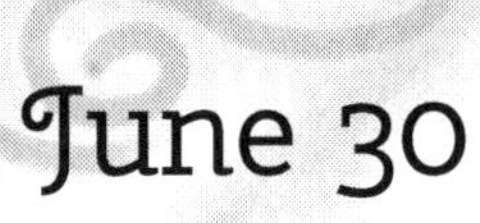

# June 30

Ah, Sovereign Lord, you have made the heavens and the earth by your great power and outstretched arm. Nothing is too hard for you.
**Jeremiah 32:17 (NIV)**

**I live in** the city, in a neighborhood where most houses are a narrow driveway apart. It is very common to look out your window and see right into your neighbor's house. I also live in a neighborhood where people love to garden. There are beautiful flowers and bushes and trees that brighten up the day.

There are also beautiful parks in my city. Yesterday I spent time walking around one of them. The air was cool and crisp. The sky was a bright blue with cotton-ball-white clouds. It was a perfect day for walking. As I gazed in the sky and noticed the trees, acorns, and pinecones around me, I marveled at the beauty and complexity of God's creation. He made all this. He made me and He loves me.

His creation is a wonderful reminder of His power. There is nothing too hard for Him! Read the verse above again. Think about it. Nothing is too hard for the Lord Creator. He loves you and is available for you. He is as close as the grass under your feet, and as big as the sky. Trust Him to help you with the hard things in your life because nothing, absolutely nothing, is too hard for Him!

*Patricia S. Becker*

# July 1

> By day the Lord went ahead of [the Israelites] in a pillar of cloud to guide them on their way and by night in a pillar of fire to give them light, so that they could travel by day or night.
> **Exodus 13:21** (NIV)

### A Heavenly Kind of Protection

**Wouldn't it be** awesome if we could go through life with a tall cloud guiding us? If we ever wondered which direction we should go, we could just follow the cloud. Then, when nighttime came, imagine the cloud turning into a giant pillar of fire that lit our path. Just think! We would never get lost!

When the Israelites left the country of Egypt three thousand years ago, they had to journey across a desert to get back to their homeland of Canaan. But they didn't have a desert map and there weren't any sign posts saying, "This Way to Canaan." So, they needed God's help—big time! It's fun to imagine a pillar of cloud by day, and a pillar of fire by night, leading a whole group of people through the desert. That's exactly what God's protection is like! The cloud symbolizes a concentration of God's holy breath. Fire symbolizes God's holy light. Together, the cloud and the fire reveal the presence of God's Holy Spirit.

When people say, "go with God," it is a phrase that acknowledges God's protection. We go through life with God's Holy Spirit leading us. If we ever forget that God is with us, we can think about the tall cloud and the giant pillar of fire that led the Israelites through the desert. It's a reminder that we are never alone.

*Carol Wimmer*

# July 2

Let everything that has breath praise the Lord.
**Psalm 150:6 (NIV)**

**The world we** live in is beautiful, isn't it? God has given us colorful sunsets, big green forests, sparkling rain, towering mountains covered in snow, and oceans that crash onto beaches. As trees grow and ocean waves tumble, they are praising God, just by doing what He made them to do!

Revelation 5:13 gives us an amazing picture of what heaven will be like: "Then I heard every creature in heaven and on earth and under the earth and on the sea, and all that is in them, saying: 'To him who sits on the throne and to the Lamb be praise and honor and glory and powers, for every and ever!'"

But guess what? We don't have to wait until heaven to praise God together! In fact, we don't even have to wait until Sunday at church.

God created us to love Him, to love each other, and to love the world around us. And we can praise Him each and every day by simply doing what He made us to do! Just like the trees of the forests praise God by growing straight and tall, and the ocean waves praise Him by rolling up on the shore, so we can praise Him by loving all around us.

How can you praise God this week?

*Bethany Wagner*
*Dedicated to Caleb Wagner*

# July 3

**Gather all of** your tears and prayers from your greatest hurts and place them at the feet of Jesus Christ. You are never alone and without hope; He sees your pain and knows your desires. Now, more than at any other time in your life, He is with you. Sometimes we must examine our lives and see why we are asking for certain things. Ask yourself if the things that we think would make our life more pleasant or easier are honoring to God. Be grateful and never forget that God often uses our trials to grow our faith in Him. Even during our darkest times, He is there for us. He knows exactly how and when to either bless us or correct us. Just because we may not fully understand why He delays in responding, this does not mean that He does not care. He loves each of us perfectly! Pray for a life that honors Him through all that you say and all that you do, in all circumstances.

*J. Richard Martinez*

I write these things to you who believe in the name of the Son of God that you may know that you have eternal life. And this is the confidence that we have toward him, that if we ask anything according to his will he hears us. And if we know that he hears us in whatever we ask, we know that we have the requests that we have asked of him.
**1 John 5:13-15 (ESV)**

# July 4

## Wisdom

**Joe had always** known from his dad that telling lies, stealing, and breaking promises were bad. He would not want to face his father's anger and disappointment. With this in mind, Joe was facing three older boys who seemed determined to do some of those evil things—and wanted Joe to join them.

Joe didn't believe it would be smart to break a window even in an old, abandoned house. Stealing was worse, but nothing would be as bad as breaking his promises to his dad.

Joe rode his bike casually down the block, trying to keep his distance from the other boys. He remembered his dad had told him wisdom came with knowing the difference between good and bad, and understanding how to decide which things mattered and with which he need not be concerned. In the Bible, Joe had read

> Take fast hold of instruction; let her not go: keep her, for she is thy life.
> **Proverbs 4:13 (KJV)**

Instructions from the Bible came with a sound warning. Joe's dad told him repeatedly not to forget God's Word. He must hold firm to it and bring it to mind when needed. Joe pedaled back to his house.

Later Joe learned that the boys had thrown rocks and broken a window. He stayed away from them and was quickly forgotten. Joe never told his dad about the boys, but somehow he was sure his dad knew about everything.

*Dottie Thornton*

# July 5

> But we have this treasure in jars of clay to show that this all-surpassing power is from God and not from us.
> **2 Corinthians 4:7** (NIV)

**I loved making** pottery in school. When I was a kid, I made a little jar for my parents, and even though it was not very attractive, they thought it was a masterpiece. Sometimes this is how we feel before Jesus. We look at our life and think we are not very attractive, but to Jesus, we are His masterpiece. This is how the great thinker and writer, George MacDonald speaks about this:

> "I would rather be what God chose to make me than the most glorious creature that I could think of; for to have been thought about, born in God's thought, and then made by God, is the dearest, grandest and most precious thing in all thinking."

Have you ever wished you were shorter or taller? Have you ever wished you lived in a different place or time? That is completely natural. However, when we are content where we are, we can be fully present in that moment, and we are open to what God wants to do in us and through us, to accomplish His purpose. How can God use you this week? How can God use your family this week?

There are opportunities all around; you simply have to be a jar of clay.

*Matthew Nash*

# July 6

Let all that you do be done in love.
**1 Corinthians 16:14** (ESV)

**Love is where** all life comes from. As John the Apostle told us, God is Love. All God's intentions and actions towards us from Adam and Eve forward have been for love's sake. Jesus died for love's sake, and love raised Him from the dead to immortality, so we could follow.

It is easy to lose sight of this in the torrent of everyday life and its often-painful lessons, but with God all things are possible. He knows full well we need Him in our every moment, so He teaches us to love our way through every day, every word, every action, every decision. It is through our faith in Him and by His Spirit in us that we can bear this fruit in our lives and be a blessing to others.

"The principle part of faith is patience."
George MacDonald

*Lorin Hart*

# July 7

**In 1635, in** France, at the age of 24, a young man entered a monastery where he would be known as Brother Lawrence of the Resurrection. A poor and uneducated man, Lawrence worked at simple jobs in the kitchen, or repairing shoes. In spite of his seemingly unremarkable life, Lawrence was a man who loved God whole-heartedly. His way of spirituality was simply to "practice the presence of God." In his own words:

> "He does not ask much of us, merely a thought of Him from time to time, a little act of adoration, sometimes to ask for His grace, sometimes to offer Him your sufferings, at other times to thank Him for the graces, past and present, He has bestowed on you, in the midst of your troubles to take solace in Him as often as you can. Lift up your heart to Him during your meals and in company; the least little remembrance will always be the most pleasing to Him. One need not cry out very loudly; He is nearer to us than we think."
>
> *The Practice of the Presence of God,* by Brother Lawrence

Brother Lawrence's simple way profoundly affected others who came to him for wisdom and guidance. Let us learn from his example!

There can be a world of difference between knowledge and experience. You know that God is with you. The challenge now is to experience the presence of God by learning to be aware of it at all times. If you lovingly seek Him with all persistence, you will find Him. Your life will never be the same.

*Sharon Edel*

I am God the Almighty. Walk before me and be blameless.
**Genesis 17:1 (NASB)**

# July 8

"...the highest wisdom must ever
appear folly to those who do not possess it."
*At the Back of the North Wind,* by George MacDonald

**Have you ever** heard someone say, "Oh, that's just plain foolishness," or, "You aren't making any sense!" The Bible tells how King Solomon asked God to give him an understanding mind so he could make wise decisions for the people of Israel. What about us? How can we know the right thing to do? How do we gain wisdom? We can start as King Solomon did, by asking God to help us. We can also listen to people who love us who have wisdom themselves. What can happen if a parent doesn't hold a young child's hand when they are near a street? The child could get hurt. Yet the child might not want to hold the parent's hand, and he might cry and pull away. The child wants to run. Holding hands seems foolish to him.

Even when we're older, we don't always understand the wisdom of obeying those who love and care for us. At times it doesn't seem to make sense. Proverbs 2:2 says, "Making your ear attentive to wisdom and inclining your heart to understanding." If something seems foolish, and it's coming from our Lord and others who love and care for you, look closely, and see if you can find the wisdom. Can you find it?

*Katherine T. Lee*

The law of the Lord is perfect, reviving the soul; the testimony of the Lord is sure, making wise the simple.
**Psalm 19:7 (ESV)**

# July 9

Rejoice in the Lord always. I will say it again: Rejoice!
**Philippians 4:4** (NIV)

**Usually, it's easy** to rejoice at the end of each summer day. We can find lots to thank Jesus for, and there is always something fun happening. But have you ever had a summer season that was not filled with the usual fun in the sun, swimming. and going away on vacation?

When I was in fifth grade, we had to move far away right around this time of the year. I had to leave my friends and all the activities that I loved. Usually summertime was full of thrills, but I was very sad. I thought my life was over and I was the most sorrowful girl on the planet. One day, I was biking along a path by our new property and came across a boy and a girl around my age, sitting on a huge rock that looked out into a meadow. The boy had his arm around the girl, who was crying. I introduced myself and learned that their dad had passed away just a week before. We talked and I told them that they had a Father in Heaven who would always be with them. I went home and told my mom what had happened. She told me our Bible verse for today, and I realized that I had lots to rejoice about. I also had something to share with those kids to give them reason for rejoicing. Even when we think our lives are ruined because of an event or circumstance, as God's children we can always rejoice!

*Holly Van Shouwen*

# July 10

"He took the rope they had tied him with—for Curdie's hindrances were always his furtherances—"
*The Princess and Curdie*, by George MacDonald

**Curdie is a** boy who meets a princess at the top of the stairs in a big house owned by a king, in a story by George MacDonald called *The Princess and Curdie*. While he is there, the princess tells him he must put his hands in the fire. As Curdie knows the princess means only good for him he does a very brave thing; he does it:

> "He rushed to the fire, and thrust both of his hands right into the middle of the heap of flaming roses, and his arms halfway up to the elbows. And it did hurt! . . . The princess told him to take them out and look at them. He did so, and found that all that was gone of them was the rough, hard skin; they were white and smooth like the princess's."

His hands weren't destroyed in the fire—they were cleansed of everything that wasn't good on the inside and out!

The book of Hebrews states that

...our God is a consuming fire.
**Hebrews 12:29** (NIV)

He consumes—or cleans out—the bad stuff in us when we let Him. All we have to do is put our hands in the fire like Curdie did. And, just like the princess, God means only good for us! So, the best thing we can do is rush to Him and thrust our whole selves into His fire. It will hurt, but we will come out clean—inside and out!

*Darren Hotmire*

# July 11

"'He took the rope they had tied him with—for
Curdie's hindrances were always his furtherances—'"
*The Princess and Curdie,* by George MacDonald

**God is a** great and wonderful weaver of life!

The threads He uses are time and people, circumstances and history. Some of His threads are dark, like winter and storms: pitch black and confusing! Some threads are unseen, like aloneness and sorrow. Along with the dark ones, He has oodles of beautiful ones, threads of white and gold and green; with these He weaves 'Good Mornings', fresh, wonders and new life, like chicks and Easter flowers, adventures and summer streams. Some of these unseen threads lace in hope and joy and love. God is a master weaver! He plans and puts His threads in place with purpose! The life we live is like a weaving; we don't see the whole picture. We often see only the working side that is full of knots and untrimmed edges. It looks tangled. But God sees the whole! He takes all the parts of life and makes something beautiful. He is working all the darks to shine the lights. In the end it will be perfect!

Consider these wonders: winter to spring; night to morning; buried seed to new sprout! Consider the night sky; without the black we would not see the stars! It is very important to remember that when life is dark and hard, you can absolutely know that God is doing something! And it matters!

He never wastes a thread.

*Blythe Followwill*
*For May*

And we know that God works all things together for good to those who love God, to those who are called according to His purpose.
**Romans 8:28 (NASB)**

# July 12

...no one will snatch them out of my hand.
**John 10:28 (NIV)**

**MacDonald lived in** a place where dangerous floods happened often, and he sometimes wrote about these in his books. In his story *What's Mine's Mine*, two people are caught in the midst of the rising waters. Ian tells Mary not to be scared, and Mary responds. The conversation goes like this:

> " I can't help being frightened!" she panted.
> "We are in God's arms," returned Ian. "He is holding us."
> "Are you sure we shall not be drowned?" she asked.
> "No; but I am sure the water cannot take us out of God's arms."

Floods happen in our lives. They may not always be made up of water—but they happen. Parents get divorced, students harass or bully, school work mounts up. Sometimes we feel like we will be swept away and drown in these types of floods.

God doesn't always keep these things from happening, no matter how much we wish He would. But He does promise that He "will never leave or forsake" us. (Dt 31:6) No matter what—God will always be there to comfort, love, guide and help us learn from these experiences. No matter what—nothing can snatch us out of his hand.

*Darren Hotmire*

# July 13

"I wonder how many Christians there are who so thoroughly believe God made them that they can laugh in God's name; who understand that God invented laughter and gave it to his children. The Lord of gladness delights in the laughter of a merry heart."
George MacDonald

**How long has** it been since you laughed until you cried or giggled until you could hardly catch your breath? It happened to me the other day! For no particular reason, I got tickled and could not stop laughing. I didn't want to stop laughing! When the giggles did finally stop, I realized I felt refreshed and full of joy. It was like a gift from God. The Bible says,

A cheerful heart is good medicine…
**Proverbs 17:22 (NIV)**

…the cheerful heart has a continual feast
**Proverbs 15:15 (NIV)**

Often life is hard and other kids can be mean. But remember, God is good. He invented laughter! Good, clean humor and a case of the giggles can help you to stay healthy. It can give you more energy and protect you from the bad things stress can do in your body. Laughter releases endorphins, which are special "feel-good" chemicals in your brain.

So, I hope you get a good case of the giggles soon! Laugh often! Laugh long! It's like medicine from God!

*Rennie Marie Sneed*

# July 14

**Wouldn't it be** wonderful if everything went our way all the time, and we always got what we wanted? What could be better? You may be thinking that absolutely nothing could be better than that!

But it actually *is* better to not get everything we want all the time. If we did, then we might not work as hard for the things we want, and we might stop appreciating them because they come too easily.

Think about a test that you may have taken and didn't do so well on, or a toy that you wanted and were told that you had to earn. You may have wanted to be upset with God for not helping you do better on the test, or not letting you have the toy right away. Instead, you can thank Him for showing you you may need to spend more time studying, and for helping you earn the toy.

When it comes time to take the next test, you may find yourself doing better, and you will likely end up earning the toy. Thank God for His help. You will better appreciate the grade and the toy because you've worked harder for them.

Even though we may not always get what we want, one thing we will always have is God's love for us. So whether or not you get the things you want, God is still worthy of your praise, because He is our loving God when things are good and even when they are not.

And the Child continued to grow and become strong, increasing in wisdom; and the grace of God was upon Him.
**Luke 2:40** (NASB)

# July 15

Blessed rather are those who hear the word of God and keep it.
**Luke 11:28 (NIV)**

**One time, a** woman in the crowd proclaimed that Mary must be very blessed to be Jesus' mother. Jesus, however, says that His mother is blessed, not simply because she is His mother, but because she hears the word of God and keeps it!

Mary was a young girl when an angel of God asked her to be the mother of Jesus. Mary must have been surprised, scared, and even a little confused. But she did not doubt that the angel had come from God, and that God wanted something of her; therefore she did not hesitate to obey. Indeed, Mary was blessed to be the mother of Jesus; but she was also blessed because she believed and obeyed! Jesus had echoed similar words from Elizabeth to Mary, quoted in Luke 1:45: *"Blessed is she who has believed that the Lord would fulfill his promises to her!"*

You are blessed if you have someone in your life who loves you and who helps you to know and love God. You are blessed if you learn to hear the word of God, and trust and obey it.

Let us thank God for the loving parents, grandparents, relatives, and any adults in our lives who help us to feel safe and loved and happy, because they are people who hear the word of God and obey it. May we too be blessed as we learn to do the same!

*Sharon Edel*

# July 16

## What Are You Becoming?

**A pretty amazing** thing happens to Curdie in George MacDonald's story *The Princess and Curdie.* The Great-Grandmother gives him a magical sort of gift of touch. When he touches anyone living, he can feel beneath their skin and feel what their souls look like. She goes on to explain what he will find out: "All men, if they do not take care, go down the hill to the animals' country; that many men are actually, all their lives, going to be beasts. . ."

The Grandmother then gives him a word of caution:

> "Ah! But you must beware, Curdie, how you say of this man or that man that he is travelling beastward...two people may be at the same spot in manners and behavior, and yet one may be getting better and the other worse...

Curdie finds this out. Some people he meets appear nice, but on the inside they are becoming snake-like monsters. However, some who look scary on the outside are becoming child-like on the inside.

What he found out is true: The real us, our souls, are all either growing better or growing worse. That is why Peter wrote

> ...like newborn babies, long for the pure milk of the word, so that by it you may grow in respect to salvation, if you have tasted the kindness of the Lord.
> **1 Peter 2:2-3 (NASB)**

Hopefully, we are longing to learn and grow from God through his Word. If not, it is much too easy to be a monster on the inside!

The question we all have to ask ourselves is: "What are we becoming?"

*Darren Hotmire*

# July 17

"You darling! Do you think I care more for my dress
than for my little girl?"
*The Princess and the Goblin,* by George MacDonald

**When God looks** at you, He is flooded with love! You are more important to Him than *things.*

Do you see the birds flying in the air? Who gave them feathers to glide on the wind? Do you see the beautiful flowers that colour the fields? Who sends the rain so they can grow?

If God provides everything for plants and animals to live, won't He provide for you, His precious child? Some people run around busying themselves, spending their whole lives worrying, trying to get more and more because they are afraid they might run out of food or things or clothes. That is behaving like there is no loving Father in heaven! But those who belong to God can have a special peace, for He knows what you need even before you ask Him!

Therefore, You are free to spend your life loving God—giving Him first place in your heart! You can be sure He will take care of everything else!

*Blythe Followwill*
*For Abigail*

"Therefore I tell you, do not worry about your life, what you will eat or drink; or about your body, what you will wear. Is not life more than food, and the body more than clothes? Look at the birds of the air; they do not sow or reap or store away in barns, and yet your heavenly Father feeds them. Are you not much more valuable than they?"
**Matthew 6:25-26 (NIV)**

# July 18

So, whether you eat or drink or whatever you do, do it all for the glory of God.
**1 Corinthians 10:31 (NIV)**

**Have you ever** seen chubby little pigs eat, and heard them squeal and snort as they shove their nose deep into their food trough? Maybe you have a puppy that goes full face into its food, scattering it everywhere with unconcern as it gobbles as much as it can. If we saw a person eat that way, we would probably say, "Eeeww, that's disgusting!"

Eating like greedy pigs wouldn't bring God glory, would it? But this verse tells us to give glory to God in *whatever* we do, even eating! We can describe giving glory with some other words that help us understand, like thankfulness, praying, and obedience. For example, God gives your parents jobs to earn money to buy food, which they use to make you good meals. How does it make you feel when someone does something kind for you? Do you want to thank them, hug them, maybe even try to be like them? That's giving glory!

Giving God glory then, is thanking Him, giving Him a hug in your heart, and learning to know Him so we love the same things He cares about. As we show kindness for others, people enjoy being with us and we can tell them wonderful things about Jesus. That gives God lots of glory! So, take time each day in 'whatever you do' to do everything kindly, thinking about how God would treat others. Then, thank Him for all things, and you will be giving Him glory all day long!

*Gwen Rushing*

# July 19

"All children, except one, grow up…You always know after you are two. Two is the beginning of the end."
J.M. Barrie

**It is told** that the fantastical boy Peter Pan never grew up. He lived a life of adventure while still being a little boy. But this is just a story; we all grow up, right? Well, there was one real-life person who never did grow up: the man Jesus. You see, He was a man, while still being a boy. And He said that any of us who want to be with Him must do the same.

Then Jesus said,

> Leave the children alone, and don't try to keep them from coming to Me, because the kingdom of heaven is made up of people like this.
> **Matthew 19:14 (HCSB)**

Of course, there is a good growing up, where you learn responsibility and hard work, but there is also a bad growing up, and that is the kind we are talking about. Ever since the time of Adam and Eve, growing up has meant doing bad things. Sadly, if you are old enough to read these words, you have probably started the bad kind of growing up already: being selfish and mean to others, telling lies, and disobeying.

But happily, we can go back to being the boys and girls Jesus is talking about. George MacDonald tells us to "just do the next thing you think God wants you to do." And if we really want it, one day Jesus Himself will secretly give us a new heart, the heart of a little child, so that we can forever be with Him.

*Joseph Dindinger*

# July 20

A friend loves at all times...
**Proverbs 17:17a (NIV)**

**When my granddaughter** picked this verse for the devotional, I thought, "Great! This will be an easy verse to write about. This is a great verse!"

Then I started thinking about it. It's not always easy. Being a friend can be hard work. I often hear kids say, "She's not my friend anymore," or "He decided to be his friend instead of mine." "I don't want to be her friend anymore because. . ." Ouch. Having friends can hurt!

In the Old Testament, there were two friends who loved each other a lot. One was the son of a king, and his friend was a warrior who was more victorious than the father king. This caused problems, and soon their friendship was at great risk, because the father king wanted to kill his son's best friend. The two friends knew they could not be together anymore, so they chose to make a covenant, a promise, that they would remain friends forever.

Although many of us do not face the dangers that these two friends did, we can learn that even though things may be rough, it is important to remain friends. Do you have a friend that you love very much, but sometimes they just plain make you mad? Think about the friendship that you have with them, and decide to be a friend that loves at all times. It will be worth the effort.

*Patricia S. Becker*

# July 21

**How wonderful it** is to gain wisdom! Wisdom is truly something that is earned, and is therefore to be cherished. Wisdom comes from life experience, but some gain wisdom from just listening and heeding the words of those they love and respect. They don't need to learn the hard way and suffer the consequences of trying to do it their way first. They listen and gain favor right away, and it makes their path very clear.

We all have times when we do it our own way first. But if you are wise, you know that there are always things you don't know. It doesn't matter how old you are. Whether you are four or fourteen or forty, your wisdom is always growing.

Studying and knowing God's Word is the first step to true wisdom. There is a light that God's Word shines into your heart, even when you've taken a misstep, that is undeniably beautiful when you find yourself lost. This brings a humility and radiance of spirit that comes only from being forgiven and set on solid ground.

*Karen Thornton*

But the wisdom that comes from heaven is first of all pure; then peace-loving, considerate, submissive, full of mercy and good fruit, impartial and sincere.
**James 3:17 (NIV)**

# July 22

**Do you know** what a habit is? The dictionary says it's something that a person does often, in a repeated and regular way. Maybe you are reading this devotional often, even every day. It is a good habit to spend time with God each day and learn more about Him through the Bible.

Daniel was a young man who the Bible says made it his habit to pray three times a day. When Daniel prayed he got down on his knees and gave thanks to God because he knew that God would hear and answer his prayers. But you don't always have to be on your knees to pray, and you don't have to pray three times a day. Prayer is talking with God, and He wants to hear from you every day.

Corrie Ten Boom once said, "Don't pray when you feel like it. Have an appointment with the Lord and keep it. A man is powerful on his knees." You probably have a schedule: for example, when you go to school, when your favorite TV show is on, and what time you go to bed.

Consider setting an appointment at a particular time each day to spend time in prayer with God. Thank Him for your many blessings. Pray for your family and friends and your country. And thank God for hearing and answering your prayers! God is always ready to listen; you will never get His voicemail.

*Barbara Hollace*

Three times a day he got down on his knees and prayed, giving thanks to his God, just as he had done before.
**Daniel 6:10b (NIV)**

# July 23

Take delight in the Lord, and he will give you the desires of your heart.
**Psalm 37:4** (NIV)

"Man finds it hard to get what he wants because he does not want the best; God finds it hard to give because He would give the best, and man will not take it." George MacDonald

"Yet I know that good is coming to me—that good is always coming." George MacDonald

**I was eating** a sandwich the other day, and my cat was VERY interested in having some of it. He was alert and attentive to my every move. Finally, I relented, and took a bit of meat out of the sandwich and dropped it in front of him. He was so intent on watching me that he didn't even notice that I had given him some. Instead, he kept hungrily inspecting my hand. There in front of him was food for him, but he didn't notice! I had to point it out to him for him to see it, and begin to eat and purr.

We are like that sometimes, with our parents, our teachers, and especially with God. We are so intent on what we think we want, on where we think it is, that we miss what is given to us, what is right in front of us. Sometimes we need it pointed out over and over before we can see it and believe it. Sometimes we object because it looks nothing like what we had expected, but if it is the right thing, time shows us how much better it is than the idea we had.

God is always giving us good things. We just have to be open to seeing them.

*B. Daniel Speake*

# July 24

We have come to know and have believed the love which God has for us. God is love, and the one who abides in love abides in God, and God abides in him.
**1 John 4:16 (NASB)**

**What is God** like? It's one of the most important questions anyone can ask. People become like the God they worship. Those who believe God is angry and vengeful will become angry and vengeful. Those who believe God is kind and forgiving will become kind and forgiving.

John was one of Jesus' closest friends. He knew Jesus better than anyone else. If you asked John what God was like, he would have told you, "God is like Jesus." Jesus loved people that no one else loved. Jesus helped people who didn't deserve help. Jesus defended people when others threw rocks at them. Jesus loved people enough to tell them the truth. Jesus did what was right, even when it hurt. Jesus cared about other people more than Himself. That's what John believed God was like. That's what he meant when he wrote, "God is love."

John tells us that whoever "abides in love, abides in God and God abides in him." The place where you "abide" is your home. The hero in *The Princess and the Goblin*, by George MacDonald, is a miner named Curdie, who spends much of the story underground in utter darkness filled with goblins. Curdie experienced the same darkness as the goblins, but did not become like the goblins because he lived like a person from the light instead of like a goblin from the darkness. When we love others like Jesus does, we remember that He is our home and others can see that He is living in us.

*Scott Dossett*

# July 25

"For a moment he became so one with the bird that he seemed to feel both its bill and feathers, as one adjusted the other to fly again, and his heart swelled with the pleasure of its involuntary sympathy."

*The Princess and Curdie,* by George MacDonald

**We were coming** out of the pizza place, when my daughters squealed aloud, "Oh look, a baby bird!" He was a young, black starling, stranded on the rocky ground under a scraggly tree in the parking lot. His little leg was broken. If we left him, he would surely die! That's how "Scott Starling" came to reside at the makeshift bird hospital at our house. After researching how to feed and care for him, we found that he loved cherry Gatorade! Soon his leg was well, and we released him in the park by our house. We rejoiced with his birdsong as he soared to a leafy refuge and perched upon a branch. He joined a group of starlings, sheltering with other birds in the trees and vines by the creek. Scott Starling found a safe place for healing. God rescues us, heals us, delivers us, and provides refuge in Him for us. We are safe "under His wings."

*Karise Gililland*

He who dwells in the shelter of the Most High will abide in the shadow of the Almighty. I will say to the Lord, "My refuge and my fortress, my God, in whom I trust." For He will deliver you from the snare of the fowler and from the deadly pestilence...under His wings, you will find refuge...

**Psalm 91:1-2, 4 (ESV)**

# July 26

> Be kind to one another, tenderhearted, forgiving each other, just as God in Christ also has forgiven you.
> **Ephesians 4:32 (NASB)**

**In the book** *Sir Gibbie,* by George MacDonald, Gibbie is wounded by a cruel man named Angus. Gibbie has every right to be angry at Angus. But Gibbie chooses forgiveness.

> "If the offence had been committed against Gibbie, then with Gibbie lay the power, therefore the duty, of forgiveness. Few things were easier to him than to love his enemies, and his merit in obeying the commandment was small indeed. No sooner had Janet ceased than he was on his way back to the cottage; on its floor lay one who had to be waited upon with forgiveness."

I don't know about you, but forgiving others is really hard for me sometimes, especially when someone has really hurt me badly. The truth is, I know that I MUST forgive them if I wish to abide in Jesus, but my feelings are overwhelmed with hurt and anger. I've found a secret weapon to forgiving, though. I don't wait until I feel like forgiving, I make myself forgive *despite* how I feel. I make myself pray for the person who has hurt me. Sometimes I even have to grit my teeth and pray, "God please bless ________". You know what happens? When I pray for the person who hurt me, my feelings begin to change and I am not hurt anymore. Praying for that person makes forgiveness easy!

*Jolyn Canty*

# July 27

**I love my** garden during springtime; it teaches me so much about God. The bulbs hidden in the earth begin to pop up, and soon a beautiful, happy tulip sneaks out between the leaves. One day I made a bouquet of red tulips. Their heavy heads bobbed on their sturdy stalks. I put them in a crystal vase and set them on my table. The next morning, I noticed that the tulips were facing the opposite direction and were now leaning and turning toward the sunlight that was streaming through the window behind them.

It is only as we lean on, and turn to, Jesus that we will increasingly reflect His goodness and truth. Every day we are greeted with the rising sun, and Jesus is the Light of The World. May we always remember to lean into the Light.

Gibbie was a boy who continually reflected Jesus' light: "Then rose the very sun himself in Gibbie's eyes aand flashed a full response of daylight—a smile that no woman, girl, or matron could mistrust." From *Sir Gibbie*, by George MacDonald.

*Jolyn Canty*

...walk as children of Light (for the fruit of the Light consists in all goodness and righteousness and truth), trying to learn what is pleasing to the Lord.
**Ephesians 5:8-10 (NASB)**

# July 28

**Jesus first reveals** His glory in rejoicing with a bride and groom at a wedding by supplying them with wine for the festivity. The rejoicing of bride and groom is a central symbol in Judaism for joy, delight, and wellbeing. Jesus came to increase our joy.

One sometimes hears of melancholy, judgmental, stern, or grim Christians. Somehow they have lost touch with a real, living union with Christ. This union, which takes place in the heart, not the head, is a source of joy and makes the things of life sweeter, not more bitter. As George MacDonald wrote, "If we will but let our God work with us, there can be no limit to God's enlargement of our existence."

*Matthew Levi*

On the third day there was a wedding in Cana of Galilee, and the mother of Jesus was there. Jesus and His disciples had also been invited to the wedding. When the wine gave out, the mother of Jesus said to Him, "They have no wine." And Jesus said to her, "Woman, what concern is that to you and to me? My hour has not yet come." His mother said to the servants, "Do whatever He tells you." Now standing there were six stone water jars for the Jewish rites of purification, each holding twenty or thirty gallons. Jesus said to them, "Fill the jars with water." And they filled them up to the brim. He said to them, "Now draw some out, and take it to the chief steward." So they took it. When the steward tasted the water that had become wine, and did not know where it came from (though the servants who had drawn the water knew), the steward called the bridegroom and said to him, "Everyone serves the good wine first, and then the inferior wine after the guests have become drunk. But you have kept the good wine until now." Jesus did this, the first of His signs, in Cana of Galilee, and revealed His glory; and His disciples believed in Him.

**John 2:1-12 (NRSV)**

# July 29

> So when you offer your gift to God at the altar, and you remember that your brother or sister has something against you, leave your gift there at the altar. Go and make peace with that person, and then come and offer your gift.
> **Matthew 5:23-24** (NCV)

**It is often** much easier to make peace with God than with our brothers and sisters. Since God is perfect, there is never anything for us to have against Him, and He always forgives us freely. This is not always so for other people, who may have something against us, or we may be hurt or angry with them.

Since God expects us to love Him completely, and to love others as we love ourselves, these verses show us how that will change our behavior. As we love God and offer our devotion to Him, we must also love others and try to live in peace with them. When you know your little sister is frustrated with you because you have been ignoring her, ask her forgiveness, and make time to do something special with her. Wouldn't it be a wonderful world if everyone did that?

*Dear Lord Jesus, I want to follow You, and live the way You showed me to. Please forgive me for the times when I am selfish or angry and do not treat others the way I want to be treated. Thank You that You are always ready to help me do better. In Jesus' Name, Amen.*

*Vicki Ryder*

# July 30

"And do you think that the words of your book [the Bible] are certainly true?" "Yes, verily; for it was made by him who cannot lie."
*The Pilgrim's Progress*, by John Bunyan

**If you have** always heard God's Word at your house, you may wonder how people could not believe it.

Actually, many people don't know about the Bible, except for what they've picked up here and there. They may not know if what they've heard is true, but they also don't know anything else. Even in your church there may be someone who hears, "Open your Bible…" and thinks, "Well, I'll open it, but I don't know why you want me to."

There are people who have never *seen* a Bible, much less read one. Many others may have seen it or read it – but they've been told what to think of it. They may have been taught that the Bible is an old book that doesn't matter. They may have been instructed to listen to other voices and not to the Bible's voice.

So not everyone *knows* that God is good. Not everyone knows He is always right, always true, never false. Not everyone knows He is holy and powerful. Not everyone knows there is such a thing as eternal life – or even what that means.

Ask God to make you strong for Him as you grow. Ask Him to teach you how to teach others the Bible so that they will also know what is true.

*Mary Lichlyter*

This truth gives them confidence that they have eternal life, which God—who does not lie—promised them before the world began.
**Titus 1:2 (NLB)**

# July 31

> Now to him who is able to do immeasurably more than all we ask of imagine, according to his power that is at work within us...
> **Ephesians 3:20 (NIV)**

**Imagine that you** want something very much, but you can't imagine ever receiving it. How would you feel if you received exactly what you want, plus so much more? You have been given more than you can possibly comprehend! It would probably seem unreal or dreamlike. Because our God is a loving God and is faithful in all of His words, our wants and needs can be fulfilled. God will work within us, to provide for us.

Our God is powerful. When we compare our thoughts and minds to God's, we realize how limited and small we, as humans, are. In fact, our brains are so much smaller and more limited than God's, we cannot even fathom how much He can do for us. The human brain simply cannot process this!

Anything that we ask our God, He can provide to us, assuming it's His will. When we are obedient and focused on the Lord, He alone is able to provide and give us our heart's desire and more. He has no limits.

*Laura Bennin*

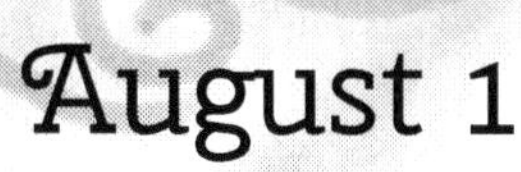

# August 1

Consider how the wild flowers grow.
**Luke 12:27** (NIV)

**Have you ever** looked at a dandelion closely? The Lord made it with many parts, each one with its own intricate design, and it has a wonderful yellow color.

Let's just think about it for a minute—the flower gets stomped on by both man and animals; bugs crawl all over it; people complain about it because it messes up their freshly cut, all-green lawns; children pick them thinking they are pretty flowers; but other people mow them or spray some kind of week killer to get rid of them.

Their existence is not without trouble, to say the least, but they still close up and sleep at night. God put them here for a reason, and He says, "Consider the lilies of the field, how they grow."

One thing this little flower has is perseverance! No matter what it faces throughout its time here, it still stands tall. When the dandelion's time is up, it disappears, and not until then.

Shouldn't we too have faith that the Lord will see us through all our trials and sorrows? Should we not lean on God, believing that no matter what comes along, He will see us through?

The Lord says "You do not receive because you do not ask! Ask in my name and you will receive and your joy will be complete!"

…pray without ceasing.
**1 Thessalonians 5:17** (ESV)

How do we ask, but through prayer?

*Susian Lambert*

# August 2

**George MacDonald's fairy** tale *Little Daylight* tells the story of a princess who, as a baby, received a curse from a wicked fairy, much the same as Sleeping Beauty did. Little Daylight's curse caused her to sleep all day long, every day, so that she never got to see the sun.

Can you imagine what it would be like to never see the sun, or to never go outside and see things in the light of day? Colors wouldn't be nearly as vivid and beautiful. For instance, the grass in your yard might be very green, but if you never saw it in the sunlight, it would look much paler, and hardly green at all. That's the kind of thing that Princess Daylight experienced.

Nevertheless, Daylight loved all the light she could see. She loved to go outside her house at night and gaze up at the moon, and sing to it, and dance beneath it. Even lesser lights are a wonderful gift, if that's all you have!

Think about the gift of light. It helps you see where you're going. Have you ever tried to walk in the pitch black, with no light? That can be very scary and dangerous! One of the writers of the Bible says:

> Your word is a lamp for my feet, a light on my path.
> **Psalm 119:105 (NIV)**

*Thank you, Lord, for the light of Your Word. Help me to love and follow all the light you've given me. Amen.*

*Daniel Koehn*

# August 3

> I have even seen servants riding horseback like princes—and princes walking like servants!
> **Ecclesiastes 10:7 (NLT)**

**Have you ever** wondered what it would be like to be a prince or a princess? Maybe you've seen one in person or read about one in a book. If you have read the story *The Princess and the Goblin*, you will know about the princess Irene and the young miner-boy Curdie.

Curdie is the son of a poor miner-family, while Irene is the daughter of a great king with a great white horse. Curdie has his tools and his mining work to do; Irene has toys and books to occupy her, and servants to wait upon her. There seems to be no question of the difference between them; one is royalty, one is not.

But as the story unfolds, we find that they are really alike in very important ways. From the beginning, Curdie demonstrates his courage many times over. Later, Irene, in an act of great courage and faith, rescues Curdie from his entrapment. And, finally, Curdie saves not only Irene, but also the king and his whole household from certain destruction. And so it is no wonder that George MacDonald brings to our attention that Curdie may be more than just a miner.

"So you see there is some ground for supposing that Curdie was not a miner only, but a prince as well. Many such instances have been known in the world's history."

To be a prince or a princess, then, depends not on clothing or station, but on how we live our lives. Handsome is as handsome does.

*Steve Fronk*
*For Zachary Edward*

# August 4

**We had some** lovely visitors this summer, a hard-working pair of robins who carefully built a nest on our front porch. Next came three pretty blue eggs, and then the helpless baby robins. But these babies were not forgotten; mother and father nourished and nurtured until they were out of the nest and bounding about our front yard.

Three weeks later, our son found an egg lying on the ground at our community swimming pool. Not knowing what should be done with it, we placed it in the abandoned nest. The very next morning, to our amazement, there was a robin sitting in the nest attempting to incubate the egg. As of today, she is still involved in her motherly ministry.

This, I think, is what George MacDonald means when he speaks of certain women who are God's mothers. They are mothers to not only their own dear children, but will take to their hearts any child in need of a mother.

I cannot tell you the end of this story, as it has yet to be written, but I believe there is a valuable lesson here about the true meaning of motherhood. If you ever feel lost or forgotten, try to remember that there is One who will never lose sight of you and never forget you. And he might just send one of his birds to look after you—or one day even send a little lost one your way!

*Steve Fronk*
*For Kathy Ann*

Can a mother forget the baby at her breast and have no compassion on the child she has borne? Though she may forget, I will not forget you.
**Isaiah 49:15 (NIV)**

# August 5

> In the same way, the Spirit helps us in our weakness. We do not know what we ought to pray for, but the Spirit himself intercedes for us through wordless groans.
> **Romans 8:26 (NIV)**

**God wants you** to pray at all times: when you are sick; when someone you love is sick; when you are sad. You can pray to ask God for things you want, like a new bike, or things you need, like a new pair of shoes. You might share your need with your friends in Sunday school if the teacher asks if anyone has a prayer request. The teacher might ask everyone to hold hands, and then speak to God for you and your friends, telling Him your needs or requests.

Maybe you have a lot you want to share with God, but you're nervous or think He doesn't hear you, so you ask someone else to pray for you. When they pray, it's called *intercession*. That means someone is praying on your behalf.

There is someone who intercedes, or speaks to God, for you all the time and knows exactly what to say; He is called the Spirit. The Spirit intercedes for you when you are so sad or so hurt you don't have the words to speak to God. The Spirit lets God know how sad you are or how hurt you are. He doesn't even use words! He uses wordless groans that express how you are feeling.

It's okay if you don't always have the words to pray.

*A.E. Sanchez*

# August 6

**What is it** to truly hope in the Lord, to trust Him completely, to lay your life and all you have at His feet, and know beyond a shadow of a doubt that He will see you through? It's not like taking orders and submitting to authority; it is a belief that you will be okay without all the certainty of orders and tasks, because your Creator holds you in the palm of His Hand.

It is learning to rest in spirit and body. It is slowing down to hear His voice. It is waking up to all the love that has always surrounded you, but that you were too busy to see. It's giving up your own plan. It's resting in His arms, and being carried on wings, and finding your strength and endurance because He loves you.

*Karen Thornton*

...but those who hope in the Lord will renew their strength. They will soar on wings like eagles; they will run and not grow weary, they will walk and not be faint.
**Isaiah 40:31 (NIV)**

# August 7

In the same way, let your light shine before others, that they may see your good deeds and glorify your Father in heaven.
**Matthew 5:16 (NIV)**

**In George MacDonald's** story *The Day Boy and the Night Girl,* a young girl named Nycteris grows up without ever seeing the sun or moon. She is locked away in a windowless room, with just a dim lamp for light. One night her lamp falls, and she is left in the dark! Thankfully, she escapes outside and discovers the glowing light of the moon for the first time. But for Nycteris—and us!—being left alone in the dark can be scary.

If you were stuck in the dark, what would you wish for? I know what I would wish for: a flashligh, something to light the way, so I could find the right path.

Today's world is often a dark place. Many people don't know about Jesus and his love for them, and they live without the hope that knowing Him brings. But Jesus tells us in Matthew 5:14 that *we* can be the light of the world. By offering kind words, loving others, showing generosity, and being good friends, we can shine a light for all to see that points the way towards Jesus.

What are some specific ways you can be a light to the people in your life?

*Bethany Wagner*
*Dedicated to Kathleen Wagner*

# August 8

**Sometimes things in** life just don't go right, do they? It's hard when we try something and fail. Sometimes we hop on our bike and crash into the curb. Sometimes we make a mistake when we're playing a song on the piano, or miss a goal in soccer. Sometimes we can't remember the answer to a question on a test, no matter how hard we study.

It's easy to be hard on ourselves when mistakes like these happen. It's also easy to compare ourselves to others, asking, "Why do they have that, and I don't?" or "Why are they so much more talented or popular than me?"

But read what the Bible has to say:

In Christ Jesus you are all children of God through faith.
**Galatians 3:26** (NIV)

God has made us His children!

1 John 3:2 echoes this truth: "Dear friends, now we are children of God, and what we will be has not yet been made known. But we know that when Christ appears, we shall be like him, for we shall see him as he is."

We are God's children. Even though we are excited for the day we will be with God in heaven, where they are no mistakes, we can celebrate the fact that we are God's children right now. We don't have to do anything or try to be perfect to be adopted into His family.

God loves us just as we are. So if you feel discouraged today, try seeing yourself as God sees you: as His precious child whom He loves.

*Bethany Wagner*
*Dedicated to Abigail Wagner*

# August 9

> However, he has given each one of us a special gift through the generosity of Christ.
> **Ephesians 4:7** (NLT)

**Most people love** receiving gifts. There are many reasons why people give and receive gifts. Some people enjoy receiving, rather than giving, and there are those who would rather give. What type of person are you—or are you both types?

Acts 20:35 reads, "It is more blessed to give than to receive." What is the greatest gift that you have been given? Have you ever thought about it? All of us have been given a gift that is above all else. That gift is Jesus.

Jesus is the reason for many things, including equipping you with your gift? What is your talent? What are you good at? We have all been given special gifts and talents, which we are to use to work in the ministry and build up the body of Christ. Some of us are given the talent of teaching, evangelizing, preaching, etc. Whatever the gift may be, you were given it because of Jesus' generosity. He has entrusted you with that particular gift, and it is important that you use the gift to glorify Him.

Next time you see something that catches your eye and you think that you'd like to have it, remember the gift that you've already been entrusted with. Use all that you have to glorify the Lord. He has trusted you and given you a gift that is designed specifically for you.

*Laura Bennin*

# August 10

**In George MacDonald's** book *Sir Gibbie*, the beauty of God's creation is always noticed by Gibbie. Although humans may be cruel to him, he never loses sight of the beauty of the Lord all around him:

> "The lambs were frolicking and in the sheltered places the flowers were turning the earth into a firmament. And now a mere daisy was enough to delight the heart of Gibbie. His joy in humanity so suddenly and violently checked, he had begun to see the human look in the face of the commonest flowers. The wind, of which he had scarce thought as he met it roaming the streets like himself, was now a friend of his solitude, bringing him sweet odors, alive with the souls of bees, and cooling with bliss the heat of the long walk."

Nature is God's gift. Remember that. Whenever you are sad, choose to let His beauty overwhelm you. See the beauty of the Lord and His great love for you in the chirping birds, the fragrant flowers, the playful puppy. Make yourself behold His beautiful creation, and let His love be upon you.

*Jolyn Canty*

Let the beauty of the Lord our God be upon us...
**Psalm 90:17** (MEV)

One thing have I desired of the LORD, that will I seek after, that I may dwell in the house of the LORD all the days of my life, to behold the beauty of the LORD...
**Psalm 27:4** (KJV)

# August 11

For God so loved the world, that he gave his only Son, that whoever believes in him should not perish but have eternal life. For God did not send his Son into the world to condemn the world, but in order that the world might be saved through him.
**John 3:16-17 (TLV)**

**In the language** that is used in the Hebrew Bible, or Torah (*the book of instruction*), the phrase *Son of God* refers to the king; specifically, the king of Israel. It is also important, though, that in Hebrew when something is "the son" of something else, it shares in the nature of that thing, for example "sons of hell" (destined for hell), "sons of a wedding" (part of a wedding party), "sons of the devil" (wicked, deceptive people). The Son of God, then, in some way shares in God's character, is in some way divine. Jesus is the Son of God in both of these ways—He is the King appointed over Israel, and He is divine.

The shocking message of the passage above is that Jesus is a king given for the sake of the world, the only true King, the only truly divine person, and He is given into the hands of the world to suffer and die to redeem creation. Jesus is a king who serves and rules by offering Himself, which is God's offering of Himself to the world. A king who sacrifices himself for his subjects is a true king, and that is the nature of the real king of all things, who is the loving ruler and servant of us all.

*Matthew Levi*

# August 12

To God belong wisdom and power;
counsel and understanding are his.
**Job 12:13 (NIV)**

**Have you ever** lost something—a favorite toy, your school backpack, or something else you needed or loved? Have you ever lost a pet? Did you feel as if no one knew how you felt and that no one could really help you?

Well, there was a man in the Bible named Job who might have felt that way. He was a very rich man whom God blessed with great wealth, including a loving family, but he lost it all.

God allowed this to happen to show what Job would do if he were to lose all that God had blessed him with. He wanted to show how faithful Job was! Many of Job's friends tried to give him advice, but what they said really wasn't what he needed to hear.

When you or your friends feel terribly sad and don't know what to do, consider this advice from the great writer George MacDonald, who learned a lot from thinking about Job. When we are afraid, he said, and just don't know what to do, we should call out to God! "What can please the Father of men better," wrote MacDonald, "than to hear his child cry to Him from whom he came, 'Here I am O God!'"

Like Job, you and your friends just need to know that God cares. Job knew that God cared and that all wisdom belonged to Him. When we seek the wisdom to deal with all the things in life that can go wrong, we go to God!

*Steven Joos*

# August 13

**Imagine that you** were a princess who had no gravity and couldn't stay on the ground, no matter how you tried! It would take many people with ropes tied around you to keep you in place so that the wind wouldn't carry you away. In the fairy tale *The Light Princess,* by George MacDonald, this is exactly what has happened, and the poor princess is doomed until a special person figures out how to save her.

In your world today, you may be a prince or princess that is suffering from being stuck in the mud, so to speak, with no close friends, or with difficulties at home or school. Or you may be just like the light princess, who never takes things seriously and thinks everything is a joke or not important as she floats above the solid ground. The writer in Psalms praises God for bringing us out of the muck and setting our lives on solid ground. Trusting Him even when things look bad or you are scared to move forward is exactly what King David did. You can read all about the trouble he got into and how God came in and saved the day; all he had to do was believe! If you feel like you need a steady hand to lift you up or bring you back down to earth, call out to Jesus. He is waiting with the strongest arms.

*Holly Van Shouwen*

He lifted me out of the slimy pit, out of the mud and mire; he set my feet on a rock and gave me a firm place to stand.
**Psalm 40:2 (NIV)**

# August 14

And the LORD God made garments of skins for the man and for his wife, and clothed them.
**Genesis 3:21 (NRSV)**

**Have you ever** done something naughty? Everyone has. What did your mother or father do? Did they tell you the consequences of your choice? Send you to your room? Did they seem angry? Sometimes, people can seem so angry it is hard to believe they still love us.

Your many-times-great-grandparents Adam and Eve did something naughty, too; they ate from a forbidden tree in God's garden. God seemed very angry, and Adam and Eve were afraid. God told them all the bad consequences of their disobedience, then sent them away. Instead of going to their room, they had to go out into the world beyond the garden. They probably worried God didn't love them anymore!

But, just like your mother or father, God only seemed angry because He was worried for His children. He knew the world can be dangerous and cold, so He made them coats to keep warm. He did still love them, after all!

In Jesus' time, the teachers said that the Torah (the first five books of the Bible) begins and ends with an act of kindness: God clothes Adam and Eve and He buries Moses. The first and last word about God, they said, was the good care He takes of us because of His love.

Think about your mother or father. What kind things do they do to show their love, even when they are angry? Are there kind things you can do to show your love, even when you are angry? We all make mistakes and get angry, but with God's help we can also make each day begin and end, just like the Torah, with an act of kindness.

*Race MoChridhe*

# August 15

Jesus, Master! Have pity on us!
**Luke 17:13**

Jesus, Son of David, have pity on me!
**Luke 18:38**

O God, be merciful to me a sinner.
**Luke 18:13**

**Listed are three** similar prayers from the Gospel of Luke. The first is from the story of the ten lepers, the second is from the story of the blind beggar, and the third comes from a parable told by Jesus. These words in Scripture help teach us how to talk to God. They are short, simple prayers that you can use when you pray. The prayers address Jesus (God) and ask Him for pity or mercy. To ask for pity (mercy) is to admit that you are not perfect and that you cannot solve a problem on your own.

A prayer for mercy does not ask for just any help, but asks for loving help. A prayer for mercy addresses One whom we trust and can expect to help. If you have read these stories in Scripture, you will know that all of these people received the mercy they prayed for. Whether you are praying alone or with others, whether praying for yourself or for others; whether you are praying because healing or for forgiveness, asking Jesus for mercy is always appropriate. There is no problem too big or too small for you to ask Jesus for His mercy. No person or situation is outside God's desire to grant His mercy. Heis waiting for you to ask.

*Sharon Edel*

# August 16

> The fear of the Lord is the beginning of knowledge, but fools despise wisdom and instruction.
> **Proverbs 1:7 (NIV)**

**Should we really** be in fear of the Lord? Our Lord is a kind Father. Knowing what He expects and requests of His children molds our earthly minds into His likeness. It is through our knowledge and discernment of the Lord that we can be faithful in our walk with Him. Fools decide not to follow or adhere to the words of the Lord.

What if everyone in the entire world did what they wanted, when they wanted, and suffered no consequences for their actions? Can you even begin to fathom the craziness that would be happening everywhere? Thankfully, this is not how our world is. We all experience consequences and are held to standards, whether we are good, bad, or indifferent. No person is exempt from consequences.

What exactly does knowledge mean? According to the Merriam Webster dictionary, knowledge is understanding or skill you get from experience or education. Knowledge of the Lord is what a wise person seeks. The Lord will guide and lead you into a life of faithfulness. Always seek to gain the Lord's wisdom in all that you do. Don't be foolish.

*Laura Bennin*

# August 17

> But Jesus answered and said, "Stop! No more of this." And He touched his ear and healed him.
> **Luke 22:51** (NASB)

**Do you ever** wonder what you will be like when you grow up or what work you will do as an adult? Do you ever wonder how many years you will live on this earth? I used to wonder what it would be like to turn sixteen, then twenty, and now I am wondering what it will be like to turn sixty.

Did you ever ask yourself, "If I knew this was the very last thing I would ever do, would I do it?"

Today's Bible verse is about the time when Jesus was arrested and taken away. Did you know that the very last thing He did with His kind hands was to heal a bad cut? Jesus left us an example that we should follow. Do the next thing that is given in this moment, this next minute, this next hour, for you to do. Do it faithfully and lovingly and patiently. Watch for things that you can do for those whom you love. Simply do each thing as it comes, as well as you can. If you make this a habit throughout each day, you will form a continuous habit of good, and you will be like Jesus.

The young lad, Gibbie, in George MacDonald's wonderful book *Sir Gibbie* loved to help every human and every living creature with whom he came in contact. He was always watching and ready. Not to be able to help was "to Gibbie like being dead," and "If anything suggested the possibility of helping further, a possibility turning entirely on the person's self, the attempt was set on foot."

*Jolyn Canty*

# August 18

I know your deeds. See, I have placed before you an open door that no one can shut. I know that you have little strength, yet you have kept my word and have not denied my name.
**Revelation 3:8 (NIV)**

**When you look** for adventure in your relationship with Jesus, do you worry about every little detail, or do you just trust and hold on for the ride? In the book of Revelation, Jesus tells the church that nothing is impossible for Him. He even says in the letter, "I know you have little strength." Have you ever felt like your strength is little?

It is a great thing that, all through the Bible, God takes people of little strength and does extraordinary things through their obedience. He tells them that they have kept His word, which means they are living by the teachings of the Bible and they have not been embarrassed to be called a follower of Jesus.

What are the open doors that God is showing you today?

Where are the places that you can seek adventure for Jesus this week? Maybe there is a family in your neighborhood that doesn't know anybody. Maybe there is someone at school that you can hang out with and get to know. You may feel like you cannot do it, but here is the reality: you can in the power of the Holy Spirit! When God opens doors to adventure for us, no one can shut them. Enjoy the adventure!

*Matthew Nash*

# August 19

## Attitude

**Myra walked into** her class with a bad attitude. She was so bored with school and her friends! "Are they really friends? Will they be there for me if I need them?" she wondered.

She was in deep thought when her teacher introduced a new girl. Her name was Marcie and she smiled all the time and at everyone. Even when pranks were pulled on her, she smiled. Then insults and rejection began, but she never said a word. Myra watched her handle these problems with ease. Finally, she could stand it no longer.

"What's wrong with you? Don't you ever get angry? Don't you know they're laughing at you?" Myra wanted to know what made this girl so different. Myra began to spend more and more time with Marcie, and she realized the smiles were for real. Marcie had a caring heart for others. Marcie invited Myra to church with her, where for the first time she heard how much Jesus loved her. Myra liked spending time with Marcie, and they became friends in a short time.

Myra began to look forward to going to Sunday School and memorizing verses. She especially liked this verse:

> Serve the Lord with gladness; come before His presence with singing.
> **Psalm 100:2** (KJV)

Then one day Myra received Christ into her heart. She could not help smiling, and the songs just flowed out of her mouth. Myra understood then how Marcie smiled, sang, and kept her cool with others. Myra's attitude was so much better that everyone noticed it, especially her parents!

*Dottie Thornton*

# August 20

…"and I will bring my people Israel back from exile. They will rebuild ruined cities and live in them. They will plant vineyards and drink their wine; they will make gardens and eat their fruit. I will plant Israel in their own land, never again to be uprooted from the land I have given them," says the Lord, your God.
**Amos 9:14-15 (NIV)**

**Tessa Scott and** her parents had moved to Savannah, Georgia over the summer to live closer to her grandparents.

About two weeks after starting sixth grade, she saw her parents watching TV after school one day: a hurricane was forming over Florida, and tracking towards Georgia. Her mom looked at her and said, "No school tomorrow. I got an e-mail from the principal."

Tessa and her family made preparations for the hurricane, but decided to move inland to stay with her grandparents.

Still, Tessa protested. "I don't want to leave home. What if when we come back, everything's gone?"

In the morning, the Scotts left Savannah, and Tessa said, "This reminds me of when Moses had to lead his people out of Israel to a different country. We are like nomads, Mom and Dad." Her mother said, "I know. Moses didn't know where he was going, but he obeyed the Lord. And the prophet Amos told the people of Israel that they would return home and rebuild what was broken. God wants us to be safe too, and to believe that we, his beloved nomads, will return home very soon."

Have you ever had to leave home to be safe?

What was it like?

*Amy Adams*

# August 21

## What to Wear, Where?

**King Solomon is** often called the wisest king who ever lived. He was also fabulously wealthy! We can be certain that King Solomon dressed himself in the finest clothing money could buy. But Jesus believed that the flowers of the field—like daisies, tiger lilies, coneflowers, and toadflax—were dressed more beautifully than King Solomon could have dressed himself. In fact, Jesus said that the flowers of the field didn't even labor or spin to create their clothing. God designed the wildflowers and Jesus appreciated their natural beauty.

Kings, queens, and lots of ordinary people have closets full of clothing: pants, skirts, dresses, robes, shoes, belts, hats, coats, scarves, wraps, boots, socks, t-shirts and underwear. Appropriate clothing is needed for personal privacy and for protection in cold or hot climates. But, too often, clothing is used to define who people are, where they live, how smart they might be, or how much money they have. Nothing is gained by judging people by the clothing they wear.

Yet, we often wonder…what should we wear? And where should we wear it?

Jesus said, "Do not worry about your clothing." Your true beauty, in the eyes of God, is in the way God designed you. Trust that you are as beautiful as the wildflowers that grow in the fields.

*Carol Wimmer*

"And why do you worry about clothes? See how the flowers of the field grow. They do not labor or spin. Yet I tell you that not even Solomon in all his splendor was dressed like one of these."
**Matthew 6:28-29** (NIV)

# August 22

When they had all had enough to eat, he said to his disciples, "Gather the pieces that are left over. Let nothing be wasted."
**John 6:12 (NIV)**

**If you remember** back to August 4th, I told you the story of a robin adopting an egg in an abandoned nest. At the time I couldn't tell you the rest of the story but now I can, at least, what I know of it.

When we left the story before, the young mother robin was sitting day after day on the abandoned egg. We were pretty sure the egg would not hatch, but wanted to let the mother do as she felt called to do. Soon an opportunity arose for us to peek into the nest. And what do you suppose we found? Three pretty blue eggs.

After some days, two little beaks appeared above the rim of the nest. Once more, when we had a chance, we peeked in to see the tiny babies resting their heads on the egg we had placed in the nest.

At the time I write this the birds have grown up and flown away. The nest still sits neatly within the upper framing of our front porch. But you may wonder what has happened to the abandoned egg. It is nowhere to be found. Was it eaten or cast out of the nest? We simply don't know.

What I think we can be certain of is that nothing in God's creation is wasted. Though something may be lost to us it has not lost its purpose in God.

*Steve Fronk*
*For Mom*

# August 23

## When No One Needs a Lamp or Light

> There will be no more night. They will not need the light of a lamp or the light of the sun, for the Lord God will give them light. And they will reign for ever and ever.
> **Revelation 22:5** (NIV)

**Did you know** that God's eternal light is greater than all of the light we can see? The sunlight only allows us to see a small portion of the light that actually exists. The light that we see is known as the visible spectrum, but there is an enormous, gigantic amount of *invisible light* that we cannot see.

It's hard to imagine being in the presence of God's invisible light, because we've never seen it! But we know that God's light contains no darkness. If there's no dark, then there's no night. Did you ever think of that? Night does not exist in the presence of God's light. The Bible talks about a time when there will be no more *night*. No one will need a lamp or the light of the sun because God will give us eternal light. Day and night will be no more.

I wonder what it would be like to never see darkness again? I wonder what God's eternal light will reveal? Will we be able to see God's face? Wouldn't it be awesome to see what God looks like? Imagine coming into God's presence and standing in God's light. Do you think we will be able to see things from a different angle, or a different perspective? Do you think we will see what God sees? Hmmm. I wonder.

*Carol Wimmer*

# August 24

**Have you heard** of the Great Chicago Fire of 1871? It killed several hundred people and destroyed more than three square miles of that city.

Horatio Spafford was a wealthy landowner in Chicago and lost a lot of money in the fire. A little later, his four-year-old son died of scarlet fever. To soften their sadness, the Spaffords decided to take a trip. Mrs. Spafford and their four daughters boarded a ship to England; Mr. Spafford would join them later after tending to some business. During the voyage, the ship sank, and all four of the girls were lost. Mr. Spafford quickly sailed to be with his wife, and as his ship traveled near the place where his daughters had died, he wrote the hymn "It Is Well With My Soul."

One of the verses is especially precious:

*Though Satan should buffet (meaning hit), though trials should come,*
*Let this blest assurance control,*
*That Christ hath regarded (seen) my helpless estate (condition),*
*And hath shed His own blood for my soul.*

Our sinful nature and the sins we commit have left us in a helpless condition. However, Jesus paid for our sins so we can be forgiven and live. In today's verse, God calls us to identify with Christ in His death *and* in His resurrection to new life. (Also see Romans 6:11.)

What a wonderful plan God has!

*William F. Powers and Jerian Powers*

I have been crucified with Christ and I no longer live, but Christ lives in me. The life I now live in the body, I live by faith in the Son of God, who loved me and gave himself for me.
**Galatians 2:20** (NIV)

# August 25

For we wrestle not against flesh and blood, but against principalities, against powers, against the rulers of the darkness of this world, against spiritual wickedness in high places. Wherefore take unto you the whole armor of God, that ye may be able to withstand in the evil day, and having done all, to stand. Stand therefore, having your loins girt about with truth, and having on the breastplate of righteousness; And your feet shod with the preparation of the gospel of peace; Above all, taking the shield of faith, wherewith ye shall be able to quench all the fiery darts of the wicked. And take the helmet of salvation, and the sword of the Spirit, which is the word of God: Praying always with all prayer and supplication in the Spirit, and watching thereunto with all perseverance and supplication for all saints.

**Ephesians 6:12-18 (KJV)**

**When I learned** these verses as a young man, I thought the important things were the individual military pieces that it describes: the shield, the helmet, the sword, and the rest. Indeed, all these *are* important, but the *most* important thing to remember is that they are all *God's* choices.

You see, the Apostle Paul reminds us here that we cannot fight the good fight of faith in our own way or in our own strength. We must trust our leader and what He says. That is what faith is—the assurance that God is right in what He says, how He leads, and in the way He equips us for the Christian life.

We can trust Him all the time. He is good!

*William F. Powers and Jerian Powers*

# August 26

"'Don't be sorry for me, Mr. Wingfold,' said her sweet voice after a few moments. 'The 'poor dwarfie,' as the children call me, is not a creature to be pitied. You don't know how happy I am as I lie here, knowing my uncle is in the next room and will come the moment I call him—and that there is one nearer still,' she added in a lower voice, almost in a whisper, 'whom I haven't even to call. I am his and he shall do with me just as he likes.'"

*The Curate's Awakening*, by George MacDonald

**Rachel was disabled.** Her body was misshapen, and pain was an everyday fact of her life. Some days she could hardly move. But she was happy nonetheless. When the curate came to visit, she gladly shared with him the source of her joy—the knowledge that Jesus was always with her, and her faith in His goodness and care.

When we are sick or injured and in pain, we can find comfort in remembering that God has promised never to leave us. And when we have experienced God's presence in our suffering, we also can share the promise of His care with others.

*Rebekah Choat*

Praise be to the God and Father of our Lord Jesus Christ, the Father of compassion and the God of all comfort, who comforts us in all our troubles, so that we can comfort those in any trouble with the comfort we ourselves receive from God. For just as we share abundantly in the sufferings of Christ, so also our comfort abounds through Christ.

**2 Corinthians 1:3-5 (NIV)**

# August 27

**In everything, there** is a moment of choice. You choose what to wear, what to eat, whether to obey your parents and teachers, and how to spend your free time. You choose whether to lose your temper or to speak kindly. There's always a moment of choice. With each choice, all day long, there is a consequence. Not wearing a jacket when it is cold can make you ill, eating too much sugar can give you a stomach ache and cavities, not doing your homework will cause you to fall behind in your studies. You get what I'm saying. At every moment there is a choice, and every choice has a consequence. The best way to make choices is to ask yourself, "What would Jesus do?" like little Gibbie did:

> "Gibbie was always placing what he heard by the side of what he knew, asking himself what Jesus would have done, or what he would require of a disciple...he always took refuge in doing something—and doing it better than before; leaping the more eagerly if Robert called him, spoke the more gently to Oscar, turned the sheep more careful not to scare them—as if by instinct he perceived that the only hope of understanding lies in doing. He would run to do the thing he had learned yesterday, when as yet he could find no answer to the question of today. Thus as the weeks of solitude and thought glided by, the reality of Christ grew upon him, till in the very rocks and heather and the faces of the sheep the felt His presence."
>
> *Sir Gibbie,* by George MacDonald

*Jolyn Canty*

...He knows enough to refuse evil and choose good.
**Isaiah 7:15 (NASB)**

# August 28

Do not fear, for I am with you; do not anxiously look about you, for I am your God. I will strengthen you, surely I will help you; Surely I will uphold you with My righteous right hand. For I am the LORD your God, who upholds your right hand Who says to you, "Do not fear; I will help you."
**Isaiah 41:10, 13 (NASB)**

"Now Curdie, are you ready?" asked Princess Irene. "Yes ma'am," answered Curdie. "You do not know what for," she replied. And Curdie said, "You do, ma'am. That is enough."
*The Princess and the Goblin,* by George MacDonald

**Curdie, a young** boy who helps his father in the mines below the castle, trusts Princess Irene, even though he doesn't know what she is sending him to do. She needs his help because she is in danger from the mountain goblins who seek to conquer the castle. Curdie trusts her completely, just like we should trust God. We might not know what He has planned for us, but we have to trust Him that He will always be with us, to have courage, and all will be well.

Just like Curdie, it is very important to trust the people in your life that love you. Always trust and obey your parents every day as they teach and help you learn important lessons, because God has entrusted them to take care of you, and they want God's best for you.

*Tegan Stark*

# August 29

How long, Lord? Will you forget me forever?
How long will you hide your face from me?
How long must I wrestle with my thoughts
and day after day have sorrow in my heart?
How long will my enemy triumph over me?
**Psalm 13:1-2 (NIV)**

**Listen how boldly** King David begins this Psalm! Did you know that you can speak that boldly to the Lord through prayer? He doesn't reject us when we are pouring out our hearts to Him and expressing our sadness, hurts, or anything else that we experience in life.

What has happened in your life today or recently that has caused you to hurt? Pour it out into the lap of God without fear of rejection in any way. We grow closer to Him when we tell Him what is in our hearts. He knows what is there already, for there is nothing that is hidden from Him. And when you truly have laid those burdens down, you have God's own promise that He will handle the situation and you will experience His peace, peace which is beyond human understanding. Then you will be able to say with the hymn writer Horatio Spafford, "It is well with my soul!"

*J.S. Donald*

# August 30

"I am content with what I have, little be it or much."
*The Pilgrim's Progress*, by John Bunyan

**"But if I** can't have that, I'll just *die!*"

Wanting better grades can push you to learn. Wanting friends can help you think about others instead of yourself. Wanting to pay your uncle the $20 you owe him can set you to earning money. But when it comes to *things*—especially other people's things—wanting what you don't have isn't always good.

Why would we make ourselves miserable by longing for what somebody else has? Three reasons are *resentment* ("It's not fair that I don't have it and he does!"), *competition* ("What do you mean, I can't have that? I'll show you!"), and *fear* ("My chance may be gone forever!").

When you've been happy with what you have until you see what somebody else has, you're coveting.

Covetousness and envy are cousins (you *envy* the person; you *covet* the thing). If you turn your brain and heart over to them, you'll never be content, ever. Look at Cain in the book of Genesis.

Maybe God has given you what you have because that's what He wants you to have right now. Maybe His plan for your future is better than your brother's new motorcycle or your friend's part in the play. Maybe saying, "No, that's not good enough!" is telling God that He's falling short. And that's not such a good idea!

*Mary Lichlyter*

Take care, and be on your guard against all covetousness, for one's life does not consist in the abundance of his possessions.
**Luke 12:15** (ESV)

# August 31

Some little girls would have been afraid to find themselves
thus alone in the middle of the night, but Irene was a princess.
*The Princess and the Goblin,* by George MacDonald

**A princess is** a girl whose father is a king. There are many more princes and princesses than you might think!

YOU may be a prince or a princess. YOUR Father may be the King.

I don't mean a king on earth that lives in a palace and wears a crown upon his head—but there is One who is the King of kings! I wonder if you know Him?

He is the most powerful! He is always present! He created the world! He defeated every enemy! He is good and kind, compassionate and gracious. He only speaks the truth; He knows the way to go. He can see through darkness, and night is just like day to Him. He knows every single thing about everything! There is no star He cannot reach; there is no problem He cannot solve! He heals the lame, gives sight to the blind, and restores life to the dead! He frees the imprisoned; He sings songs to the sorrowful. He is the highest name and the wisest counsellor. Can you guess His name?

He is Jesus Christ, King of Kings!

All who belong to Him are royal, chosen, and holy: a people for God's own possession—children who are true princes and princesses belonging to His Royal family!

*Blythe Followwill*
*For Jordan*

But you are a chosen race, a royal priesthood, a holy nation, a people for God's own possession.
**1 Peter 2:9a (NASB)**

# September 1

"Nature is not our mother; nature is our sister. We can be proud of her beauty, since we have the same Father; but she has no authority over us."
*Orthodoxy*, by G.K. Chesterton

> You are the LORD, you alone. You have made heaven, the heaven of heavens, with all their host, the earth and all that is on it, the seas and all that is in them; and you preserve all of them; and the host of heaven worships you.
> **Nehemiah 9:6 (ESV)**

**We don't own** the earth to do anything with it we please.

Many Christians say it's our job to be stewards of the earth. A steward takes good care of somebody else's property. God's Word says that the earth is the Lord's, and so is everything in it.

Some people say the earth is our mother ("Mother Earth"... "Mother Nature"), and we must care for it with the love and devotion a child has for its mother. That sounds as if nature is God. Is that true? No.

There's nothing God *didn't* create. He created the earth, the hippos, the butterflies, the swordfish, the weeping willows, and the people. He made cars, smart phones, and other inventions, by creating people with the abilities to invent them.

Long ago, people worshiped nature. They worshiped animals, thinking they were gods. They worshiped the sun because of its power. They worshiped stars, believing the stars controlled their lives. ( Some people do this today as well.)

Christians worship only the *Creator* of nature.

So thank God for the earth! Learn about it and take care of it. Know that it comes from our Savior.

*Mary Lichlyter*

# September 2

**Do you like** it when things change, or does it make you nervous?

Here are some examples of change: you are at school and come home to find your bedroom has been rearranged by your mom; your classrooms have all been switched because of flooding in one of the school halls; your mom cannot pick you up at school today so your neighbor will be picking you up.

How would those situations make you feel? They would make me feel nervous and a little out of control. I'll tell you a secret: even adults don't like change very much. We all like it when we know what's going on, right?

Well, one thing you can know for sure is that there will ALWAYS be changes in your life!

Things constantly change: you grow, your family moves, your puppy gets big, you go up a grade, you make new friends, and so on.

There is one thing that NEVER changes, though. Would you like to know what it is?

> Do not be afraid or discouraged, for the LORD will personally go ahead of you. He will be with you; He will neither fail you nor abandon you.
> **Deuteronomy 31:8 (NLT)**

Did you see it? Jesus will *always* be with you, even through all the changes in your life. The Bible says He will never leave you. Not only that, but He will also "go ahead of you!" That means He already knows about the change, and is getting things ready for you.

Isn't this great news? Now all you need to do is to trust Him as your Savior and follow Him!

*Alba Rice*

# September 3

> Be very careful, then, how you live—not as unwise but as wise, making the most of every opportunity, because the days are evil. Therefore do not be foolish, but understand what the Lord's will is.
> **Ephesians 5:15-17** (ESV)

**These verses offer** us great wisdom on how to be wise, if we listen to them. What does it mean to be careful how you live? Does it mean to be afraid? Does it mean to be so cautious you do nothing? I believe it means to think carefully, intentionally, about what you are doing and why. If you are in a family, God requires you submit to your parents and that your parents love and attempt to discipline you without exasperating you (see Ephesians 6).

Some people find they can live as they like while ignoring this advice, and lots of them do. But then they cannot be wise. They cannot make the most of every opportunity apart from the grace of the Gospel because they cannot overcome evil. None of us can, without God's grace.

We cannot overcome the evil of our own hearts or anyone else's. This means we are living in evil days. When you see evil you may get angry, you may fear for yourself or someone else, you may become sad. All of these responses are legitimate. Yet, when we remind ourselves of the good that God has done in history, in the lives of His people, and in our own lives, we free ourselves to be wise and not foolish. We free ourselves to have the wisdom to overcome evil with good, to forgive and seek forgiveness, and to love instead of hate.

*Amy Farley*

# September 4

**In *The Princess and the Goblin*** by George MacDonald, a young boy named Curdie grows up near a towering mountain. Curdie and his father are miners, and they delve deep, deep, deep into the mountain's caves and caverns looking for silver. Curdie goes on many adventures on and in the mountain as he encounters goblins and magic and the Princess Irene. Throughout the whole story, Curdie and Irene fight goblins, solve mysteries, and explore the many twisting caverns inside the mountain.

By the end of the story, both Curdie and Princess Irene have changed. They are braver, and have learned many lessons. But while the events of the story twist and turn, one thing stays the same throughout the whole book: the mountain.

Have you ever seen a big, towering mountain? Just as in the story, mountains stay the same day after day. Only big, rare events like earthquakes or eruptions can change their shapes suddenly.

Our Savior Jesus Christ is like a mountain. The Bible tells us,

> Jesus Christ is the same yesterday and today and forever.
> **Hebrews 13:8** (NIV)

As our lives twist and turn, He stays the same. As we make friends and lose friends, begin new adventures and finish them, He stays the same. We can always count on Him to be faithful, loving, and fulfill His promises to be with us every moment of every day.

*Bethany Wagner*
*Dedicated to Betty Wagner*

# September 5

So from now on we regard no one from a worldly point of view...
**2 Corinthians 5:16 (NIV)**

**In George MacDonald's** story *A Rough Shaking*, the young Clare Skymer has taken into his care the even younger Tommy. At one point in the story they find themselves in a very dangerous situation, chased by an angry blacksmith, but trapped by a formidable garden-wall. Can they find a way to safety? It's certainly worth reading the book to learn the whole story of their adventures.

But right now I would like us to look at a comment that Mr. MacDonald makes about the garden-wall itself.

> "In a few moments they were safe in the thicket at the foot of what had been their enemy and was now their friend—the garden-wall. How many things and persons there are whose other sides are altogether friendly! These are their true selves, and we must be true to get at them."

If there is a friendly side to everyone we meet, it seems like a good idea to get to that side as soon as ever we can. And fortunately, we are given a clue to making our way there. It seems to lie mostly with *us*. If we will think rightly about them, as God thinks, and work hard to be as true as we can be ourselves, we will likely find the friendly side of others. And that must be a better place to live, don't you think?

*Steve Fronk*
*For Emily Elizabeth*

# September 6

## A Whisper Voice

A whisper voice can start your day.
Wake up, sleepy, come and play.
Outside the wide world waits for you,
there is so much to see and do.

A whisper voice is how you call
a sleeping kitten in a ball
to wake up from his morning nap
and climb into your cozy lap.

A whisper is for when you see
the smallest duck in a family
who stops as they go marching by
and looks at you right in your eye.

A whisper is for when you see
a tiny spider in a tree
drop on a slender silver string
into the air and swing and swing.

Whisper when a butterfly
comes floating out of the blue sky
and folds its orange wings to rest
a little while upon your chest.

Whisper when the setting sun
turns golden and the day is done.
It slips away into the night
and leaves behind the white
moonlight.

With a whisper you can say
goodbye to a very happy day.
While you're drifting off to sleep,
whisper as you count the sheep.

And whisper, if you feel afraid,
to God, who all your playthings made,
for He can hear the softest sound
and with His love He will surround
you, gently, like a whisper.

*Diane Adams*

After the earthquake came a fire, but the LORD was not in the fire. And after the fire came a gentle whisper.
**1 Kings 19:12** (NIV)

# September 7

> Do not be anxious about anything, but in every situation, by prayer and petition, with thanksgiving, present your requests to God. And the peace of God, which transcends all understanding, will guard your hearts and your minds in Christ Jesus.
> **Philippians 4:6-7** (NIV)

**Our minds can** play tricks on us at times. We start worrying about things that have not yet happened! That's silly, isn't it? But God understands you and cares about what is worrying you or making you anxious. Philippians 4:6-7 tells us what to do when our minds trick us into worry. First, God commands us not to be anxious about anything, because He is in charge and takes care of us. We, too, need to command our minds, telling ourselves not to be anxious. Second, God wants us to pray and tell Him how we are feeling. He cares about everything that bothers you. Leave everything in His hands. He will help you win when your mind wants to play tricks on you and make you worry.

*Heavenly Father, thank you for caring about me and how I feel. Help me not to worry about things that have not even happened yet. In Jesus name. Amen.*

*Jose del Pino*

# September 8

**School is back** in session with old friends to see, new adventures to share, and division, percentages, and haikus to learn. It's exciting to be back into the swing of things, catch up on the summer activities, and take on new challenges in the year ahead. As I spent much of each summertime in Vacation Bible School, I often started my first few school days wondering how I could possibly say something that would produce "fruit" that Jesus would be proud of. Not that I wanted to hand out bananas and mangos, but I felt like I should somehow tell my friends and schoolmates about all that I had learned about God and how much he loved everyone and wanted to be in our lives.

Even at your age, you can have an impact on your school, and preach the good news without standing on a pulpit. Jesus taught us to show His love and tell people we know about the good things that He has done for us. I remember when the teacher asked us on the first day one year what we had learned over the summer, and we each took turns telling about something we had done or experienced over those long, hot days of fun. I put up my hand and even though I was scared, I stood up and told the truth. "I learned that I am loved more then I can imagine," I said. Later that day, a friend asked me how I knew that. Do you see what a wonderful opportunity that was? How might you answer a question like that?

*Holly Van Shouwen*

Go into all the world and preach the gospel to all creation.
**Mark 16:15** (NIV)

# September 9

> Love is patient, love is kind. It does not envy, it does not boast, it is not proud. It does not dishonor others, it is not self-seeking, it is not easily angered, it keeps no record of wrongs. Love does not delight in evil but rejoices with the truth.
> **1 Corinthians 13:4-6** (NIV)

**Love, a young** girl from Rwanda named Esther told me today, is the most powerful force on Earth. Esther grew up without a mother and father, because they were killed in the 1994 war in Rwanda. She has forgiven the people who did that, because of how Jesus forgave her. The love of Jesus is big enough to do this! The love that you show people every day is a reflection of Jesus' love.

Try something right now: take the verse above, and everywhere you see the word "love," put in your name instead. Was it difficult? How did you feel after doing it? It is hard, because as much as we try on our own to love exactly like Jesus, we fall short. Thank God that we have grace. The power of grace and love can take away our sin when we surrender to Jesus.

Make a list of five people this week whom you can *show* that you love,not just tell them. You may have heard the phrase: actions speak louder than words. It is really true! I know that you can bring love to others, because you have been loved by God.

*Matthew Nash*

# September 10

**There is something** magical about watching the sunrise on a cold crisp morning, when you can see your breath, and the cold air makes your toes retreat for shelter. Everybody connects with God best in different places, but for me it is most definitely outdoors. I remember when I was taking a morning hike up in the Sequioa National Forest in California, and I was struck by how massive the tree trunks were. It made me rejoice that we have such a creative God.

George MacDonald said, "God is so true and good and strong and beautiful! The God of mountain lands and snowdrops, of woman's beauty and man's strength—the God and Father of our Lord Jesus Christ."

Where do you best connect with God in a special way? Find some time today, even if it starts with just five minutes and then grows from there. We will always struggle to know God without a steady diet of time with Him. There is no substitute, no app, no quick fix. It is often when we slow down that we most understand the heart of God.

*Matthew Nash*

In his hand are the depths of the earth, and the mountain peaks belong to him. The sea is his, for he made it, and his hands formed the dry land.
**Psalm 95:4-5** (NIV)

# September 11

> "Teacher, which is the greatest commandment in the Law?" Jesus replied: "'Love the Lord your God with all your heart and with all your soul and with all your mind.' This is the first and greatest commandment. And the second is like it: 'Love your neighbor as yourself.'"
>
> **Matthew 22:36-39 (NIV)**

**Christ spent the** whole of Himself showing love to God and His neighbors. He asks us to do the same. While this is a simple principle, it can be very difficult to always follow. Learning to do so brings the greatest level of happiness in our lives.

George MacDonald said, "For as these are *the* two commandments of life, so they are in themselves *the* pleasures of life." To help us learn this pleasure, all of his stories are full of characters who show love during their daily interactions with people. Through these examples, we learn new insights into being like Christ, and truths such as:

"In thinking lovingly about others, we think healthily about ourselves."

"Love is divine...most divine when it loves according to needs and not according to merits."

"It is a small thing to be wronged, but a horrible thing to wrong [another]."

"A very great part of the disputes in the world come from our having a very keen feeling of our own troubles, and a very dull feeling of our neighbour's."

"The man here that doeth most service, that aideth others the most...is the man who standeth highest with the Lord...and his reward and honor is, to be enabled to the spending of himself yet more for the good of his fellows."

*James House*

# September 12

> But go and learn what this means: "I desire mercy, not sacrifice." For I have not come to call the righteous, but sinners.
> **Matthew 9:13 (NIV)**

**George MacDonald once** said that "justice and mercy are simply one and the same thing; without justice to the full, there can be no mercy, and without mercy to the full, there can be no justice." But sometimes it's really hard to show mercy, and therefore give justice, when someone has really hurt us, or hurt someone we love and care for.

Jesus had invited those that were thought of as "sinners" and, therefore, unworthy, to be his dinner guests along with his disciples. This made many people angry—they couldn't understand it! They thought they were better than the sinners, and deserved more of Jesus' attention. But, with this verse, Jesus was trying to teach them that showing mercy, even to those who may not seem like "good" people, was more important than rigidly following rules and giving up pleasures to make ourselves seem better.

When I was a teacher, I once witnessed a young girl who was teased all morning for wearing new glasses. By lunchtime, she was nearly in tears and sat by herself to eat. She then noticed that one of the bullies had forgotten his lunch and, because he had nothing to trade, none of his companions shared their lunches with him. She looked down at her own food and thought for a moment. She then walked over and handed the child who'd teased her half of a sandwich from her own lunch. Despite the pain and humiliation she'd suffered, she demonstrated both mercy and justice.

*Lisa Lynott-Carroll*

# September 13

> Be wise in the way you act toward outsiders; make the most of every opportunity.
> **Colossians 4:5** (ESV)

**Paul writes often** of *wisdom*. This time he is telling members of the body of Christ to watch, be mindful of, be careful about, and think about the way people who don't know Jesus see them.

Why would we worry about that? Why should we care what other people think of what we do, or how we live?

Sometimes we have to do what we know is right even if people disagree with us, but that is not what Paul is warning about here. Paul is telling his friends who love Jesus that the world outside their church is watching to see if they really live like the Gospel, like Jesus. How do we love each other? Are you respectful of your parents and grandparents, and even your brothers and sisters? Do you make jokes at other people's expense, just so someone will laugh?

What opportunities do we have to show people about Jesus? I suspect we have more opportunities to *show* them than to *tell* them. What about the student who always sits alone at lunchtime? What would happen if you sat next to them? What about the one who is always whispered about? Do you ever speak up against the whispers?

Jesus came to show us and the whole world how much God loves us. How does how you act show people about what God has done for you? Think about it!

*Amy Farley*

# September 14

"The principal part of faith is patience."
George MacDonald

And it shall come to pass, when I bring a cloud over the earth, that the bow shall be seen in the cloud:
**Genesis 9:14 (KJV)**

**The story of Noah** and the ark is about a man told to do a thing—build an ark—who went about doing it no matter what. Many people believe it took over a hundred years to build the ark and gather the animals into it. It had to have taken a long time, but Noah and his sons patiently did the building as God told them to. It was to be of a specific wood and specific size and be caulked and ready to float. Noah patiently did as God told him.

Meanwhile, God was being patient with all of mankind. Noah was a preacher and was telling the people that a flood was coming, but the people of the earth were wicked and cruel to one another. They would not listen. Still, God was patient and sent a message of peace through His servant Noah.

When the flood finally came and washed away all the violent people and the animals not taken into the ark, the world was, in a way, made new. When the land was dry enough for Noah, his family, and the animals to leave the ark, God gave Noah a special sign of His everlasting promise of peace to mankind. It was the rainbow, the promise that God would never again destroy the earth with a flood. Noah had faith in a patient, loving God.

*Linda S. Storm*

# September 15

**In one of** George MacDonald's fairy tales, a wicked fairy places a dreadful curse on a baby princess named Daylight. Thankfully, however, a good fairy steps forward and declares that the curse will last only "until a prince comes who shall kiss her without knowing it." But how could such a thing happen? How could a prince kiss this unfortunate princess without knowing it?

Evidently, a power greater than the prince was guiding his steps, for the prince did unknowingly fulfill the prophecy. But the prophecy would never have been fulfilled through him if the prince hadn't done his part. When he kissed Daylight, it was a compassionate act. He didn't recognize her, for at that moment she didn't look like a princess at all, but like an old, suffering woman, about to die. He had found her forsaken in the forest and picked her up in his arms to carry her to a place of help. What if the prince had not had a compassionate heart? He wouldn't have thought to show such pity and tenderness toward an old, helpless woman, and the curse would not have been broken through him.

The Bible says:

> ...for it is God who works in you, both to will and to work for his good pleasure.
> **Philippians 2:13 (ESV)**

When you do what is pleasing to God, God lives and works in you. So be compassionate and generous today, and God will be at work in you, just as he was in the prince, possibly even breaking a curse in someone's life.

*Daniel Koehn*

# September 16

## Belonging

**When we sit** down in the evening for supper, we can look around us and see our family. Sometimes, there are special days when more of our family comes over to share a meal with us. Sitting there, we know we are part of that family.

There are times when we eat at church, and it feels like we are sitting down with family. We can find family all around us: our friends, schoolmates, neighbors, and even people we meet as we go about our life.

A good prayer we can pray every day is to imagine everyone we know and see, everyone we hear about, even those people we see in pictures or on the television, as a member of our family.

Surrounding us with His love is our Heavenly Father, who is God. All of us are members of God's family, those who are in Heaven, and those who are here with us on Earth.

The Bible teaches us that all of us have God's name as part of our own. At the end of our own name is the title, God's-Son or God's-Daughter.

All of us belong to the family of God. We are in His family.

We all come together in unity under the love and the name of God, the Father.

Keep this thought very close to your heart, and whenever you need someone to talk to, someone from your own family, always remember that you can go to God, the Father of us all.

*Julia Marks*

...I kneel before the Father, from whom every family in Heaven and on Earth derives its name.
**Ephesians 3:14-15 (NIV)**

# September 17

## In His Image

And we all, who with unveiled faces contemplate the Lord's glory, are being transformed into his image with ever-increasing glory, which comes from the Lord, who is the Spirit.
**2 Corinthians 3:18 (NIV)**

**At creation, man** was created in God's image and likeness. *So God created mankind in his own image, in the image of God he created them; male and female he created them.* Genesis 1:27 (NIV) However, after the fall (when Adam disobeyed God), the glory of God left Adam and Eve. Jesus restored all that was lost by Adam. Now we are being transformed into the likeness of Christ.

We are to be a reflection of God's nature. We are to alter our vocabulary and lifestyle to conform to His. We look into the Bible to determine His nature and character, and as we invite Him into our lives, He comes in and gives us a new nature. We let go of our natural sinful attitudes and we are transformed continually to conform to the likeness of Christ. Jesus was God who came in human form with all the frailties of human nature, yet He lived an overcoming life by the Holy Spirit. He has equipped us to do the same!

*Prithika*

No, in all these things we are more than conquerors through him who loved us.
**Romans 8:37 (NIV)**

# September 18

## Blessings

**As Alahna reluctantly** walked into her new Sunday School class, she was very unsure of herself: her looks, her dress, her whole being. Already she was missing her old church and friends. The teacher was reading the Bible where The Lord said,

> (See) if I will not open you the windows of heaven and pour you out a blessing, that there shall not be room enough to receive it.
> **Malachi 3:10 (KJV)**

Alahna was sure her blessings came only one at a time.

Alahna took a seat beside a girl with long black hair, because she had such a warm friendly smile. After asking if anyone wanted to share a way God had blessed their life, the girl raised her hand. Alahna listened intently as the girl, Nikki, told of losing her family in an accident when she was young. She felt so blessed by her new family and the home she had. Alahna was very uncomfortable.

As soon as class was over, a man with a wheelchair came to the door. As he lifted Nikki and placed her in the chair, she turned and gave Alahna a radiant smile. "Will I see you next Sunday?" she asked. Alahna nodded a "yes" as she gave the girl her most sincere smile.

Some blessings may come slower than others, but, God blesses us in His way and in His time. He wants us to look for our blessings each day.

Alahna learned that growing in the Lord was to accept herself as she was. Today's blessings were many, but the blessing of a friend was the best.

*Dottie Thornton*

# September 19

> We can rejoice, too, when we run into problems and trials, for we know that they help us develop endurance. And endurance develops strength of character, and character strengthens our confident hope of salvation.
> **Romans 5:3-4** (NLT)

**Sometimes bad things** happen. Sometimes we have to go through things that are not very fun. The Bible says that we should be happy about those times. But why? Since it is a difficult thing to understand, C.S. Lewis told a story in the *Chronicles of Narnia* to help us understand.

Eustace Scrubb was not a nice boy. He was so mean he even picked up a talking mouse by the tail and swung him around in circles. He thought that was funny! He was a bully of the worst kind.

But then something happened—he was turned into a dragon! Eustace did not like being a dragon. One minute he was a boy, the next minute he was a big, clumsy monster. He couldn't walk easily and he couldn't talk. He couldn't eat like a boy, run like a boy, or do anything that boys like to do. Even though he could have bullied his friends even more as a dragon, he realized he would much rather just be a boy again.

Eustace went through a lot of hard times as a dragon. But he learned how to be nice and how to help other people. By the time he was changed back into a boy he had learned how to not be a bully.

This is why the Bible says to "rejoice when we run into problems." With God's help problems can make us into better people.

*Darrel Hotmire*

# September 20

## Living with Time and Eternity

**Did you know** that human beings are the only creatures on earth that measure time? Animals understand day and night, and know about changing seasons, but they don't know how to measure the passage of time or think about the future. Animals live in the present moment—every moment.

Many people wonder when time began, or when the heavens and earth were created. People also wonder when time will end, or *if* time will end. Humans live with measured time, but we also have eternal time set in our hearts. The clock, which measures temporal time, is a clever human invention that helps organize our days. It can also cause us to feel stressed or pressured, especially when taking a timed test or playing a timed game.

Eternal time is unmeasured time. It has no beginning or end. Every second of our temporal life also belongs to our eternal life—like two co-existing realms of time. Since we cannot know when our time on earth will end, we live with the trust that God is making everything beautiful in His time. That includes us. So, the best thing we can do with our time is to be happy and do good while God is making us beautiful! What makes you happy? What does *doing good* mean to you?

*Carol Wimmer*

He has made everything beautiful in its time. He has also set eternity in the human heart; yet no one can fathom what God has done from beginning to end. I know that there is nothing better for people than to be happy and to do good while they live.
**Ecclesiastes 3:11-12 (NIV)**

# September 21

> Listen, I tell you a mystery: we will not all sleep, but we will all be changed—in a flash, in the twinkling of an eye, at the last trumpet. For the trumpet will sound, the dead will be raised imperishable, and we will be changed.
> **1 Corinthians 15:52** (NIV)

**God loves music!** More specifically, the Bible can easily show that God really loves trumpets! Today, the Jewish people celebrate the Feast of Trumpets, remembering how Joshua and his army of priests blew trumpets that caused Jericho to crumble down, and how people were called to go to the temple with trumpets. He used it to proclaim to all of Israel the liberty that He had given them in Leviticus, and we know that when Jesus returns, a trumpet will blast as we meet Him in the sky to begin our lives in heaven with Him.

I was in band when I was in school and I always wanted to play the trumpet and trombone. I ended up with flute and clarinet. I loved to be a part of the whole musical symphony that would ring through the class, giving each type of instrument time to showcase its special sound. When the trumpets had their turn, I would close my eyes and listen to the royal sounds coming from the shiny horns as if they were making a message clear. As our verse for today states, the ultimate royal trumpet will sound and raise the dead in Christ, and we will be called together to be with Him in paradise forever! I often try to imagine what that sound will be like, and the beauty of the song. That's a concert I do NOT want to miss.

*Holly Van Shouwen*

# September 22

For the eyes of the Lord are upon them that love him. He is their mighty protection and strong stay; a defense from heat, and a cover from the sun at noon, a preservation from stumbling and an help from falling.
**Ben Sira 34:16 (KJVA)**

**Summer was ending,** and James was beginning a new school tomorrow. The summer had been awesome, moving to the farm, but his mom wanted James to make some new friends, too.

James was a loner, and he was okay with that. He liked to play by himself, read, and work on the farm. Today James was reading *The Princess and Curdie*, a story by George MacDonald. James loved to read fantasy, and he enjoyed the characters' adventures.

James went into the kitchen and asked his mom, "Why can't I be brave like Curdie?" Before Mom could answer, he read, "'So he began to think about his father and mother in their little cottage home high in the clear air of the open mountain side, and the thought, instead of making his dungeon gloomier by the contrast, made a light in his soul that destroyed the power of darkness and captivity.' Curdie found a way to destroy the darkness," said James. "I wish I could!"

Mom said that James was brave, and added, "How about talking to God and telling Him what you're afraid of? God has got you covered." James asked, "He has my back?" "Yes," said his mom. "Picture God walking next to you, being your strength and power. You'll be as brave as Curdie."

What do you do when you are afraid?

Have you tried talking to God?

*Amy Adams*

# September 23

## The Joy Ahead

**There are many** wonderful things about this world. There are many things that make our lives fun and exciting. We have friends and family who we love dearly and enjoy being with. The beauty of creation is spread out all around us. We have the privilege of living on a planet that is able to meet all of our needs in a way that no other planet yet discovered would be able to.

However, even with all of the things that make our lives here special, at the end of the Bible, we find John asking that Jesus would come back and bring us to our eternal home with Him. As amazing as our lives here are, for those who love and follow Jesus Christ and trust Him as personal Lord and Savior, this is only the beginning. John was willing to leave the world to go to the place that God has planned for the future.

C.S. Lewis wrote about this at the end of *The Chronicles of Narnia* in *The Last Battle,* and told about a future where "every chapter is better than the one before."

As amazing and beautiful as life on earth is, it is only the beginning. Spending an eternity with God is the ultimate joy. We should be excited when we think about our future. It is very bright.

*Zak Schmoll*

He who testifies to these things says, 'Yes, I am coming soon.' Amen. Come, Lord.
**Revelation 22:20** (NIV)

# September 24

"To the glory of His name let me witness that in faraway lands, in loneliness (deepest sometimes when it seems least so), in times of downheartedness and tiredness and sadness, always, always He is near. He does comfort, if we let Him. Perhaps someone as weak and good-for-nothing as even I am may read this. Don't be afraid! Through all circumstances, outside, inside, He can keep me close."
Amy Carmichael

"Always, everywhere God is present, and always
He seeks to discover Himself to each one"
*The Pursuit of God,* by A.W. Tozer

**There are times** in our lives when we feel like we are in a faraway land. Perhaps our family, friends, or others do not understand us. Maybe we have said or done something that has caused hurt in our relationship with someone—or even between us and God. Take heart. He is always faithful and His love is everlasting. Return to Him if you have gone astray and He will give you rest and peace. Seek comfort from Him if you feel like you are alone. Ask Him to show His love and mercy to you. He is the faithful one who will never leave you nor forsake you.

*Laurel Shepherd*

In a far-off land the LORD will manifest himself to them. He will say to them, "I have loved you with an everlasting love. That is why I have continued to be faithful to you."
**Jeremiah 31:3** (NET)

# September 25

Jesus answered, "I am the way and the truth and the life. No one comes to the Father except through me."
**John 14:6 (NIV)**

**Some days it** is so hard to know what to do. Friends pull you one way. Parents tell you to do things. You have homework for school. Where do you begin?

Jesus answers all these questions by telling you a simple answer: go to Him. Jesus is the Way, the Truth, and the life. So start with Him. Sit down and pray. Journal your conversation to help you stay focused if your mind wanders. Ask Jesus your questions. He will help you know if you should listen to friends. He will help you finish your schoolwork with a clear mind. He will help you obey your parents. How wonderful it is that you do not have to find your way alone, that Jesus is there with you every step.

The answer is simple; following it is not always so simple. However, you can do it when you focus and try. Do not step out with answers to friends or actions to work until you have first talked to Your Savior to find your way. He is there to walk with you, make your decisions easier, and your load lighter. Talk to Him; He will show you the way!

*Michelle Blackmon, Ed.D.*

# September 26

**When you wake** in the morning, how do you decide what to do first? How do you decide where you are going for the day? Sometimes, it seems like it's not your choice. Some days you go to school because that is what you have to do. Some days you go to church; be grateful for parents who allow that for you. So you may feel as if where you go is not your decision.

But it is.

You choose to go where God wants you, or not go where He wants you. When you choose His will, He comes with you. So, choose where you go and bring God along with you. How is your day different knowing you choose to bring God with you? How do you feel knowing you bring a piece of heaven along with you? That is a lot of power!

Wherever you go, take God with you. You will change your destination by adding a piece of heaven. Stay where He wants you; go where He wants you. Let God be your God, let Him have the details, your day will be so much better when you do!

*Michelle Blackmon, Ed.D.*

But Ruth replied, "Don't urge me to leave you or to turn back from you. Where you go I will go, and where you stay I will stay. Your people will be my people and your God my God.
**Ruth 1:16** (NIV)

# September 27

The kingdom of heaven is like treasure hidden in a field. When a man found it, he hid it again, and then in his joy went and sold all he had and bought that field.
**Matthew 13:44** (NIV)

**Gibbie crawled about** in the dirt, clawing at it with his hands, ignoring everything—even someone calling his name. Then suddenly he jumped to his feet with a yell, laughing. He had found what he was so intently looking for, a purple glass earring. He rubbed it on his sleeve until it glistened, then tucked it safely into his pocket—not to keep, but to return it to Mysie, the baker's daughter, who had lost her mother's earring that morning (summarized from *Sir Gibbie* by George MacDonald).

In our Bible verse, a man found a treasure of great wealth. The man, not even thinking about seeking for treasure, found one, and then hid it again, and sold everything to make it his own. You could say that man was greedy, while Gibbie was not, and you'd be right. But while we should all be generous like Gibbie, Jesus is making a different point. The treasure the man found is like finding the kingdom of heaven, and we need to seek the kingdom with everything we've got. In the story, Jesus tells us that the kingdom of heaven—knowing God's love and loving God—is worth far more than anything else we have.

*Frank Mills*

# September 28

And now, dear brothers and sisters, one final thing. Fix your thoughts on what is true, and honorable, and right, and pure, and lovely, and admirable. Think about things that are excellent and worthy of praise.
**Philippians 4:8 (NIV)**

**One of the** greatest blessings in life is to have a mother and father who love you and always seek to do their best for you. We are told by George MacDonald in *The Princess and Curdie* that the miner-boy Curdie had parents just like this. Here's what he says about them:

> They were the happiest couple in that country, because they always understood each other, and that was because they always meant the same thing, and that was because they always loved what was fair and true and right better, not than anything else, but than everything else put together."

What, do you suppose, helped them to love that which is best so deeply? I suspect it had a great deal to do with how they chose to use their minds. God has given us a great freedom in what we think about. MacDonald says elsewhere that our imaginations are given us that, "… alone one may meet many, sitting still may travel far, and silent make the universe hear."

By placing our thoughts on those things that are right and admirable we will begin to see their beauty and to love them. Now it's your turn. Can you think of some good things to think about?

*Steve Fronk*
*For My Grandchildren*

# September 29

> Store your treasures in heaven, where moths and rust cannot destroy, and thieves do not break in and steal. Wherever your treasure is, there the desires of your heart will also be.
> **Matthew 6:20-21** (NLT)

**A lot of** money is spent on advertising on TV and all around us. A thing can look very appealing, and soon we may want what is advertised. The longing can become so great, you think you just cannot be happy unless you have that thing you have set your heart on. These verses point out that *things* do not last very long. They do not bring real contentment and happiness. Jesus is the only One who can do that, and He says to store our treasures in heaven, where nothing or no one can take them away. What does that mean, and how do we do it?

You can probably think of some people you know who think a lot about making money and spending it. They often love to collect things, and then spend time admiring what they have. Now think about people who focus on serving Jesus and others. Their lives are very different, aren't they? Everyone needs money to live, but some don't live for money. Their treasure is Jesus. Jesus said, "You cannot worship God and money." (Matthew 6:24) That makes the choice clear, and we need to pray for His help to stay true to Him.

*Dear Jesus, As I make my choices, please help me to remember that You are my treasure, and everything in my life should please and serve You. Thank you for loving and helping me.*

*Vicki Ryder*

# September 30

God is our refuge and strength, an ever-present help in trouble. Therefore we will not fear, though the earth give way and the mountains fall into the heart of the sea, though its waters roar and foam and the mountains quake with their surging.
**Psalm 46:1-3 (NIV)**

**What a great** promise this is! God is beside you always to help you in any trouble that you face. I've heard several different preachers say that we should claim the promises in the Bible and personalize them. So you can say, "God is MY refuge and strength, MY ever-present help in trouble. So I will not fear....."

You can take the promise even further. Most of us will not see the "earth give way and the mountains fall into the sea." Thank God that we won't see troubles like that, though we may feel like what we're experiencing is that bad. But you can still take this verse and appy it to your problems. Have your friends treated you poorly? Then you should say, "God is my refuge and strength, my ever-present help in trouble. So I will not fear, though my friends treat me badly and I feel alone." The Lord is beside you and will step into the troubles you face to comfort you and guide you through them.

*J.S. Donald*

# October 1

"Then the great old, young, beautiful princess turned to Curdie.
'Now, Curdie, are you ready?' she said.
'Yes, ma'am,' answered Curdie.
'You do not know what for.'"
*The Princess and Curdie,* by George MacDonald

**Once there was** a little girl who was asked to do a very hard thing, a very scary thing, something she was afraid would hurt. Her daddy, who was big and strong and good, took her in his arms to pray. The little girl looked up into his face and asked, "Daddy, will it hurt?" He looked into the eyes of his daughter, whom he loved dearly, and said, "Yes, it will hurt. But we will pray and ask your Father in Heaven to help you." The little girl believed her father; she trusted him because she knew he loved her. Later, when everything was over, she said earnestly, "I was berry-berry brave to me." She was only three, yet she trusted her daddy even when it was scary. She knew her earthly father loved her. She believed he would not lead her where it was not good.

Some things that are good for us hurt. Some things we are asked to do in life are scary—things like having to have a shot or an operation. But when the person with you is good, and strong, and true—you trust them!

God is good and strong and true! He will give you the very trust to trust Him with.

*Blythe Followwill*
*For Esther*

Blessed is the man who trusts in the Lord and whose trust is the Lord.
**Jeremiah 17:7** (NASB)

# October 2

**One is never** too young or too old to talk about love, and it is important to know that there are different kinds of love. There is father love: easy to please, but difficult to satisfy. There is mother love: always protective, comforting, and nurturing. And there is romantic love: a longing to know someone fully and to be fully known by them. Everyone needs all three kinds of love, but trouble sometimes comes when we mix up where we try to get each kind.

The most confusing of all is romantic love. That is why the Bible says you should

> Guard your heart above all else, for it is the source of life.
> **Proverbs 4:23** (HCSB)

Our hearts are precious and should not be given away carelessly, as author George MacDonald warns in his novel, *Phantastes:*

"Alas! how easily things go wrong!
A sigh too deep, or a kiss too long,
And then comes a mist and a weeping rain,
And life is never the same again."

We shouldn't be afraid of love, but neither should we rush into it. Here is the best advice that I've found:

> Promise me, O women of Jerusalem, not
> to awaken love until the time is right.
> **Song of Solomon 8:4** (NLT)

But how do you know when the time is right? That is a matter of prayer, wise counsel, and circumstance.

Even when you've weighed the matter on your very best scale, there's always a risk your romance may fail; nevertheless, give love a chance.

*Michael Gailey*

# October 3

"Then [the maid] went from the room, and in a moment returned in royal purple, with a crown of diamonds and rubies…The king rose and kneeled on one knee before her…But she made them all sit down, and with her own hands placed at the table seats for [the servants]. Then in ruby crown and royal purple she served them all."
*The Princess and Curdie,* by George MacDonald

Blessed are those slaves whom the master will find on the alert when he comes; truly I say to you, that he will gird himself to serve, and have them recline at the table, and will come up and wait on them.
**Luke 12:37 (NASB)**

**Imagine that a** very special person is coming to visit. With delight, you spend extra time cleaning and arranging everything just so. You prepare delicious foods, tea, cakes, and homemade ice cream, and invite all your friends and neighbors to come for the big day. But most of all, your heart swells with joy and anticipation!

Jesus Christ is that very special person who is coming to your house! He is the King of Kings and Lord of Lords, robed in light and crowned with glory. But when He sees how you have longed for His coming, and how you have prepared yourself and your neighbors to receive Him, His heart will swell as He joyfully embraces you. Then, as He pleads for everyone to sit down, He will put on an apron and treat you all with honor as He serves you with His own hands.

*Thaine Norris*

# October 4

## Waiting for The Morning

As regular as the clock
Yet with sudden impulse
My eyes open before the light—
Waiting for the morning.

The mountains & the trees
Standing regal & unmoving
Begin to glow & reach for the sky—
Waiting for the morning.

The sky dawns
indescribable colors
That change with every
blink & turn

Waiting for the morning
With laughter & rush of steps
We move so as not to miss
its brilliance
As light cascades over
hill & dale—
Waiting for the morning.

With hearts lifted in
urgent longing
Light having been sown to
ready the soul—
We wait for the morning.

**I walk four** miles, six days each week. The mornings call to me, and with great delight I hop out of bed to greet each new day. It thrills my soul every time I see the glow of light that rests between the land and the sky just as the sun is about to rise. The Bible tells us,

> The path of the righteous is like the morning sun, shining ever brighter till the full light of day
> **Proverbs 4:18 (NIV)**

As we walk with Jesus each day, the path we follow in this life will become brighter and brighter when we desire most that the light of His glory will be seen in us.

*Dianne Platter*

# October 5

> Have I not commanded you? Be strong and courageous. Do not be afraid; do not be discouraged, for the LORD your God will be with you wherever you go.
> **Joshua 1:9 (NIV)**

**Have you ever** felt lonely or small? Can you think of a time when you just didn't feel like you were good enough? I think everyone at some time or another has felt small, lonely, and like they didn't measure up. We can be pretty hard on ourselves sometimes, and life doesn't seem to stop giving us situations where we feel out of place.

The thing to always remember is that God created you specifically and for a purpose. You are part of a tapestry woven through generations in your family, and through history, for this time and place. There are no accidents. You are here for a reason and you can never give up on the beautiful life with which God has blessed you.

Yes, sometimes, at points in life, the reason and purpose won't be as clear. But keep being you. Don't back down to anyone. Stand strong and know that your God never "slumbers or sleeps." He is always with you!

*Karen Thornton*

# October 6

Love is patient, love is kind. It does not envy, it does not boast, it is not proud.
**1 Corinthians 13:4** (NIV)

**If you have** brothers and sisters, you know that there are challenging moments. You don't always get along. Maybe you want to play the same game, or play with the same toy. How do you settle it? Do you always want to have your own way, or do you let your brother play with it instead? Maybe you are the oldest child, and when your sister was born, it was hard to share your parent's attention with a newborn baby. Once you had your parents all to yourself, and now you have to share!

The Bible tells us that love is *patient and kind.* Kind means being nice to your brother or sister, your friends, or your parents. Love means that we are not always thinking about ourselves first. What does that mean? It means that you let your brother play the game, or help your mom set the table, even when it's not your turn. Love means we don't brag about getting all the answers right on the test when our friend is struggling with math.

What can you do to be kind today? Max Lucado said, "God loves you just the way you are, but He refuses to leave you that way. He wants you to be just like Jesus." Every time we choose to be kind and patient, we become more like Jesus. Make the best choice today, and if you are unkind, apologize and try again.

*Barbara Hollace*

# October 7

"'You are Curdie,' she said.

'And you are the Princess Irene,' he returned.

'Then we know each other still,' she said, with a sad smile of pleasure. 'You will help me.'

'That I will,' answered Curdie. He did not say, 'If I can'; for he knew that what he was sent to do, that he could do.'"

*The Princess and Curdie*, by George MacDonald

**When God sends** His people out, He often asks them to do the impossible!

Why? Does He want His people to fail? No! Not at all! He wants His people to find their confidence in Him. This is a mystery!

When you are a Christian, God has put the life of Jesus Christ in you! You have His power! We don't understand this power until we face difficult things. When facing really hard things, we find not that *we* can do it, but that He can! And He does! God may ask His children to go when it is too far, to carry what is too heavy, to love the unlovely, to finish what they have not yet begun, to give more than they have, to keep going when they are worn out—God calls us to do the impossible. Why does He do that? Because He loves to prove that he is the Living God, and His life in you is a miracle! When the Lord calls you to do the impossible, it is not because you can, but He can and He wants you to get comfortable with that! He is faithful to do all that He calls you to do!

*Blythe Followwill*

The one who calls you is faithful, and he will do it.
**1 Thessalonians 5:24** (NIV)

# October 8

Do you not know? Have you not heard? The Everlasting God, the LORD, the Creator of the ends of the earth does not become weary or tired. His understanding is inscrutable. He gives strength to the weary, and to him who lacks might He increases power. Though youths grow weary and tired, and vigorous young men stumble badly, yet those who wait for the LORD will gain new strength...
**Isaiah 40:28-31** (NASB)

**In the book** *Sir Gibbie* by George MacDonald, there is a lovely elderly lady named Janet. She is frail. Her age and health keep her from leaving her cabin much, but she is a beautiful example of how we should be, even in our youth. She didn't let anything keep her from learning from Jesus and studying her Bible.

> "Not for years and years had Janet been to church. She had long been unable to walk so far; and having no book but the best, and no help to understand it but the highest, her faith was simple, strong, real, all-pervading. Day by day she pored over the great gospel until she had grown to be one of the noble ladies of the kingdom of heaven—one of those who inherit the earth and are ripening to see God. For the Master, and His mind in hers, was her teacher. She had little or no theology save what He taught her. To Janet, Jesus Christ was no object of so-called theological speculation, but a living Man who somehow or other heard her when she called to Him, and sent her the help she needed."

You don't need to be elderly to read your Bible and to let Jesus teach you! Always remember that you can talk to Him about anything and seek His help for any need that you have.

*Jolyn Canty*

# October 9

**Have you got** a baby brother or sister? Where were they before they were born? Inside Mummy's tummy. Where was baby Jesus before He was born? Inside his Mummy's—Mary's—tummy.

What if I told you that Jesus "was" a very, very long time before that? The Bible tells us

> In the beginning the Word already existed. The Word was with God, and the Word was God. He existed in the beginning with God. God created everything through Him, and nothing was created except through Him...The Word became human and made His home among us. He was full of unfailing love and faithfulness. And we have seen His glory, the glory of the Father's one and only Son.
>
> **John 1:1-3, 14** (NLT)

Jesus is called "the Word" here. We know that because "the Word was God" and "the Word became human."

From the very beginning, Jesus—the Word—has always been! In fact, God created the world by speaking the Word; by speaking Jesus!

And it gets better! The Creator came to live with those He had made!

Why?

To live the perfect life that we can not live. Sinless Jesus took our sin on Himself, dealing with it once and for all on the Cross. After Jesus got rid of the sin that made us God's enemies, the Father adopted us into His family, where we truly belong.

You see, the Word became a Child so that we could become God's children. God the Father and His Son made this plan before the world began. They've been looking forward to your adoption all that time! They have loved you with a forever love!

*Agnes Priddle*

# October 10

**Have you ever** been camping?

When the weather's good, settling down in a cozy sleeping bag under canvas is great!

But when a storm rolls in and the wind whips the canvas back, letting the rain soak everything, and the temperature drops, it isn't long before we want to go home.

Now imagine your body is that tent.

The good things that happen to us are like the warm, comfortable nights. We feel loved, happy and strong. But the sad, bad things of life are like the storms. We are battered by troubles, drenched in tears, and numbed by the coldness of sin—sin in the world and in us. In the stormy times, we want to go home.

For those trusting in Jesus, there is good news! The Bible says, when our bodies die, we will be "'swallowed up by life,'' enter God's house and live with Him forever.

For we know that when this earthly tent we live in is taken down (...when we die and leave this earthly body), we will have a house in heaven...We grow weary in our present bodies, and we long to put on our heavenly bodies like new clothing... While we live in these earthly bodies, we groan and sigh... it's not that we want to die and get rid of these bodies...we want to put on our new bodies so that these dying bodies will be swallowed up by life. God Himself has prepared us for this, and as a guarantee He has given us His Holy Spirit.

**2 Corinthians 5:1-2, 4-5 (NLT)**

*Because of David, who is at home with God.*
*Agnes Priddle*

# October 11

> You are the light of the world. A town built on a hill cannot be hidden. Neither do people light a lamp and put it under a bowl. Instead, they put it on its stand, and it gives light to everyone in the house. In the same way, let your light shine before others, that they may see your good deeds and glorify your Father in Heaven.
> **Matthew 5:14-15 (NIV)**

**Did anybody ever** tell you that you are a good kid? What did you do to get that praise? Perhaps you like helping out at home, setting the table, cleaning your room, or shoveling the driveway. It feels good to do good and get a thumbs up!

But who are we doing good for? Is it for Mom or Dad? Could it be for God? Would you answer, "Absolutely! I like to make God happy!" Could you turn it around, and in your joy, say, "Thank you God!" for His gift to you of wanting to do good? Can you praise God? He desires to give all good gifts to His children. Don't you think it's a good idea to give God a thumbs up, too?

When you do good for God and others, your inner light is shining, brightening the way. You might be surprised at what your light can do, especially with God's help right behind you. Then, you might want to shine that light back at God, the Creator of all good things, for all the world to see!

What happens when you "shine your light?"

*Amy Adams*

# October 12

"It was the joy of having saved that
caused Gibbie's merriment thus to overflow."
*Sir Gibbie*, by George MacDonald

"Whoever drinks of the water that I shall give him shall never thirst; but the water that I shall give him will become in him a well of water springing up to eternal life."
**John 4:14 (NASB)**

**It's easy to** become irritated when someone is bugging you. When Mom calls and wants you to make your bed or take out the garbage, but you are busy doing your own thing, it's easy to be frustrated. So how should we respond when we are interrupted from what we are doing to help someone else?

There is a very old saying that I think we can apply to these situations. It comes from a book called *If*, by Amy Carmichael: "If a sudden jar can cause me to speak an impatient, unloving word, then I know nothing of Calvary love. For a cup brimful of sweet water cannot spill even one drop of bitter water, however suddenly jolted."

The idea is that if you are filled with sweet water and you are bumped or your plans are upset, only sweet water will spill out. Of course, the opposite would be that if you are filled with bitter water and you are bumped or interrupted, then only bitter water will spill out.

So how can you be filled to the brim with sweet water? The answer is actually quite easy. Follow the footsteps of Jesus. Drink in His words and let Him fill you with His "well of water springing up to eternal life." Whenever you are bumped or your plans are interrupted, ask Him to fill you with His sweetness so that you can respond to your mom, or friend, or anyone with sweet, not bitter water.

*Jolyn Canty*

# October 13

### Faithfulness

**Jensen had a** choice to make: he could let his baseball team down, or he could let his grandparents down. He always went to church with grandparents on Sunday; and while his team had never before played a game on Sunday, it had changed the schedule because there had been so many games cancelled due to storms. But he had promised his grandparents to go with them, and they had said there was a surprise for him.

It was a battle he fought over and over. The guys said he was their best first baseman and their fastest runner. His grandparents said they understood, but he had seen the look on their faces. He had been saved six months ago and in his heart he knew his choice. He thought about this verse from the Bible:

> ...for this day is holy unto our Lord: neither be ye sorry; for the joy of the Lord is your strength.
> **Nehemiah 8:10b (KJV)**

Sunday morning as Jensen sat with his grandparents, the pastor said he had a very important speaker. As he called the man's name, Jensen almost jumped out of his seat. Not only was he a great ball player, he was Jensen's favorite player! Jensen listened to his testimony of how God had blessed him. He said being faithful was always best, and his joy was in the Lord.

With an autograph in one hand and a handshake in the other, Jensen had never been so excited. The joy of the Lord made Jensen glad he had chosen to come to church. Hearing later that the game had been cancelled again, Jensen was twice as grateful he had been faithful to his wonderful Lord.

*Dottie Thornton*

# October 14

Where, O death, is your victory?
Where, O death is your sting?
**1 Corinthians 15:55 (NIV)**

**In George MacDonald's** book *At the Back of the North Wind,* Diamond befriends the North Wind and travels with her as she goes about her work. There are times when she needs to do something that seems very bad and will cause a lot of pain and suffering for many people. Diamond comes to learn that even in circumstances and events that cause sadness and make our hearts hurt, something good is being worked out on the other side.

In our lives we experience the death of family members and friends, and it can seem as though God isn't there, isn't watching, and is not full of love as He says He is. The hurt (the North Wind) comes up suddenly and causes havoc and chaos in an instant. We know our lives will never be the same. Jesus knew this pain; He took it on Himself for all of us at the cross, and because He did, we can rest, even when we are full of tears. Learn this Bible verse so that you can rest knowing that death is not forever for those who love Him and love God our Father. There will be many times when you will go through things and see things that you don't understand, but trust that God has made everything perfect according to His will, even when you can't see it just yet.

*Holly Van Shouwen*

# October 15

**Dancing, Dancing, Dancing!** This is what the boys and girls ages ten to eighteen were doing while we watched. We were in Rwanda and they were performing their country's traditional dance for our group on my birthday. I began to think of the verse above and how God rejoices over his children.

So often, we picture God as the angry neighbor who keeps the ball if it goes over his fence just one more time, when he is more like the Father that will read his daughter one more story even though he already read five!

God delights in us more than we delight in him, and He has given us everything we need for a life rich and full of joy.

"God's love is ever in front of his forgiveness. God's love is the prime mover, ever seeking to perfect his forgiveness."
George MacDonald

Tell someone today that they are loved and rejoiced over by God.

*Matthew Nash*

The Lord your God is with you, the Mighty Warrior who saves. He will take great delight in you; in his love he will no longer rebuke you, but will rejoice over you with singing.
**Zephaniah 3:17** (NIV)

# October 16

**Donal Grant grew** up a shepherd on the mountain, in a humble home in which he learned love and duty and unshakeable faith in God. Although as a young man he left his native place to become a tutor to a nobleman's son, he did not leave behind his firm beliefs and his trust in the Lord.

Donal soon became aware that there was some mystery about the household in which he was working, and upon further investigation learned that his employer had done, and was still doing, wicked things. The young lady of the house was, in fact, in great danger.

Seeing she had no other protector, Donal understood his God-given duty to watch over Lady Arctura. When things were at their worst, "he thanked God and took courage" and devoted his strength to rescuing her and keeping her safe from that day on (as told in *The Shepherd's Castle,* by George MacDonald).

The Bible calls us to be strong, loving, courageous, and firm in our faith. Donal Grant's story can help us to see what this kind of life might look like.

*Rebekah Choat*

> Be on your guard; stand firm in the faith; be men of courage; be strong. Do everything in love.
> **1 Corinthians 16:13 (NIV)**

# October 17

**I like getting** good instructions.

The Lord gives us good instructions in 1 Peter:

> But in your hearts revere Christ as Lord. Always be prepared to give an answer to everyone who asks you to give the reason for the hope that you have. But do this with gentleness and respect.
> **1 Peter 3:15** (NIV)

This one verse has three parts, a perfect plan of action for sharing hope in a world desperately in need of the Lord's kind of hope.

Jesus is hope, just like Jesus is love.

Every one of us has God's hope, and that hope is to be shared. I love that.

First, Peter points out that before we can share the hope God has given us, it is important to know we ourselves love and trust Him, for He is our hope and the foundation of all hope.

Second, we are to do our best to be ready to share our hope; what is Jesus doing in your life and heart right now, and in this week? If you don't know, just ask Him.

Third, the Lord tells us exactly how to share what He is doing in our lives, "with gentleness and respect." We are sharing, not force-feeding. It is so much easier and less stressful to humbly offer our gift and to leave the results to the Holy Spirit.

The Lord intends our witnessing to be easy, natural, and a normal part of our day-to-day lives. I love that, too.

Jesus keeps giving us hope so that we can give hope to someone today, and again tomorrow.

*Richard Zepernick*

# October 18

## But They Laughed At Him

**It's never a** good feeling when someone laughs at us. It can feel like an arrow piercing our heart. It can even cause us to cry. If we laugh at someone else, we must understand that our laughter can hurt their feelings, too. It can cause them to feel insecure, or less valued as a friend. Laughing at people can cause *invisible* injuries.

One day, Jesus entered a house where a young girl had died. A noisy crowd of people were playing funeral music on their pipes. So, Jesus said to them, "Go away. The girl is not dead. She is sleeping." But they laughed at him.

How did Jesus handle their laughter? He ignored it! Jesus came to earth to heal people. That was His mission. So, in spite of their laughter, Jesus went to the girl and healed her. He didn't let their laughter stop Him.

Did you know that we also have the power to heal or comfort others? If people laugh at you, it is wise to simply ignore them and remember your mission of healing. Don't let laughter stop you. The world just might need the specific gift of healing only you can offer!

*Carol Wimmer*

… a synagogue leader came and knelt before him [Jesus] and said, "My daughter has just died. But come and put your hand on her, and she will live." When Jesus entered the synagogue leader's house and saw the noisy crowd and people playing pipes, he said, "Go away. The girl is not dead but asleep." But they laughed at him.
**Matthew 9:18, 23-24 (NIV)**

# October 19

Blessed are the peacemakers, for they will be called children of God.
**Matthew 5:9** (NIV)

**Tommy rolled his** eyes at his younger brother and said, "You're a little weirdo! Get away from me."

This really hurt Allen's feelings. Allen couldn't remember a time when Tommy didn't make fun of him or pick on him. It made him angry. He started thinking about ways to pay him back for being so mean.

Then he thought about how his grandmother had told him that when someone did something bad to him, he should try doing something nice. It didn't make a lot of sense to Allen; nothing else, however, had ever worked with Tommy.

"What could I do for Tommy?" Allen wondered. He thought about it for a while, then went to the kitchen. Tommy had not taken out the trash yet. That was one of his chores. Allen tied up the trash bag and replaced it with a clean one, and carried the trash to the dumpster.

As he walked back in the house, Tommy asked, "Hey, did you take the trash out?"

"Yeah," answered Allen.

"Ah, thanks, I guess," shrugged Tommy.

When Allen was talking at dinner, Tommy started to make a comment, then seemed to change his mind. He was just a little bit nicer to Allen that night.

It's always tempting to try to find some way to get even. But try being the peacemaker. Things will probably get much better, although it might not happen all at once; some things take time.

And best of all, you will be called a child of God.

*Debra Baker Davis*

# October 20

It is a sin to despise one's neighbor, but blessed is the one who is kind to the needy.
**Proverbs 14:21 (NIV)**

**Sometimes it's hard** to care about our neighbors. Maybe they are loud, or their dog is loud, or they keep their lights on late at night and it shines in our bedroom window. They are not always nice to us, and it makes us angry or hurts our feelings. Sometimes they are just plain scary.

Maybe their yard is filled with trash, or the grass isn't mowed. Perhaps the house needs paint or a new porch. It might even have a broken window. We wonder what's wrong with them.

Of course, not all neighbors are like that. And I expect this verse isn't talking just about the folks that live on our street. Our neighbors could include our classmates, friends at church, teammates at sports, and even family members.

It is a sin to despise them. Despise means to dislike very much, to look down on, to treat someone as though they are not important. Have you ever felt like someone treated you that way? It can really hurt.

We are told that blessed (happy!) is the one who is kind to the needy. Helping someone who is in need is a wonderful thing. Maybe a neighbor needs help with their yard, or a classmate needs help with their homework. Is there someone in your class that could maybe use the coat that you have outgrown?

Be on the lookout for those who may be in need. What can you do to be kind to them? Once you figure it out, do it! You'll be glad you did.

*Patricia S. Becker*

# October 21

> And he said to him, "Truly, truly, I say to you, you will see heaven opened, and the angels of God ascending and descending on the Son of Man."
> **John 1:51 (NRSV)**

**In Genesis 28:10-12** Jacob has a vision of angels ascending and descending on a ladder to heaven. When he awakes, he exclaims, "This is the place of God, and I didn't know it!" That is, of course, Jesus' point here. What Nathanael, the simple, rustic Israelite to whom Jesus is talking, will eventually see, is that Jesus is the "place of God." Jesus is the holy ground where we have access to God. When you look at Jesus, you see what God is like and can draw near to Him.

George MacDonald wrote: "No manner or amount of belief *about* Christ is the faith of the New Testament." It is not our beliefs *about* Jesus that save us (though what we believe of Him is, of course, important), rather it is our belief *in* Him. It is our trust in Him, our love of Him, our dependence on Him that transforms us.

*Matthew Levi*

# October 22

> Go, eat your bread with enjoyment, and drink your wine with a merry heart; for God has long ago approved what you do.
> **Ecclesiastes 9:7 (NRSV)**

**Have you ever** heard someone say that doing something bad "makes baby Jesus cry?" They just mean that God created us to do good, and it makes Him sad when we don't. When we look at Jesus, we remember He suffered and died to set us free, and it makes us sad to think of times we used that freedom to do something that wasn't very nice.

But when we look at Jesus, God reminds us also that, just like He made us to do good, He made us to be happy! Jesus gave His life so that we could become more like Him, doing things that make God smile.

The Olympic runner Eric Liddell was asked once why he ran. "God made me fast," he said, "and when I run, I feel His pleasure." When we do the things that make us really happy—not just that make us laugh, or that seem fun for a little while, but the things that really make us happy deep inside—we can feel those things making God happy, too, and knowing that we make God happy makes us the happiest of all!

Every day, do something—even just a little something—that helps you feel God smiling!

"When I was five years old, my mother always told me that happiness was the key to life. When I went to school, they asked me what I wanted to be when I grew up. I wrote down, 'happy.' They told me I didn't understand the assignment, and I told them they didn't understand life."

John Lennon

*Race MoChridhe*

# October 23

"The value of a life can only be estimated by its spiritual relationship to God."
Oswald Chambers

**Saul was a** tall man. God appointed him to be the first king of Israel, because that is what the people wanted—they wanted a king like the countries around them. The problem was, they already had a king—the LORD God! But they wanted someone they could see; someone like themselves, but "better!"

At first, Saul followed the Lord's instructions and was blessed. However, after about two years, Saul found his country surrounded by the armies of the Philistines, a powerful enemy. Samuel, God's High Priest, sent word to Saul that he, Samuel, would come and make prayers and sacrifice for the Israelite people. That was Samuel's job as High Priest; God had said so. But Saul became impatient. When Samuel didn't show up exactly on time, Saul offered the sacrifice himself! Samuel came soon after and told Saul that because he had disobeyed, God would take his kingship away. And that happened just a few years later.

The person God chose to be king after Saul was a young, red headed boy, who did not look at all like a king. You may have heard of him: his name was David. Though he was just a young shepherd boy, he had something Saul did not have: a heart that loved, obeyed, and trusted God!

*Linda S. Storm*

They ran and brought him out, and as he stood among the people he was a head taller than any of the others.
**1 Samuel 10:23** (NIV)

# October 24

"The saint who satisfies the heart of Jesus will make other saints strong and mature for God"
Oswald Chambers

And let us consider how we may spur one another on toward love and good deeds
**Hebrews 10:24** (NIV)

**Hayden's friend, Joey,** was older and stronger, but when they played together, Joey was kind and considerate. One day a new boy moved to the neighborhood. Lee was rough. He used bad language and would actually hit the children he played with. He threw tantrums and threw rocks. He wouldn't share his toys. He just did not play well with others. It was not long until the boys decided not to play with Lee.

Hayden and Joey were playing one day, throwing the football, when Lee came running up and grabbed the ball away from them. At first the boys were angry, but then they went and asked Hayden's mom for advice. "Did you ask Lee to play football with you?" she asked. "No," said the boys. "Maybe you should!" Mom said.

Reluctantly, the boys went out to where Lee was angrily spiking the football. Joey called to Lee, "Hey, would you like to play catch with us?" "Why would I want to play with you?" Lee snarled. "Because," said Hayden, "we want to play with *you!*" Then he smiled and put his hands in the air to catch the football. Wonder of wonders, Lee tossed the football to Hayden and smiled back. Soon the boys were all playing together and having a great time. Little Hayden had taught both Lee and Joey a good lesson. Loving one another leads to happiness.

*Linda S. Storm*

# October 25

**As a Christian**, you know the basics of moral law: you should not lie, cheat, steal, or hurt others. Additionally, you know that Christians should go beyond the bare minimum and should love their enemies, forgive those who hurt them, "turn the other cheek," and lay down their lives for others.

But sometimes Christians begin to think that what they should not do to others, they must let others do to them! They think they simply have to put up with being hurt by others. This is not what God wants! We are to resist evil with good (Rom. 12:21), but not ignore it or allow it to happen to ourselves or others when we can prevent it in a lawful way.

At one point in Jesus' preaching, people became angry with Him. *They picked up stones to stone him, but Jesus hid himself, slipping away from the temple grounds.* (John 8:59) Jesus did not allow them to do the harm they intended. Jesus continually laid down his life for us; but he did not always allow Himself to be bullied. It was only when His mission on earth was complete that, for our sake, He would submit to evil that He might overcome it for the sake of all.

It is not the Father's will for you to suffer needlessly. You are a temple of God, and should be protected and respected. When necessary, ask others for help. God intends not only for you to help others, but for others to help you!

*Sharon Edel*

Do not take advantage of each other...
**Leviticus 25:17 (NIV)**

# October 26

**Consider these details** that the Gospels give us regarding Jesus:

- He attracted large crowds.
- By the age of twelve, he challenged leaders.
- Learned men came to question him and were amazed.
- He healed the sick and drove out demons.
- He stood up to Jewish leaders, speaking harshly, but truthfully.
- He protected and cared for women, children and those society ignored.
- He forcefully drove out from the Temple those who were taking advantage of the people.

These are not the characteristics of a timid man!

Know that you have been given the Spirit of Jesus, full of strength and goodness to do what is right.

Perhaps you think that kind of strength is for heroes or kings, characters in stories, but not for ordinary people. But the Spirit of God is indeed for us who are the children of the Great King. Let us, therefore, live as such!

Here is an example to make you smile and to encourage you. Author George MacDonald, in his fairytale *The Wise Woman,* gives us this description of a princess:

> "A princess is able to do what is right even should she unhappily be in a mood that would make another unable to do it…Whoever does what she is bound to do, be she the dirtiest little girl in the street, is a princess, worshipful, honorable. Nay, more; her might goes farther than she could send it, for if she act so, the evil mood will wither and die, and leave her loving and clean."

*Sharon Edel*

For the Spirit God gave us does not make us timid, but gives us power, love and self-discipline.
**2 Timothy 1:7 (NIV)**

# October 27

> For the word of God is alive and active. Sharper than any double-edged sword, it penetrates even to dividing soul and spirit, joints and marrow; it judges the thoughts and attitudes of the heart.
> **Hebrews 4:12** (NIV)

**My grandsons like** swords. One of them likes to draw them with different designs or markings. He often makes swords out of paper or cardboard and sometimes even wood. Of course, they aren't very sharp, but that's not really his intention. He just likes making them.

My grandsons also love to have their video games' characters use them. Their video game characters have light sabers, fire swords, heavy swords, and some made of materials that I have never heard of. It is always a great honor and accomplishment for the character to wield a sword!

Not only is it important for the swordsman to handle his sword well, but the sword blade must be sharp. It must be able to pierce and cut accurately.

Did you know that the Bible, God's Word, is a sword? It is so sharp it can reach the deepest parts of our hearts. It teaches us how much God loves us, and it shows us the way to live. It points out the things in our lives that we must get rid of: anger, selfishness, gossip, disobedience to parents, and more. It also teaches us how God can give us love, joy, peace, patience, kindness, goodness, faithfulness, gentleness, and self-control. (See Galatians 5:22) That is a powerful sword!

*Patricia S. Becker*

# October 28

> ...Jesus said to them, "My Father is always at his work to this very day, and I, too, am working."
> **John 5:17** (NIV)

**In this verse,** Jesus holds up the Sabbath Rest for us to think about. God's gift of Sabbath had become in some way more a restriction than a blessing, and Jesus wants to set that straight.

Jesus also wants to show us that the Lord never misses an opportunity to work character into our hearts and blessings into our lives.

The religious people of Jerusalem made accusations against a man who had been an invalid for 38 years; they were outraged because he obeyed Jesus' Sabbath command, "Pick up your mat and walk."

The Lord challenges us to both obey Sabbath Law and at the same time to understand that "The Sabbath was made for man, not man for the Sabbath." Mark 2:27 (NIV) They sound like contradictions, but God will make it clear if we keep asking Him.

I love how the Lord jam-packs John 5:17 with so many blessings. In it, Jesus affirms He and the Father are one, doing the same things.

Best to me is what Jesus reveals about the nature of the triune God; He cares about you, and you are never a burden from which He must rest. He never tires of you. The Lord is ever ready, ever willing and able to do for you, and for others, all that you need, and far more.

Be ready for Jesus to be there for you, and for Him to ask you if you truly want what He has to offer you. Be ready also because Jesus will soon call you to action.

*Richard Zepernick*

# October 29

"If you love only those who love you, what reward is there for that? Even corrupt tax collectors do that much. If you are kind only to your friends, how are you different from anyone else? Even pagans do that."
**Matthew 5:46-47** (NLT)

**How can you** love someone who doesn't love you? Don't we want to lash out at people who say and do unkind things to us? Yes, and that is why Jesus said, "Your love for one another will prove to the world that you are my disciples." (John 13:35)

So how does a person become Jesus' follower? Romans 3:23 says, "Everyone has sinned. No one measures up to God's glory." So what can we do? John 3:16 says, "God loved the world so much that He gave His one and only Son. Anyone who believes in Him will not die but will have eternal life." Romans 10:9 says, "Say with your mouth, 'Jesus is Lord.' Believe in your heart that God raised Him from the dead. Then you will be saved." Will you accept and follow Jesus now? Pray a prayer like this from your heart:

*Dear God, I know I have sinned, and I'm sorry. Please forgive me and change my heart. I believe Jesus died for me and rose from the dead. I want to follow Him all my life and obey Him. Thank you for making me part of Your family and for loving me. In Jesus' Name, Amen.*

Now you are changed inside, and a child of God. Read your Bible daily and talk to Jesus. It is important to find a church that loves and teaches about Him. Share your decision with them and be baptized. And keep following!

*Vicki Ryder*

# October 30

"Cast thy care on Jesus, when the way is long;
He can turn thy sorrow, into joyful song."
Fanny J. Crosby

**Cares and worries...**every day we pick up things that we either worry about or care about.

Now imagine if those cares and worries are rocks and stones. Rocks and stones come in all sizes, just like worries and cares. The Lord Jesus Christ cares about everything that we care about, regardless of their sizes! He knows that if we try to carry all our worries they will become a great weight, like stones pressing down on us, making joy feel very far away. Sometimes those weights are worries, sometimes fears, and sometimes they are troubles we are having. Big or small, Jesus cares for them all and He is here to help! He will comfort and cheer us on.

Every day I make a list of my cares, and then I pray about each one and give them all to the Lord.

If you were to pull out of your pockets all your worries, sorrows ,and cares, what would they be? No matter how big or small your stones, Jesus wants to have them all. He is the one person you can always talk to; His consolations will cheer your soul and He will carry your stones.

*Blythe Followwill*
*For Samuel*

When the cares of my heart are many,
your consolations cheer my soul.
**Psalm 94:19 (ESV)**

# October 31

**A man came** to a pumpkin patch looking for a certain pumpkin, one exactly right for the purpose he had in mind! He scoured the fields, looking under leaves, lifting up vines, and walking down the rows. He was looking for ME! He chose me, and took me home.

He chose us in Him before the foundation of the world, that we would be holy and blameless...
**Ephesians 1:4** (NASB)

Before settling in, I confessed, "I've got a LOT of gooey gunk inside." I was a little nervous, but I knew it had to go. So he got busy. Gently, he cut a hole in my top and carefully scooped out the ugliness inside. He worked patiently, until I was wonderfully clean.

If we confess our sins, He is faithful and righteous to forgive us our sins and to cleanse us from all unrighteousness.
**1 John 1:9** (NASB)

Then he began to carve his image on my face! He gave me eyes, he gave me a nose, and he gave me a mouth with a smile.

God said, "Let us make man in Our image, according to Our likeness..."
**1 John 1:9** (NASB)

I was ready! His plan was complete! He filled me with light, so I would shine! His hope is that all those lost in the darkness might find their way home—home to Him.

God, Who said, "Light shall shine out of darkness," is the One who has shone in our hearts to give the light...
**2 Corinthians 4:6** (NASB)

*Blythe Followwill*
*For Landon and Theo*

# November 1

> Forgive us our sins, for we also forgive everyone who sins against us.
> **Luke 11:4a (NIV)**

**I learned the** Lord's Prayer as a child; but I did not understand the meaning of all the words. As I grew, I learned to better understand the prayer, as well as my faith. I remember learning that "forgive us our trespasses as we forgive those who trespass against us" carried a bit of a warning. It meant that if we wanted God to forgive our sins, we had to be willing to forgive others! This is certainly a valid understanding, and the way that I understood it for many years of my life.

However, one day as I heard the Gospel of Luke being read, I heard these words: *Forgive us our sins, for we also forgive everyone who sins against us.* I was shocked and excited! I checked the Scripture and verified what I had heard. For the first time, it occurred to me that when I was praying the Lord's Prayer, I was supposed to be actively forgiving anyone who may have hurt me. I was saying, "Right now, I forgive anyone who has hurt me!" This forever changed the way in which I pray, as I now realize that if I am to pray these words, I must *mean* them!

When the whole congregation prayed the Lord's Prayer, I wondered if they all knew what they were really saying. How exciting would it be if everyone who prayed the Lord's Prayer made it a heartfelt and honest act of forgiveness! Might it not just change the world?

*Sharon Edel*

# November 2

**In George MacDonald's** book *At the Back of the North Wind,* a little boy named Diamond befriends the North Wind, who appears to him as a kind, wise, and beautiful lady. She often carries him as she goes about her work of sweeping clean the streets or filling the sails of a ship. At one point, out in the dark of night, she appears to abandon him. When she returns he asks:

*"Why did you leave me, dear North Wind?" "Because I wanted you to walk alone," she answered… "You had to be taught what courage was. And you couldn't know what it was without feeling it."* She encourages him to try to be brave, but he responds, *"But trying is not much."*

North Wind responds: *"A beginning is the greatest thing of all. To try to be brave is to be brave. The coward who tries to be brave is before the man who is brave because he is made so, and never had to try."*

Think about the people you most love and admire. Are they kind, good, or brave? Know that they were not born that way, nor did they become that way without effort. Each and every one of them made a beginning. Each one tried, not once, not twice, but perhaps hundreds and thousands of times!

Holy men and women are often known for particular virtues or gifts, such as wisdom, understanding, knowledge, fortitude, piety, love, hope, faith, peace, patience, and kindness. To what gift is God calling you?

Today, determine to make a beginning.

*Sharon Edel*

I do believe; help me overcome my unbelief!
**Mark 9:24** (NIV)

# November 3

> Let your conversation be always full of grace, seasoned with salt, so that you may know how to answer everyone.
> **Colossians 4:6 (NIV)**

**What does it** mean to season your conversation with salt? Just the right amount of salt makes things taste better, but too much does the opposite. That's where grace comes in. Salt can remove stains, soothe aches and pains, even take away odors. Our speech should be the same; it should remove guilt, soothe the soul, and never be foul.

Another key word in the verse above is *grace.* Grace is unmerited favor. If we respond with grace, perfectly seasoned to have compassion to the person we are speaking with, and not judging them, we are loving them unconditionally.

By expressing tolerance rather than judgement, thankfulness rather than complaint, and kindness rather than bitterness, we show the grace that God gave us through Christ. When we allow for the frailties of others, we take away the stains of judgement and bitterness with the beauty of tenderheartedness, kindness, and forgiveness.

*Karen Thornton*

# November 4

You have searched me Lord, and you know me.
You know when I sit and when I rise.
You perceive my thoughts from afar.
You discern my going out and my lying down.
You are familiar with all my ways.
Before a word is on my tongue, you, Lord, know it completely.
You hem me in behind and before,
and you lay your hand upon me.
Such knowledge is too wonderful for me,
too lofty for me to attain.

**Psalm 139:1-6 (NIV)**

**We moved to** Delaware Avenue after my dad died. Mom was ready to move. She had great faith in God, and that gave her courage. One day Mom saw me jumping after my shadow, and asked me what I was doing. I told her I was chasing my shadow. Then I followed her in to eat lunch.

After lunch, we watched a video of Lucille Ball and Harpo Marx copying each other's moves, standing in front of each other. It was like my shadow following me!

After the video, Mom read Psalm 139 to me, and when she was done, she said, "God is our shadow, following us wherever we are, in good times and bad times. He is walking beside us, in front and in back." I shouted, "Yes! God stands behind us as a shadow, and in front of us, leading the way with His light!"

What can you do, knowing God is in front of you and behind you?

*Amy Adams*

# November 5

> Faith is the confidence that what we hope for will actually happen; it gives us assurance about things we cannot see.
> **Hebrews 11:1** (NLT)

**George MacDonald gives** a wonderful illustration of faith in *The Princess and the Goblin*. On one occasion, Princess Irene's great-great-grandmother gives her a mysterious ring. The older lady takes a very special ball of thread and attaches one end of it to the ring. She then places the ball of thread in her cupboard. The thread is so fine that it cannot be seen; it can only be felt. The grandmother tells the young princess that if she's ever afraid, she must take off the ring and put it under her pillow. Then she must feel for the thread with her finger and follow it wherever it leads, even if it seems to be leading in a strange direction, for her great-great-grandmother holds the other end of it, and it will certainly lead the princess back to her eventually.

Faith is like that. There's something unseen at the root of it. It begins in your heart, in the secret place where you hear the still, small voice of God and choose to obey him, even though you can't see Him. Faith connects you to God, just like Irene's thread: He's at the other end of it. Follow His lead, even when it's difficult and you don't understand. He'll make you a blessing to others and will ultimately bring you home to Himself.

*Daniel Koehn*

# November 6

## Giving

**Mason was on** a mission. The bag in his pocket was filled with all the money he had saved to buy a new skateboard. He had saved not only his allowance, but also money made from doing extra chores: raking, picking up trash, and running errands for his dad.

His Sunday school teacher had recently read the class this verse:

> ...for God loveth a cheerful giver.
> **2 Corinthians 9:7 (KJV)**

Well, he would be a cheerful *getter* as soon as he got that skateboard!

In the car beside his mom, Mason could see himself on the new board. He would do jumps and spins just like the older boys. He wished his legs were longer; they made it all look so easy.

He sat on a bench waiting for his mom outside the store. Hearing a sound, Mason saw a boy in a motorized chair. The boys talked long enough to find out they had a lot in common, they both liked baseball games, ice hockey, and "American Ninja"—but Tyler couldn't walk.

As Tyler told about the benefit given to make money for his treatments, Mason decided to help. Donating all the money he had really did make a difference, a cheerful difference. Mason knew he could earn more money doing errands and chores. The skateboard he wished for was not important. He wished now for his friend to get better.

*Dottie Thornton*

# November 7

May the God of hope fill you with all joy and peace in believing, so that by the power of the Holy Spirit you may abound in hope.
**Romans 15:13 (ESV)**

**When we are** young, it may seem like our strength and luck will last forever, that by our own power we can achieve whatever we set our mind to, and it's true that we can do a lot by our own will and strength. If we are truly lucky though, we'll hit a wall, run out of strength and will, and find ourselves empty, in desperate need, and finally look for help. When that day comes for you, if it hasn't already, I hope you look for the God of hope, and let Him make Himself known to you and fill you with the joy and peace that cannot be lost or destroyed.

"Attitudes are more important than facts."
George MacDonald

*Lorin Hart*

# November 8

> If anyone will not welcome you or listen to your words, leave that home or town and shake the dust off your feet.
> **Matthew 10:14** (NIV)

**"Shake it off!"** People sometimes use this phrase to mean: "Don't worry about it! It's not your fault! Move on!" This is the idea expressed in this verse.

Jesus instructs His disciples to go out and share the good news by word and action. But He knows that some people will respond inhospitably, so He instructs His disciples to shake the dust off their feet!

As we strive to live as disciples and to share our faith with others, it would be wonderful if everyone treated us pleasantly and was excited about following Jesus, too! But we will sometimes meet with rejection or perhaps even hurtful behavior from others.

Of course, you already know that we are to love and pray for those who do not know Jesus and for those who hurt us. But Jesus does not want us to become disheartened or discouraged when the result of our efforts to spread the gospel seem disappointing.

Do not abandon the struggle, no matter the outward appearance. Remember that in time, God can still bring all of His wayward children to faith. Jesus' instructions are for you to move on to your next duty. Each day brings new and numerous opportunities, God's plan designed especially for you. Do the duty entrusted to you by Jesus; then shake off any fears, frustrations, or defeats, and let God take care of the rest.

*Sharon Edel*

# November 9

"After he has gathered his own flock, he walks ahead of them, and they follow him because they know his voice."
**John 10:4 (NLT)**

**In George MacDonald's** *At the Back of the North Wind,* a little boy named Diamond becomes friends with the North Wind. She takes him on many exciting—and sometimes dangerous!—adventures, but he always knows that no matter what, she will keep him safe.

One dark, stormy night, a long time since his last adventure with the North Wind, Diamond is just falling asleep when he hears something:

> "All at once he said to himself, 'Am I awake, or am I asleep?' But he had no time to answer the question, for there was North Wind calling him. His heart beat very fast, it was such a long time since he had heard that voice. He jumped out of bed, and looked everywhere, but could not see her. 'Diamond, come here,' she said again and again; but where the here was he could not tell."

Diamond goes on to look for the North Wind, following her voice even though he can't see her, because he trusts her.

In the verse above, Jesus says that God is a shepherd, and we are His sheep. Even if it's a dark night, or wolves are hiding in the woods, sheep follow their shepherd because they recognize his voice and know he will protect them. In the same way, we can follow God even when the future seems scary, because we know we can trust God and that He loves us!

*Bethany Wagner*
*Dedicated to Glen Wagner*

# November 10

> If your brother or sister sins, go and point out their fault, just between the two of you. If they listen to you, you have won them over. But if they will not listen, take one or two others along, so that 'every matter may be established by the testimony of two or three witnesses.' If they still refuse to listen, tell it to the church; and if they refuse to listen even to the church, treat them as you would a pagan or a tax collector.
>
> **Matthew 18:15-17 (NIV)**

**What do you** do when you have a major conflict with someone who refuses to do the right thing? Jesus gives a practical approach as an example of how we can handle such a situation. The first step is to try to talk to the person and work it out between the two of you. If this is unsuccessful, Jesus suggests getting others who have authority involved. If the person still refuses to do the right thing, then what? What does it mean to treat them as a "pagan or a tax collector"?

At the time when Jesus lived, Jews avoided pagans and tax collectors, as these people frequently did not mean them well! Although we know that Jesus loved everyone, and He himself did not avoid pagans or tax collectors (Matthew was a tax collector!), He was conveying a common-sense practice: Stay away from people who are likely to cause you trouble!

You may not get along with everyone, or you may not be able to change someone intent on wrongdoing. Sometimes you need to stay away from such people, until or unless they change.

*Sharon Edel*

# November 11

But encourage one another daily,
as long as it is called "today"...
**Hebrews 3:13a (NLT)**

**When you're a** kid it is hard to figure out what God wants you to do. You may wonder what you can do to serve God every day. You might be thinking that you will have to wait until you are older, because there isn't anything you can do now.

You know to read your Bible and pray for your family and others every day. You know that you are to obey your parents and even get along with your brothers and sisters—even though it is hard sometimes. But is there something more?

Today's Bible verse tells us there is something.

It comes from the Book of Hebrews, written for all Christians, young and old alike. It gives us guidance on how we are to live as Christians.

Look at the verse again. It tells us that we are to encourage one another as long as it is called "today," which is another way of saying that we are to do this every day. So what does "encourage one another" mean? It means to:

- Say nice things to others
- Be supportive of someone who is sad
- Thank your parents for the things they do for you
- Tell them you love them
- Congratulate your brothers and sisters when they accomplish things
- Be kind to others

God says do this every single day, not just when you feel like it. Ask Him to help you look for opportunities every day to encourage anyone you are around– this will please God and you will be doing what He wants "today."

*Dan Schuch*

# November 12

See that you do not use the trick of prayer
to cover up what you ought to do.
Oswald Chambers

**Prayer – a trick?** Is praying phony, then? No! But sometimes we use prayer in a tricky way.

Here's how: I'm told to do something that I clearly should do – tell the truth, be kind to the kid down the street, go to church. But I stall by saying, "Oh, wait. I need to pray and see if God wants me to."

When I already know what God wants, I don't need to ask again. I just need to do what He says—now!

When we pull that sort of trick, we usually want to get out of doing something but keep looking good. God sees through it, though. In Mark 7:11, Jesus talked about the religious principle that adults must help their needy parents. Some people were saying, "Sorry, I can't help them! I'd have to spend money on them that I've already promised to the church!" (Unhappily, their leaders were letting them get away with this, too.) What do you suppose God think of money given to the church by someone who turns his back on his own parents' needs?

Trying to wiggle out of obeying God shows that your heart needs a tune-up (or a transplant). So, if you discover yourself going in that direction—and we all do at some point—stop right there and beg Jesus to turn you around.

*Mary Lichlyter*

The Lord detests the sacrifice of the wicked,
but the prayer of the upright pleases him.
**Proverbs 15:8 (NIV)**

# November 13

> I eagerly expect and hope that I will in no way be ashamed, but will have sufficient courage so that now as always Christ will be exalted in my body, whether by life or by death.
> **Philippians 1:20 (NIV)**

**Have you ever** felt very sorry for something you have either done or forgotten to do? That is what it means to be ashamed. People may disagree with us in things we think are right. They may accept ways of behaving that we know are against the way God, in His word, tells us to live. People might make fun of us for what we think, or what we choose to do or not do.

The Apostle Paul writes to the Christians who gather in Philippi that he prays for "sufficient courage" to honor Jesus even as his body is in prison in Rome where they have the power to let him live or to kill him. That would be a scary situation, wouldn't it?

Why does he "expect and hope" that he won't be ashamed? Paul expects that God will be with him even in prison. He knows that God has brought him through his life and will not abandon him even in death. He has faith and courage to keep doing what God requires, even though he is in jail.

We can read about characters in great books who are faced with hard choices about how they will live. Who will we be when we are asked to do the right thing, even if it is unpopular, even if other people think we are wrong?

Have the courage to follow Jesus.

*Amy Farley*

# November 14

"You must learn to be strong in the dark as well as in the day, else you will always be only half brave."
*The Day Boy and the Night Girl,* by George MacDonald

I keep my eyes always on the LORD. With him at my right hand, I will not be shaken.
**Psalm 16:8 (NIV)**

**In the fairy** tale *The Day Boy and the Night Girl,* a selfish witch steals two babies. She raises the boy to rejoice in the daylight, but never allows him to experience the nighttime. She raises the girl to live in the night but never to see the day. Naturally, each loves what is known but fears the unknown.

However, both figure out (is God working here?) that there must be more goodness in the unknown part than they realize. As they meet, they try to help one another, although each is terribly afraid—and finally decide they must marry and help one another all their lives.

It's usually easy to be brave about what you believe you can handle! But when life seems out of control, fear and even terror may take over. Remember that God is Ruler of the hard times as well as the comfortable ones. Ask Him to show you what is good about whatever you're facing. Ask Him to lead you by the hand through it. He wants to, and He will give you everything you need for your task, although you may be surprised how He does it.

*Mary Lichlyter*

# November 15

Trust in the Lord and do good; Dwell in the land and cultivate faithfulness.
**Psalm 37:3 (NASB)**

**I have a** little garden, and in it I have planted potatoes, squash, tomatoes, and cucumbers. I love my little garden, and even the littlest gardens require faithful attention. They need to be watered and weeded, talked to and loved. If I don't, the seeds won't grow because they could get thirsty and die, or the weeds will grow wild and steal all the nutrients in the dirt. This is what it means to cultivate the ground: you take care of it.

In George MacDonald's story *The Princess and Curdie,* we meet the boy, Curdie, and his hard-working mother and father. They are wonderful examples of people who purpose to do good and take care of the little they have and anyone who happens to come along their way. They treat their life like a garden, cultivating faithfulness by doing good for all those around them.

What kind of "garden" has God given to you? It may be that you are cultivating kindness and being a good neighbor, or helping a friend at school. Ask God to show you where you need to be cultivating faithfulness and He *will* show you!

*Annie Mae Platter*

# November 16

**Have your parents** ever asked you to taste something you do not think you will like? Sometimes we stay away from foods we *think* we are not going to like, or we do not try to do certain things because we are afraid. That is why the Bible, God's Word, tells us to taste and see—or find out—that the Lord is good! God doesn't want us to let anything keep us away from Him, in the same way that there is nothing that will keep Him away from us! Sometimes we may hear wrong ideas about God on TV or from our friends at school; things that are just not true. God wants you to get to know Him personally and find out that He is an *amazing* God! Even if you think God will not forgive you, remember Jesus came and died for our sins, so that we would not be afraid to come to Him for forgiveness. Once we have given our life to Jesus, there is nothing we can do that will keep Him away from us.

*Heavenly Father, I know you are good. Help me pray and come to you and find out for myself that it is true. In Jesus name. Amen.*

*Jose del Pino*

Taste and see that the Lord is good;
blessed is the one who takes refuge in him.
**Psalm 34:8** (NIV)

# November 17

"Children are grateful when Santa Claus puts in their stockings gifts of toys or sweets. Could not I be grateful to Santa Claus when he put in my stockings the gift of two miraculous legs?"
*Orthodoxy*, by G.K. Chesterton

[Give] thanks always and for everything to God the Father in the name of our Lord Jesus Christ.
**Ephesians 5:20 (ESV)**

**Wait – Mr. Chesterton** isn't saying Santa is God! In this book (written over a hundred years ago), he described how he, an atheist, became a Christian. At one point, he started really noticing things around him which he had taken for granted—including his own life. He felt thankful, and reasoned, "Since I'm thankful, there *must* be someone real to thank!" (And he found out Whom to thank, too.)

What have you thanked God for? Of course, food, home, school, church, country, relatives, friends, sunsets. How about your shoes? What about bugs? Before you run away from that spider, take a good look. Can you be thankful for such a complex, interesting creature (if it's not in your house)? Pretend you're an artist; think about all the different shades of brown around you, and blue and green and red.Are you thankful for smiles, laugh, and fears?

Get a paper and pencil and hunt for things to be grateful for. Write them all down. If you're a good detective, the number will surprise you.

Why does this matter? Because God has done so much that we don't even notice. Make a habit of noticing and being thankful. Someone has written that the Biblical standards that God gives us for our behavior are based on gratitude.

*Mary Lichlyter*

# November 18

Even my close friend, someone I trusted, one who shared my bread, has turned against me
**Psalm 41:9** (NIV)

## When Friends Turn Against Us

**One of the** saddest times in life is when a friend turns against us. This psalm was written about three thousand years ago, so losing a close friend is nothing new. Yet, when it happens to us, it hurts. It *really* hurts. All of the bandages in the world cannot bind up our wounds or stop a heart from hurting. Nothing seems to help.

After a friend turns against us, a million questions can pop into our minds, "Why?" "What did I do wrong?" "Could I have done anything different to keep the friendship?" It's natural to ask these questions, because our deepest desire is to be loved. It's also natural to become angry if someone turns against us. We can even imagine doing something mean or saying something hateful to get even. But hurting someone out of revenge doesn't help us feel better. Once we say or do something unkind, we often feel worse because we can never undo what we've said or done.

If a trusted friend turns against us, the best thing we can do is let the friendship go. Then, we can ask God to heal our wounds and take care of the person who hurt us. Is this easy? No. Forgiving someone who has turned against us is one of the hardest things we will ever do. But forgiving is the fastest way to heal. Then, we can become a good friend for someone else who needs one.

*Carol Wimmer*

# November 19

**Mr. Drake had fallen** on hard times, but continued to take care of his daughter and the orphan child he had taken in as well as he could with very little money. When he unexpectedly inherited a great fortune, he immediately began to use it to improve the living circumstances of a great number of the poor working people of the town. (As told in *The Lady's Confession*, by George MacDonald.)

The Bible teaches that we are to care for widows, orphans, the poor, and the mistreated; not only when we have more than enough ourselves, but always. No matter how little we have, Jesus will show us ways to share His love with others, and it will please Him to see that we help more when we are able to.

*Rebekah Choat*

Speak up for those who cannot speak for themselves, for the rights of all who are destitute. Speak up and judge fairly; defend the rights of the poor and needy.
**Proverbs 31:8-9** (NIV)

# November 20

"As he sat, with his eyes on the peak he had just chosen from the rest as the loftiest of all within his sight, he saw a cloud begin to grow. The next moment a flash of blue lightning darted across the sky. The clouds swept together, and then again burst forth the lightning. He saw no flash, but an intense cloud illumination, accompanied by the deafening crack, and followed by the appalling roar and roll of the thunder. He clung to the rock with hands and feet. It was an awful delight that filled his spirit. Mount Sinai was not to him a terror. To him there was no wrath in the thunder...Gibbie sat calm, full of awe, while the storm roared and beat and flashed and ran about him."

*The Baronet's Song,* by George MacDonald

**Some people are** very frightened of thunderstorms, and storms in the mountains can be quite fierce, indeed. Other people feel the wonder and power of God in a storm, as Gibbie did not long after he reached Glashgar, the mountain his father had known as a young man. Gibbie was not yet formally acquainted with God, but he recognized His presence all the same.

We may sometimes be in circumstances that feel stormy and scary, but we can be sure that God is right there with us in the middle of it all.

*Rebekah Choat*

The clouds poured down water, the skies resounded with thunder; your arrows flashed back and forth. Your thunder was heard in the whirlwind, your lightning lit up the world; the earth trembled and quaked.

**Psalm 77:17-18 (NIV)**

# November 21

This is how we know what love is:
Jesus Christ laid down his life for us.
**1 John 3:16 (NIV)**

**Have you ever** read George MacDonald's fairy tale *The Light Princess?* It's a story about a beautiful young princess who was cursed as an infant, so that she lost all her gravity. This affected both her body and her soul. Her body suddenly had no weight, so she began to float in the air. They had to attach ribbons to her to keep her from drifting away in the wind. Can you imagine? Her soul also lost its gravity. She couldn't think a serious thought. She couldn't even cry. Whenever she heard a very sad story, she would just laugh. It was very disturbing.

The curse was broken in a very peculiar way. It happened through the choice of a young prince. The princess had lost something very dear, and this young prince offered to give his life. He cared more about the princess than he did about himself, even though the princess was incapable of loving him back, since she had no gravity in her soul. As the light princess saw the prince drowning, a strange change came over her: gravity rushed back into her soul and her body, and she became capable of loving him. That selfless act from the prince broke the curse!

Did you know that God cares about you that way? He cares more about you than He does about Himself. That's love.

*Daniel Koehn*

# November 22

**Discipline is choosing** between what you want *now,* and what you want *most*. This was illustrated wonderfully when a group of researchers told a group of kids that they could choose between one cookie now, or two cookies in five minutes. What do you think most kids chose? You probably guessed it—most of the kids said, "one cookie now."

When athletes or musicians want to become professional at their skills, they invest thousands of hours of work, sweat, sacrifice, and discipline to achieve their goal. One study said it was close to ten thousand hours to become a "professional." That is real discipline!

What are some goals or dreams you have for your life? Think about this great quote from University of Michigan Football coach, Jim Harbaugh: "If nobody laughs at your dream, it's not big enough."

Today in history, both John F. Kennedy and C.S. Lewis died. Both of these men are known for doing great things. They were men of discipline, who put aside their own interests for the interests of others. They left a legacy with their lives.

What do you want to be remembered for? What kind of story do you want your life to tell?

For the Spirit God gave us does not make us timid, but gives us power, love and self-discipline.
**2 Timothy 1:7 (NIV)**

# November 23

"Don't measure God's mind by your own. It would be a poor love that depended not on itself, but on the feelings of the person loved... For my part, in the worst mood I am ever in, when I don't feel I love God at all, I just look up to His love. I say to Him, 'Look at me. See what state I am in. Help me!'...And the love comes of itself; sometimes so strong, it nearly breaks my heart."
*David Elginbrod,* by George MacDonald

**Have you noticed** how wrong we can be about other people? You may think, "My teacher hates me. She yelled at me yesterday." "He was my best friend, and now he's off playing with the new kid. I guess he's not my friend any longer." Then, the next day or the next week, you find your friend still friendly and your teacher smiling.

There are better ways to evaluate people than by your moods. When you don't know all the facts, don't let your emotions push you around. Just hold your judgment until you know what's what.

Happily, God is not moody. He doesn't feel up or down, accepted or rejected. When He has to judge, He always judges rightly. He is always the same loving, caring, mighty, awesome, perfect Lord. Do you belong to Him? Then He always loves you, whatever else may be happening, however you may feel.

*Mary Lichlyter*

But you, O Lord, are a God of compassion and mercy, slow to get angry and filled with unfailing love and faithfulness.
**Psalm 86:15** (NLT)

# November 24

Do you see a man skillful in his work? He will stand before kings; he will not stand before obscure men.
**Proverbs 22:29 (NIV)**

**The pursuit of** excellence is a divine assignment. Just think about it; somewhere deep inside of us, we aspire to be the best we can be. Why? Because we are made in God's image, and He is perfect.

We are fallen and not perfect, of course, but we know what perfect is. We are attracted to it, we admire it when we see anything close to perfect in nature, art, mathematics, science, or in human kindness, and at our best we aspire to it in our work. Sometimes we can mistake perfection for a taskmaster, and it can be dispiriting; however, although God wants us to be mindful of perfection, He also wants us to be forgiving of our failures. He promises us that when we aspire to do our best, work to develop skills, and become masters of our efforts, we will be blessed with the recognition of leaders in our fields.

"Attitudes are more important than facts."
George MacDonald

*Lorin Hart*

# November 25

**Wee Gibbie had** no mother, and his father, rather than taking care of Gibbie, needed to be taken care of himself. The boy's greatest joy, in fact, was looking after his father, and helping others whenever he could. After Sir George's death, Gibbie watched over his father's friends until something horrible caused him to run away from the city. He went into the mountains, but soon

> "his heart had begun to ache…for not once since he set out had he had an opportunity of doing anything for anybody…and not to be able to help was to Gibbie like being dead."
>
> *The Baronet's Song*, by George MacDonald

He had nothing to give anyone: no money, no belongings, hardly even any clothes. But Gibbie helped people as naturally as breathing. The ways he helped might not seem important—finding lost things, seeing that people got home safely, keeping an ornery cow out of the corn. But in the Kingdom of God, helping is important.

The Bible mentions Joanna and Susanna, who helped support Jesus and the disciples (Luke 8), and tells of a disciple named Tabitha who was always doing good and helping the poor. (Acts 9) The Apostle Paul wrote that helpers are appointed by God to be part of the church.

Even you can help someone, sometime, in some way, and it will matter to God.

*Rebekah Choat*

> And in the church God has appointed first of all apostles, second prophets, third teachers, then workers of miracles, also those having gifts of healing, those able to help others, those with gifts of administration, and those speaking in different kinds of tongues.
>
> **1 Corinthians 12:28 (NIV)**

# November 26

**We should be** best known by how we live and love. Unconditionally love and forgive those who may have hurt you, hate you, or are just difficult to love. Honor God, as you purpose in your heart to try and view others as He does. Each person is worth every tear we shed and every prayer we make. Often, the person who is hurting you is hurting on the inside. Try seeing them as we all are, children who are each growing in our relationship with God at a different rate. It is very difficult to hate someone for whom we are praying. Ask God for a testimony of faith in Him that shares the same love that we were shown by Him.

The greatest healing will definitely take place when the offender comes and asks for forgiveness, but since those times are few and far between, trust that when we forgive someone who may have hurt us, God is honored. He alone can change hearts and minds. People know when we genuinely love them as they are, but still care enough to pray for their salvation. Our desire for others should be that not one of our family, friends, or enemies should perish in the lake of fire, but rather that they will be transformed through His awesome blood that He shed on the cross for all of us. It is a great thing when even those who do not love us have nothing but good things to share about how we treat them.

*J. Richard Martinez*

She opens her mouth with wisdom, and the teaching of kindness is on her tongue.
**Proverbs 31:26** (ESV)

# November 27

"I have given Him [Christ] my faith, and sworn my allegiance to Him; how, then, can I go back from this, and not be hanged as a traitor?"
*Pilgrim's Progress*, by John Bunyan

**You may hear** in the news (or a movie) of some sneaky traitor selling state secrets. But what is a traitor? It's somebody who turns against his or her own nation or ruler and helps the enemy instead. Treason is one of the worst of crimes—right up there with murder.

But you don't need to sell state secrets to be a traitor. Anyone can be faithless: betray people who have trusted them, use people to get what they want, be treacherous. Treachery is double-dealing; it's disloyalty. When you let somebody depend on you, and then turn around and work against that person, you have let him or her down in the worst way.

Traitors lose friends. Don't be one! You'll certainly never want to trust anyone who has betrayed you!

But there was Someone who was betrayed by the very people He came to rescue. They acted like His friends, and then they turned against Him. Many even rejoiced when His life was done.

But Jesus rescued them just the same.

And once He had rescued them, He began to make them different from the inside out. He didn't wait until they changed to rescue them; He rescued them *first.*

*Mary Lichlyter*

...But I will not remove from him my steadfast love or be false to my faithfulness.
**Psalm 89:33 (ESV)**

# November 28

**What is required** of a Christian? Jesus tells us,

> "'Love the Lord your God with all your heart and with all your soul and with all your strength and with all your mind'; and, 'Love your neighbor as yourself.'"
> **Luke 10:27 (NIV)**

Notice that we do not love our neighbor, or even our self, in the same way that we love God. Love for God is greater than, and comes before, any other love. This should remind us that any love, if it interferes with our love for God, is out of order.

How do we love ourselves, and therefore our neighbors? We love in imitation of God, whom we recognize as Love Itself, who wants what is good and just and right for us so that we might be His children in word, deed, and truth. Therefore we do not spoil ourselves, allow ourselves to behave badly, or act selfishly. We strive to build our character in faith, hope, and love; to grow up into the full stature of Christ Jesus, who lived every gift of the Spirit: love, joy, peace, patience, kindness, and gentleness.

Of course, growing into Christ will take time. We will make mistakes, and should surely be merciful and forgiving to ourselves, so long as we are willing to make amends and try again.

If we treat ourselves in this way, so should we treat others. We should hope for and expect the best from them. While we are willing to forgive, of course, we do not accept or allow others to constantly treat others or ourselves badly, or to influence us to join in bad behavior. If this happens, we must seek help from those God has put in authority over us.

*Sharon Edel*

# November 29

**You might sometimes** feel that you don't know or understand many things, and of course, it's true. It is true for grown-ups, as well, although they often have a hard time realizing and admitting that this is the case. But none of us need to be ashamed because we haven't yet learned all that we are able to.

Thomas Wingfold, though a grown man and a minister, found that he had not even known how much he didn't know until a friend helped him to see it. But once he was made aware, he set out at once to learn all he could through studying his Bible and discussing it with his wise friend, Mr. Polwarth (as told in *The Curate's Awakening*, by George MacDonald).

Mr. Wingfold's actions set a good example for us. Rather than worrying about all that we don't know, we can begin right away to try to learn more. The best way to start is by reading God's Word and talking about it with people who can help us to understand it better—maybe our parents or grandparents, our Sunday School teachers, and our pastors. We may also find that stories written by Christian men and women, such as George MacDonald, C.S. Lewis, Madeleine L'Engle, and many others can illustrate how God's people ought to live.

*Rebekah Choat*

Teach me, O Lord, to follow your decrees; then I will keep them to the end. Give me understanding, and I will keep your law and obey it with all my heart. Direct me in the path of your commands, for there I find delight.
**Psalm 119:33-35** (NIV)

# November 30

**In George MacDonald's fairy** tale *The Wise Woman,* a mysterious woman carries the spoiled young princess Rosamond away to her cottage in order to try to make something good of her. Rosamond has been used to getting everything she wants in the palace, and she has been very disobedient to her parents. But now, in the wise woman's cottage, she is told that she must keep the fire blazing and the cottage tidy and dusted while the wise woman is away. The princess, unused to obeying anyone, does not do the things the wise woman tells her. In fact, she soon gets bored with nothing to do. We are told that,

> "In truth she would have been glad of the employment, only just because she had been told to do it, she was unwilling; for there *are* people—however unlikely it may seem—who object to doing a thing for no other reason than that it is required of them."

Why is obedience so important? The biggest reason is that Jesus himself was completely obedient to His Father throughout His life, and even in His death, and if we want to learn to walk with Jesus, we must learn His way of thinking and doing things. He was humble, and He cherished the commands of His Father. He didn't brush them aside and say, "No, I want to do my own thing." His obedience showed that He trusted his Father, whose commands always lead to love.

Jesus said,

> Here I am…I have come to do your will, my God.
> **Hebrews 10:7** (NIV)

And He will enable us to say and do the same thing!

*Daniel Koehn*

# December 1

**Have you ever** had to prepare for someone to arrive? Perhaps you had to clean your room before your dad came home, or put your toys away before your friends came over, or maybe you had to get yourself ready by putting on your shoes or combing your hair.

Why is it important to be ready? One reason is that if you are not ready, you might miss something important. What if a baseball player isn't ready when the ball is thrown to him, or a flute player isn't ready when it's time for her entrance?

In *The Gifts of the Child Christ*, George MacDonald tells the story of a little girl named Phosy (her real name was Sophie, but she mixed up the sounds in her name). Phosy was quite young and had evidently never heard of Santa Claus. Can you imagine that? Instead of expecting Santa Claus, she had come to think that each Christmas Eve, Jesus was born anew, and came to every house as a little baby.

If you knew that Jesus was going to come to your house as a little baby this Christmas, how would you get ready for Him? If you knew that Jesus wanted to come into your heart and make His home there, how would you get ready for Him? In the Bible, Jesus says,

> Look, I am coming soon!
> **Revelation 22:12** (NIV)

Let's be sure to be ready for Him so we don't miss anything important!

*Daniel Koehn*

# December 2

"Any man can make mistakes, but only an idiot persists in his error."
Marcus Tullius Cicero

Whatever you do, do well....
**Ecclesiastes 9:10a (NLB)**

**You just got** your math homework back, and you have to do the problems you missed all over again. Why can't you just move on? There's plenty more math in the book!

Sorry—you can't. Math facts are built one on the other. You have to understand the problems you have now before you can begin to understand the next ones. And it's the same in spelling, reading, skating, computers, cooking, and car repair.

Maybe you think, "Well, *those* kids are good at math (or whatever) because they're just lucky." No; "luck," if it's anything, is just the point where opportunity meets preparation. Instead, *those* kids learn, try, make mistakes, go back, and learn again. They do a lot of work you don't see.

Real life operates that way, too. Learn, try, make mistakes, go back, and learn again. It's worth the work.

Like it or not, working to be truthful now makes you stronger and able to tell bigger, harder truths next year. Being patient with your sister now helps you later, when you have to be patient with kids you babysit or coach. Memorizing Scripture now helps you learn not only more Scripture down the road, but also many other things you need to know by heart.

If (or when!) you blow it, go back, figure out where you went wrong, and try again. Take the time to make it right. You may feel like an idiot about having to go back, but it's often the best way to go forward.

*Mary Lichlyter*

# December 3

"Our Creator is infinitely good, and his will is love. To submit to one who is 'too wise to err [make a mistake], too good to be unkind,' should not be hard."
Charles Haddon Spurgeon

**What does *everybody***, of every age, color, country, language, and income, have in common? They sometimes feel invisible—like a nobody.

Some kids work hard to be the best at something, just to get noticed. Some join a clique or a gang. Some brag about what they have or who they know. Some kids do destructive things, because it gets attention. They wonder, "Does anybody care? Does anybody see me? Am I worth anything?"

Yes, you're worth something! You matter! You have a purpose, even if you don't know what it is. You are NOT an accident or a mistake. You're in this world because God wants you here.

In some countries, sparrows are caught and sold (very cheaply) as snack food. Jesus says His Father knows each little bird, and cares about every single one. And He says to you, "Don't be afraid; you are more valuable to God than a whole flock of sparrows."

Does that surprise you? Did you know the Son of God was so *kind?*

But it's true—He can't be outdone when it comes to kindness and grace. He knows everything, He is mighty, He is powerful, He is just, He is righteous—and He cares about YOU. You're *never* invisible. Talk to Him. Read His Book and find out what He says about you.

*Mary Lichlyter*

The LORD who made you and helps you says: Do not be afraid…my chosen one.
**Isaiah 44:2 (NLT)**

# December 4

> They triumphed over him by the blood of the Lamb and by the word of their testimony; they did not love their lives so much as to shrink from death.
> **Revelation 12:11** (NIV)

**Do you like** a good story, with dragons and swords and heroes? The Bible is full of stories, told and retold to show us truth. In Revelation chapter 12, we find the story of Christmas from Heaven's perspective. Instead of seeing a quiet stable, straw, and sheep, we see a seven-headed fiery dragon ready to devour the infant boy, and the epic battle that follows.

A few years ago, on December 4th, a young doctor from Uganda died because he chose to take care of very sick patients with Ebola virus. Dr. Jonah loved Jesus, and believed that Jesus called him to love others, even if it risked his life. Some people only saw another sad funeral. But in Heaven, this was part of the great announcement that salvation has come; the accuser has been cast down.

When God's people do not fear to love, to work for justice, even in the hardest circumstances, then God's kingdom triumphs.

Perhaps you know someone who has died, or it makes you sad to think about people dying. George MacDonald wrote, "How strange this fear of death is! We are never frightened at a sunset." Yes, there is a period of sadness as the color fades to night, but we know that the sun will rise again in the morning. We will see Dr. Jonah again in the resurrection, and you will see those you love, because Jesus has won.

*J. A. Myhre*

# December 5

And suddenly there appeared with the angel a multitude of the heavenly host praising God and saying, "Glory to God in the highest, And on earth peace among men with whom He is pleased."
**Luke 2:13-14 (NASB)**

"They were all looking for a king
to slay their foes and lift them high;
Thou cam'st, a little baby thing
That made a woman cry."
*The Holy Thing,* by George MacDonald

**We are entering** a season that people love to celebrate with friends and family. Christmas time is a joy-filled experience for some people. Others have a hard time during this time of year, because they miss a loved one or dear friend. For some people it is a mix of both.

Two thousand years ago there was joy and sorrow when Jesus was born into our world. Joy because He was going to save mankind from themselves, and sin and sorrow because it would cost Him His very life to do it.

I think that it is good to celebrate and give gifts and enjoy good food together. It is also to remember that Jesus did not just come to be born; He came to die. Without His sacrifice, we would never know the deep, deep love of God.

Merry Christmas!

*Matthew Nash*

# December 6

"A free will is not the liberty to do whatever one likes, but the power of doing whatever one sees ought to be done, even in the very face of otherwise overwhelming impulse. There lies freedom indeed."

*Miracles of Our Lord,* by George MacDonald

**I'm free!** Nobody's going to tell me what to do!

Wait. I'm not that free. I still have to care for my pets, because I love them. And I still have to do what Mom says. But I don't have to listen to anybody else! I'm free—I make the choices!

Am I free not to obey the law of gravity? What *is* free will, then?

It doesn't mean I choose everything.

Last time I was with my friends, I guess I didn't use my free will. I didn't want to go to that place, but they made me. Well, they said I really should go, so I did. It wasn't my fault I got home late; it was theirs!

Well, I could have done what I should have, I suppose Why didn't I? But—it seemed important to listen to them. Wait a minute —where did my freedom go? I feel all tied up!

Maybe freedom isn't doing what I want. What I want changes every minute. Am I free when I do what God says, or is that slavery? Some people say so.

But He created me! If I belong to Jesus, am I unfree? Or is there freedom in obeying a King who loves me so much?

*Mary Lichlyter*

...If the Son sets you free, you are truly free.
**John 8:36** (NLT)

# December 7

"Love is the first comforter..."
*Paul Faber, Surgeon,* by George MacDonald

...Verily I say unto you, inasmuch as ye have done it unto one of the least of these my brethren, ye have done it unto me.
**Matthew 25:40 (KJV)**

**A very wise** man once told a story about a tiny violet, who lived under a tree with big leaves. One day the little violet looked up through the leaves, and for the first time saw the big blue sky. Soon, a rather mean, snappy dog came along, and the little violet asked the dog, "What is that up there, that is blue like me?" The mean dog replied, "Oh, that is a great giant violet that has grown so big that it can crush you!" Well, the little violet folded up her petals and hid herself as best she could. She was so frightened! The next morning, along came a little lamb, and the violet asked, "Dear lamb, will the great big violet up there come and crush me?" "Oh, no!" answered the lamb, "it won't crush you! His love is much greater than your own love, even as he is much more blue than you are in your tiny form." And the violet understood that the great big violet was so blue, so that he might have more love, and that the big violet would protect the little violet from everything in the world which might hurt her!

May we all grow to have the compassion of the lamb, and may we be assured that our deeds, whatever they may be, are done as though offered to our Lord, Jesus Christ—and strengthen the divine spark within each one of us.

*Claudia Brown*

# December 8

"Get a place for prayer where no one imagines what you are doing. Shut the door and talk to God."
Oswald Chambers

When you pray, don't be like the hypocrites who love to pray publicly...where everyone can see them. ...That is all the reward they will ever get. But when you pray, go away by yourself, shut the door behind you, and pray to your Father in private. Then your Father, who sees everything, will reward you.
**Matthew 6:5-6 (NLT)**

**Jesus said harsh** things about some religious leaders. That they prayed in public wasn't wrong; what was wrong was their pride in being seen praying! Apparently, having people watching and admiring them was more important to them than God was.

A prayer may be short or long; it can have fancy words or simple ones; it can come from a prayer book or right out of your head. But the focus of every Christian prayer should be Jesus—nothing else, no one else.

Unhappily, we can lose that focus, forget about Jesus, and try to impress other people instead. When we do that, we're performing, not praying. Performing is fine on the stage, but not for following Christ every day of your life.

So pray privately when you can—just God and you. Not that you can't *ever* pray with family or friends—but God wants you not to be distracted by what others might think of you.

*Mary Lichlyter*

# December 9

"Love is the opener as well as the closer of eyes."
George MacDonald

Love must be sincere. Hate what is evil; cling to what is good.
**Romans 12:9** (NIV)

**Have you ever** known someone who is phony? Maybe they say they are your friend, then spread bad stories about you. You've never done that yourself, have you? I certainly hope not, because the Lord tells us that love, if it's really love, must be real. He said, "Love one another." That is how the world knows we are followers of God; because we love one another.

Another thing that love will do is make us hate what is evil around us and love the things that are good. Love for our brothers and sisters will help us to see the good in them and correct the bad, if we have the chance. For instance, Johnny may be a nice boy, and polite to his parents and teachers, but say bad things to his classmates. What would you say to him?

If I had a friend like Johnny, I would tell him I like the way he is polite to his parents and teachers. I would praise him for that, but then I would lovingly tell him that it is hurtful when he says bad things to his friends. I would tell him that Jesus does not like us to be that way to other people. More than anything, I would try to see the best in Johnny, and help him see the best in himself!

*Linda S. Storm*

# December 10

**Today we celebrate** George MacDonald's birthday: December 10, 1824. Happy birthday, George!

Jesus said the most important command is

> ...You shall love the Lord your God with all your heart, with all your soul, and with all your strength.
> **Deuteronomy 6:5 (NKJV)**

That's an all-encompassing command! Not only are we to love God with every part of ourselves, but with *all* of every part. Did you know that's impossible apart from God? He is the only One who loves that completely. One of the things sin does in us is tie us to our "self," our "me." We think most about what is best for "me," and we make decisions to serve our "me" first and foremost, to the neglect of others.

But God is completely free from all that. He thinks about what is best for others, and He makes decisions that serve others first and foremost. That's what we see in Jesus. He came to earth not for Himself, but for us, because we were in need. To meet that need, He laid down all His comforts and rights, and even His own life. He was completely free from His "me." He loved us with *all* of every part of Himself.

God wants to make His home inside you and me. He wants to put His very Life in us. And when He does, we will begin to find that Life setting us free to love completely. We will soon look upon Him in the same pure love in which He looks upon us. Then we will look outward upon others and love them that way too!

*Daniel Koehn*

# December 11

> Listen! I am standing and knocking at your door. If you hear my voice and open the door, I will come in and we will eat together.
> **Revelation 3:20 (CEV)**

## Knock, Knock...

**There is something** really satisfying about sharing a meal together with family or friends. We laugh together, enjoy the feast set before us, and really get closer together. In the verse above, Jesus says He is knocking at the door of our hearts. If we respond to His knocks and invite Him into our lives, He says He will come in and we will eat together. Imagine sharing a meal with the king of the universe! In the words of George Macdonald, "Few delights can equal the mere presence of one whom we trust utterly." Jesus is so powerful and yet so personal. He knows us inside out: "You are the one who created my innermost parts; you knit me together while I was still in my mother's womb." Psalm 139:13 (CEB)

Jesus created us, formed us, and He knows every care and concern in our lives. We cannot pretend with Him. His eyes penetrate to the depth of our souls. We cannot put on a brave face, an air of sophistication, or any kind of mask to hide our true feelings and nature. God looks right through us and judges the desires and intents of our hearts. Once we bare our souls before our maker, He applies the balm of Gilead which soothes, heals, and restores our relationship with Him. Open up your hearts and welcome Christ into your life. The best relationship you can have is one with Jesus.

*Prithika*

# December 12

"She only knew there was no fear in her, and everything was so right and safe that it could not get in."
*The Princess and The Goblin,* by George MacDonald

**Take a glass,** and pour water into it ever so slowly, making it reach all the way to the top, and then keep adding to it drop by drop until you think it is completely filled; try adding beyond all that you think is possible, and keep going! You will discover that the surface water molecules are attracted to the inside water molecules and they hold together, like holding hands, creating a sort of net that allows you to fill the glass so copmletely that it goes beyond its absolute capacity, being held together beyond the edge.

When we are filled with the love of God, He so fills us up that there is *no* space for anything else! Pray that you come to know how full you really are; the breadth and length and height and depth of who Jesus Christ is inside. That truth is beyond our understanding! He fills us up beyond our absolute capacity. He leaves no room for fear. You feel this fullness when you are filled with singing, when songs and praise and joy flood your heart. He fills us with His love like water: beyond the brim!

In Him we are filled—completely.

*Blythe Followwill*
*For Jo*

So that Christ may dwell in your hearts, through faith; that you may know the love of Christ which surpasses knowledge, that you may be filled with all the fullness of God.
**Ephesians 3:17a, 18-19 (ESV)**

# December 13

"Mercy cannot get in where mercy goes not out."
*The Hope of the Gospel,* by George MacDonald

**What is mercy,** anyway? The dictionary says it's compassion or forgiveness you show to someone you *could* punish. Given the choice, it's choosing not to hurt. And that's very important to God.

Mercy is a power move. It takes a strong person to choose it. When you're attacked with words, for instance, thinking up a sarcastic comeback may sound strong, but it's really puny compared to forgiveness.

"Forgive HER? After what she said? She doesn't even want forgiveness! She doesn't even know what it is!"

But God forgave you (and me) when we didn't know what forgiveness was. We didn't know we needed His mercy. We thought we were the good guys! There was a lot we didn't know. But He was merciful, and forgave us, and changed us, and taught us the truth.

That's what we must do for the difficult people around us: choose not to hold their words or actions against them, want God's best for them, and treat them better than they deserve, knowing that God will take them in hand. Of course, there may come a time when we must stand up to defend *others* who are being mistreated, but when the ill use is toward us, we must take the mercy route.

Ask Jesus to make you that strong! Ask Him to teach you how to be merciful every time you are badly treated (even if it's your brother or sister who needs your mercy!).

*Mary Lichlyter*

If you forgive those who sin against you, your heavenly Father will forgive you.
**Matthew 6:14 (NLT)**

# December 14

But we all, with unveiled face, beholding as in a mirror the glory of the Lord, are being transformed into the same image from glory to glory, just as from the Lord, the Spirit.
**2 Corinthians 3:18** (NAS)

"To follow Jesus is to be learning of him, to think his thoughts, to use his judgments, to see things as he sees them, to feel things as he feels them, to be of the same heart, soul, and mind, as he is."
George MacDonald

**In order to** get to know Jesus, we do the beholding and He does the transforming. To *behold* means to see, to view, to look with attention, to learn and to know.

In the Bible, the Greek word *Metamorphoó* means to *transform*. The word *metamorphosis* is used to describe the beautiful change that happens as a caterpillar becomes a butterfly, or a tadpole becomes a frog. Pretty cool, huh?

So, how can you behold Jesus and God and get to know them?

You can see God and learn about Jesus in the Bible, because the Bible is God's Word, speaking to us. You can behold God by talking with Him in prayer, and also by listening. We are His sheep and He says His sheep know His voice. You can behold God by worshiping Him. You can sit quietly, thinking about Him, all the while being aware and thankful of His presence.

You can behold God in nature, His creation!

Remember, our part is looking at God; He does the transforming. He changes us and makes us look like Him!

*Rennie Marie Sneed*

# December 15

> Delight yourself in the Lord; and He will give you the desires of your heart.
> **Psalm 37:4 (NASB)**

**Only ten days** until Christmas!!! Have you filled out your Advent calendar? Eaten the chocolate? Moved the magnets? There are many wonderful ways to build the anticipation for the day when we celebrate Jesus' birth—and get to open presents! Presents are wonderful; both to give and to get. Christmas presents and dreaming of fun is a delight in life. To "delight" in something or someone means that they bring you great joy and pleasure.

Too many people, grown up and children alike, get so caught up in gifting, they forget what we are really supposed to be excited about. It's just like the two little girls in my favorite story by George MacDonald, *The Wise Woman*. A princess and a farm girl were both spoiled rotten. They got everything they wanted and didn't delight in ANYTHING. It wasn't until the Wise Woman took them away that they learned what "delight" means. This Christmas, remember to delight first in the great Giver of the best gift, His Son, Jesus, and see what surprises God has in store for you. You can be sure He will bring your heart great delight.

*Annie Mae Platter*

# December 16

"A man might flatter, or bribe, or coax a tyrant;
but there is no refuge from the love of God."
*Justice (*from *Unspoken Sermons),* by George MacDonald

**Imagine a boy** named Shane, who lies a lot. He knows it's wrong, but he does it anyway. A lie can be a very convenient sort of thing, but lies build up until they become a wall keeping Shane closed in. He'd like to get back to the truth, he thinks.

Shane could go to his Savior, Jesus, and say, "Please—do anything it takes to get this lying out of me!" But… "*Anything* it takes? God might do something awful! He might make me do something hard!"

What did the snake tell Eve in the garden? "Do what I say and you'll have what you want. God can't be trusted. God doesn't love you." We've all inherited that thinking. Talk about lies!

Jesus loves Shane too much to let him stay walled up, because Shane is His.

Now, if Jesus were only a judge or a ruler, He might not care so much. Judges can be bribed; so can other leaders. But Jesus is also God—too perfect to do anything that isn't holy and that isn't the best for Shane. If that means Shane must go through troubles to be rescued, Jesus will walk right through those troubles with him.

*Mary Lichlyter*

God is not a man, so he does not lie. He is not human, so he does not change his mind. Has he ever spoken and failed to act? Has he ever promised and not carried it through?
**Numbers 23:19 (NLT)**

# December 17

But those who trust in idols, who say to images, 'you are our gods' will be turned back in utter shame.
**Isaiah 42:17 (NIV)**

**It is easy** to take our eyes off God and focus on other things, whether we intend to or not. When you think about your favorite band, Barbie, superhero, or movie star, what comes to mind? How do those images make you feel? Do you wish that you could be like them, and have what they have? Imagine how great your life would be: all the fame, looks, money, friends, cars, power, and so on. But in time, those materialistic things will fade and go away. What will you have left? How much will you miss those things?

Idols are things that distract us from God. They are things that we put above God. We have eternity with God, and need to always remember that. With God we have eternal life. He is with us forever, but if we aren't trusting Him and are instead worshipping idols (which means making something other than God the center of your life), there will be consequences, just as there were for the Israelites, when they left Egypt and were wandering in the desert. Because they had worshipped idols, the Israelites were made to wander for forty years! Yes, God did keep His word and eventually brought them to the Promised Land, but see how much more difficult their lives became because of their unfaithfulness. Reap the blessings that God has to give you *today*. *Trust* in the Lord and put your faith in Him and in Him alone.

*Laura Bennin*

# December 18

When I was a child, I often had trouble sleeping. Sometimes I had frightening dreams; other times I just couldn't fall asleep. I might have been upset about something that had happened at school, or nervous about an upcoming event; some nights I was very sad and lonely.

I learned this Bible verse when I was about nine years old:

> Finally, brothers and sisters, whatever is true, whatever is noble, whatever is right, whatever is pure, whatever is lovely, whatever is admirable—if anything is excellent or praiseworthy—think about such things.
> **Proverbs 9:10** (NIV)

My mother helped me make a plan to follow when I wasn't able to sleep. I would recite this verse in my head, and then I would think about specific things that would fit in the categories it mentions. For instance, "whatever is true" could include the Bible, the things my Sunday School teacher told me, and the biographies (life stories) of historic people that I liked to read; "whatever is lovely" could mean the flowers growing in our yard, a piece of music that I enjoyed listening to, my grandma's face, and many other things.

The very next verse in Philippians 4 ends with, "And the God of peace will be with you." Each night as I focused my mind on the excellent and praiseworthy things God had placed in my life, He helped me to grow calm and peaceful so that I could rest.

> …for he grants sleep to those he loves.
> **Psalm 127:2b** (NIV)

*Rebekah Choat*

# December 19

"Music originated from God and was created solely for his worship, his glory, and his pleasure." *Crushing the Devil: Your Guide to Spiritual Warfare and Victory in Christ*, by Pedro Okoro

"Music awakens my spirit...(and)...promotes spiritual, physical and emotional well-being." *Think Great: Be Great!*, by Lailah Gifty Akita

"When we lift our hands in praise and worship, we break spiritual jars of perfume over Jesus. The fragrance of our praise fills the whole earth and touches the heart of God." Dennis Ignatius

"Praise and worship is such a powerful device, able to dismantle every shackle and able to breakdown every wall." "It should be our heartbeat and should never depart our lips. 'Let us come before him with thanksgiving and extol him with music and song' (Psalms 95:2)." Euginia Herlihy

**God inhabits the** praises of His people. Praise awakens us to His goodness and presence. When people praise Him, the worship goes up to Heaven like a sweet perfume. He desires that we praise Him with all of our heart, mind, soul, and strength; through singing songs, spoken words, art, music, and dance. Praise Him with sincerity and truth. Let your love for Him and the joy He gives you overflow in your praise to Him. When you do, even those who are against you will be ashamed and silenced.

*Laurel Shepherd*

O Lord our God, the majesty and glory of your name fills all the earth and overflows the heavens. You have taught the little children to praise you perfectly. May their example shame and silence your enemies!
**Psalm 8:1-2 (TLB)**

# December 20

**Did you know** that winter is the best season to look at the night sky? Why? Because during winter we have the longest nights and a sky more transparent than usual!

During summer, the warm moisture-filled atmosphere causes the sky to appear hazy at night. During winter, however, the cold air cannot hold as much moisture, making winter nights clearer. This allows us to see the stars in all of their beauty.

Go ahead! Bundle up, make some hot chocolate, and go outside to look at the stars. You will be amazed at the number of stars you will see. Actually, if you fix your eyes on a certain spot in the sky you will find that eventually you might be able to see even more stars!

Can you imagine if someone asked you to count the stars? There is no way you could do that; there are just too many!

Are you ready to be shocked? Read on:

> Look up and see: who created these? He brings out the starry host by number; He calls all of them by name. Because of His great power and strength, not one of them is missing.
> **Isaiah 40:26 (HCSB)**

Yes, you read that right. God knows not only how many stars there are, but also their names! That, my friend, is amazing!

That same amazing God wants you to know that He loves you. Even though He is in charge of that great, big universe, He still cares about you. Would you like to know how much He cares about you? Read John 3:16!

Now go outside and look at the stars!

*Alba Rice*

# December 21

The end of a matter is better than its beginning, and patience is better than pride.
**Ecclesiastes 7:8 (NIV)**

**The fact that** you exist is a big deal. There will be days when you do not understand why you are here or why you matter, and that's okay. All things are revealed in God's timing, and His clock does not work like our conventional man-made clocks. God's clock is always the "right" time: the battery does not go dead, nor is its performance hindered by extreme or adverse conditions. It knows your beginning and your end.

You may wish you were older, bigger, or taller, but be patient. The way you are is God's design. He made you just the way you are meant to be. The enemy might whisper falsehoods in your ear, like, "You're too short to play football," or "You're not tall enough to be a model." But the enemy is a liar!

The very thing you feel is holding you back in some way could be the perceived weakness God will use to make you strong. With God all things are possible. Maybe you will become the best short football player on the field, or become the first runway model who isn't tall!

Be patient, and don't let your pride get in the way. Pride is full of self. Don't forget who gifted you with the ability and instilled the discipline to fine-tune your gifts and skills.

Patience is your ability to accept what comes your way without flying off the handle, sulking, or being upset while you wait. Be patient with life, and don't let pride push you into doing things.

*Kim S. Hawkins*

# December 22

> God will be the sure foundation for your times, a rich store of salvation and wisdom and knowledge; the fear of the Lord is the key to this treasure
> **Isaiah 33:5-6** (NIV)

## A Sure Foundation and A Rich Store

**Here are some** interesting facts: the Bible uses the phrase "Do not be afraid" 78 times and "Fear not" is used 170 times. Yet, the Bible also says, "fear the Lord" 205 times. Now, if we aren't supposed to be afraid, why would we fear the Lord?

In this verse from the prophet Isaiah, we are told that God is our foundation, and that the fear of the Lord is the key to salvation, wisdom, and knowledge. Wow! So, if we fear God, we will always have a foundation to stand on and a key to the treasure. But, what does "fear God" really mean? Is God scary? Should we be afraid of God?

Fearing God is a type of respect. We fear God in the same way that we fear a raging fire, high winds, or very deep water. For example, we enjoy sitting by a campfire, but we understand its power. We are thankful for a gentle wind, yet we know that hurricanes or tornados have tremendous power. We like to dive into deep water, but we learn to swim because we respect the power of the water and we don't want to drown.

In the same way, we fear God because we respect the power of God. That type of fear gives us a sure foundation for our life on earth. It unlocks the door to a rich storehouse of salvation, wisdom, and knowledge. Now, that's a treasure!

*Carol Wimmer*

# December 23

## Love

**As Jan sat** in Sunday School, the teacher read this verse,

> And walk in love, as Christ also hath loved us, and hath given himself for us an offering and a sacrifice to God for a sweetsmelling savor.
> **Ephesians 5:2 (KJV)**

Then she told the girls to see how many examples they could find of love being shown, and to make a list of them for next Sunday.

Jan watched a young mother as she told her son she loved him when he left to go to school. Her parents voiced, "Bye, love you!" to each other as they went their way. Jan said, "I love you," as she picked up Miss Kitty and held her. Miss Kitty purred her thanks. The pastor left a message for the family and told them he loved them. The youth pastor called to remind Jan's department of an outing, and ended with, "Love you guys." Her elderly neighbor, Mrs. Jackson, thanked Jan for picking up her paper for her and said, "I love you, dear."

As Sunday finally came, Jan was eager to share what she had found. One by one, the girls read their lists. Jan read Ephesians 5:2 again. Then she humbly told how she came to know and understand what real love was all about. She told about asking for forgiveness of her sin and receiving Jesus into her heart. His love for her was a great sacrifice by God to cover her sin.

Jan found the greatest example of love had been before her all the time. God's love will never fade or go away.

*Dottie Thornton*

# December 24

**I am certain** that during this Christmas season you have been hearing much regarding the story of the birth of Jesus. I would like to share with you something that you may not have heard. It is a poetical prophecy taken from an Old Testament book called Wisdom.*

You may be familiar with the idea that many Old Testament passages, which were written before Christ came actually provided hints of the Savior to come. Even when the writers spoke of Old Testament happenings, there was often a second meaning which pointed to Christ! It's a bit like unwrapping a present. You see a beautifully wrapped box; but there is so much more inside the box!

I would like for you to unwrap this present. I think that if you know Jesus, you will be able to see for yourself (or maybe with just a little help from a parent or older friend) the many ways in which this beautiful passage refers to Jesus! Imagine the night of Jesus' birth, and read on!

> It was then, while everything was wrapped in a gentle silence, and half a night had already passed, that your all-powerful word had leaped down from heaven, the royal throne. Like a fierce warrior, he had entered the land that was marked for destruction. He carried with him your unchanging declaration like a sharp sword... he reached the sky while still standing on the ground.
>
> **Wisdom 18:14-16 (CEB)**

**The Book of Wisdom is considered apocryphal by some Christians and may not be in your Bible. You may still appreciate the beauty of this passage.*

*Sharon Edel*

# December 25

**Jesus was full** of *steadfast love*. Steadfast love means full of true, unfailing, reliable, unflinching love. Jesus revealed that the Father is full of such love. God came to earth as Jesus to show His steadfast love for us.

In Jewish thought, words are creative forces and the universe is made by God's speaking. The Word that God speaks makes our world, and that Word is what holds the world together and gives it its purpose. The Word is the inner meaning and structure of the world. That meaning, that order, became flesh, or in other words became a person—Jesus—so that we could understand God's Word. The Word became a person; the truth became a story.

On Christmas, we celebrate this event, which is the center of history. The Word that orders the stars became a baby so we could see its face.

*Matthew Levi*

And the Word became flesh and dwelt among us, and we have seen his glory, glory as of the only Son from the Father, full of steadfast love
**John 1:14 (Author's Translation)**

# December 26

And Mary said, "My soul magnifies the Lord and my spirit rejoices in God my Savior."
**Luke 1:46-47** (ESV)

**One way to** pray is to think and imagine what a Scripture verse is about. Imagine the first day after Jesus was born. Did Jesus always sleep in the manger, or did Mary snuggle up next to Him and nurse Him to sleep before she laid Him in the manger?

How much did Jesus weigh? Probably less than ten pounds. Maybe your mother has a ten pound sack of flour and you can get an idea how heavy a young baby is, although holding a real baby is much more pleasant than holding a sack of flour! Jesus was a real baby. Jesus was and is our God. Even when you are grown up, this will be confusing in a wonderful way.

When Mary first said, "My soul magnifies the Lord, " Jesus was living inside Mary. What do you do when you rejoice—do you shout, or jump up and down? You can shout or jump to the Lord for giving us Jesus. You can speak out loud that you are thankful that Mary said "Yes" to the Lord God. God takes delight in you as you talk to Him, sing to Him and think about Him. God delights in your making good choices, just as Mary made a good choice to say "Yes!" to God.

*Patrecia Jacobson*

# December 27

**Have you ever** read a really great story? Maybe it's a story full of adventure and courage. Or maybe it's a story about brave heroes and heroines traveling to magical lands and meeting talking animals. What's your favorite story? Why?

Stories we read in a book can be exciting—sometimes we can't wait to turn to the next page! But did you know you are in a story right now?

In the Bible, God tells us that He is the author of our stories. He knows everything about you, because He made you. He also knows every one of your days, before they even happen. He knows what you are afraid of, what makes you happy, and what makes you sad. He knows when big challenges will come your way.

Psalm 139:5 says, "You hem me in behind and before, and you lay your hand upon me." God, the author of our stories, has walked with us in the past, and continues to walk ahead of us into the future. Because of this, we can be *excited* about the future!

We are characters in the greatest story ever told—the story of God's love for the whole world.

*Bethany Wagner*

...All the days ordained for me were written
in your book before one of them came to be.
**Psalm 139:16b** (NIV)

# December 28

> And there appeared to [Zechariah] an angel of the Lord… Zechariah was troubled when he say him…But the angel said to him, "Do not be afraid, Zechariah, for your prayer has been heard, and your wife Elizabeth will bear you a son, and you shall call his name John. And you will have joy and gladness…And Zechariah said to the angel, "How shall I know this?"…And the angel answered him, "I am Gabriel, who stands in the presence of God, and I was sent to speak to you and to bring you this good news. And behold, you will be silent and unable to speak until the day that these things take place, because you did not believe my words…"
>
> **Luke 1:11-25** (ESV)

**Would you like** to see an angel? Zechariah did see one! How did he feel? Full of fear. It seems odd that Zechariah, who was a priest of God, was afraid, even in the safety of God's temple.

Zechariah and Elizabeth had been faithfully praying all their lives. Gabriel came to tell Zechariah good news about his future son. But did Zechariah give thanks, or exclaim how wonderful this news was? No, he questioned. Perhaps because Zechariah was a priest, God was especially strict with him regarding his disbelief. But what happened to Zechariah is a good lesson for us to remember. Since he couldn't talk for a while, he had more time to pray and thank God in his heart. Let us take time to thank God today for all the blessings He has given us!

*Patrecia Jacobson*

# December 29

The angel went to her and said "Greetings to you who are highly favored! The Lord is with you!"
**Luke 1:28 (NIV)**

**When I was** your age, I had a tough time with the days just after Christmas; my birthday was during this time. I never seemed to get the same birthday parties as others, because friends were away for the holidays; or the same gifts, because of what I'd just gotten for Christmas. I just felt left out sometimes!

One year, my grandparents were over for Christmas, and my birthday was just a few days later. I was sulking over not having a party and was sitting alone in my room. My grandpa came in to see me and asked what was wrong. I said in a low voice, "I feel left out; no one knows it's my birthday." Grandpa put his arm around me and chuckled. "Holly," he said, "when you were born I asked God to give you a special gift; did you know that?" I perked up a little and asked, "What gift?" He took my hand in his and explained how the whole family had prayed for me to come into the world at Christmas because there had been no children around for a long time. He prayed that I would have a fiery spirit and the gift of being able to speak the truth. It was a known fact that I often said it like it was, and this had sometimes gotten me into trouble. "You prayed that I would speak the truth?" I asked as I began to see myself in a different light. I *was* special. Smiling, he said, "The Lord is with you, Holly; never forget how important you are to Him and to us."

*Holly Van Shouwen*

# December 30

**New beginnings are** always invigorating. They give us hope and buoy us up. I hope that in the new year to come, you are blessed, and that you also know the blessing you are to the people in your life. I hope that you know your worth and value in Christ.

I hope that you know what it is to be truly loved by an amazing Heavenly Father. No matter your history and how life has disappointed you, know that you have a Father who loves you unconditionally. He longs to know you. Spend time with Him. Talk to Him. He will never fail you.

I also pray that, in the midst of the turmoil swirling around us in the world today, you have peace: not some earthly, shifting peace, but a peace down to your soul, the peace of Christ that grounds you and keeps you strong.

You are loved!

*Karen Thornton*

The Lord bless you and keep you; the Lord make his face shine on you and be gracious to you; the Lord turn his face toward you and give you peace.
**Numbers 6:24-26 (NIV)**

# December 31

**At the end** of Paul's first letter to the Thessalonians, Paul sounds like a parent giving instructions to his children before leaving. He tells them to obey and to be helpful and to stay out of trouble—not in those exact words, but the idea is the same!

But Paul includes these lovely "orders" as well:

> Rejoice always, pray continually, give thanks in all circumstances; for this is God's will for you in Christ Jesus.
> **1 Thessalonians 5:16-18 (NIV)**

What kind of instructions are these? These are the hopes of a Father for his children; His will for His sons and daughters.

Our Father desires our happiness (Rejoice always!); He desires that we keep in regular communication with Him (Pray continually); and He encourages us to have an attitude of appreciation (Give thanks in all circumstances). These are three practices that we must strive to make our own:

1. Rejoice Always: We may not always *feel* joyful, but we can try to cultivate an attitude that is positive, cheerful, and makes others feel comfortable around us. True joy blooms, not from the events of our lives, but from the love we receive and give in Christ Jesus.

2. Pray Continually: You are always thinking, aren't you? Simply direct those thoughts to God, and you will be praying continually! (Remember to take time to listen, too!)

3. Give thanks in all circumstances: Think about all that has been given you; all of the good people who love you, all of the beauty and goodness which you are able to enjoy. Thank God and thank others.

May all of God's children strive for joyfulness, prayerfulness, and thankfulness, and so fulfill God's will for them in Christ Jesus!

*Sharon Edel*

# Author Index


| | |
|---|---|
| Adams, Amy | January 18, February 27, March 19, April 18, 21, August 20, September 22, October 11, November 4 |
| Adams, Diane | September 6 |
| Akers, Ginger | March 14 |
| Becker, Patricia S. | March 5, June 30, July 20, October 20, 27 |
| Bennin, Laura | January 2, April 5, May 6, June 9, July 31, August 9, 16, December 17 |
| Blackmon, Michelle | September 25, 26 |
| Blair, Lisa | January 5, February 18, April 4, May 2, 7, June 26 |
| Brown, Claudia | December 7 |
| Canty, Jolyn | January 12, February 5, April 11, May 1, June 6, July 26, 27, August 10, 17, 27, October 8, 12 |
| Choat, Rebekah | January 27, February 8, March 11, 18, April 7, August 26, October 16, November 19, 20, 25, 29, December 18 |
| Davis, Debra Baker | October 19 |
| del Pino, Jose | January 14, September 7, November 16 |
| Dindinger, Joseph | July 19 |
| Donald, J.S. | June 4, 5, August 29, September 30 |
| Dossett, Scott | July 24 |
| Edel, Sharon | February 23, 28, March 6, 10, 30, 31, April 9, 10, 20, 23, 26, 27, 29, May 26, 27, June 11, July 7, 15, August 15, October 25, 26, November 1, 2, 8, 10, 28, December 24, 31 |
| Farley, Amy | February 16, May 16, September 3, 13, November 13 |
| Followwill, Blythe | January 23, 26, February 1, March 1, 20, April 25, May 22, 30, June 8, 27, July 11, 17, August 31, October 1, 7, 30, 31, December 12 |
| Footit, Kathy | June 2, 3 |

| | |
|---|---|
| Fronk, Steve | January 10, February 21, March 17, May 11, 23, June 23, August 3, 4, 22, September 5, 28 |
| Gailey, Michael | April 14, October 2 |
| Gililland, Karise | May 28, July 25 |
| Harrison, Angela | June 7 |
| Hart, Lorin | January 6, July 6, November 7, 24 |
| Hawkins, Kim S. | December 21 |
| Hollace, Barbara | April 28, July 22, October 6 |
| Hostmeyer, Phyllis | January 9, February 19 |
| Hotmire, Darrel | September 19 |
| Hotmire, Darren | March 24, July 10, 12, 16 |
| House, James | June 1, September 11 |
| Jacobson, Patrecia | January 25, March 8, December 26, 28 |
| Joos, Steven | August 12 |
| Kadlub, Sharon | May 9 |
| Kasa, Kirstin | June 21 |
| Koehn, Daniel | August 2, September 15, November 5, 21, 30, December 1, 10 |
| Koehn, Renita | March 25, 26, 27, 28 |
| Lambert, Susian | August 1 |
| Lee, Katherine T. | July 8 |
| Levi, Matthew | January 8, February 2, March 3, June 12, 13, 19, July 28, August 11, October 21, December 25 |
| Lichlyter, Mary | January 17, 19, 21, 22, February 4, 6, April 1, 13, 16, 24, May 31, July 30, August 30, September 1, November 12, 14, 17, 23, 27, December 2, 3, 6, 8, 13, 16 |
| Livingston, Heidi | April 12, May 5 |
| Lynott-Carroll, Lisa | January 3, September 12 |
| Marks, Julia | September 16 |
| Martinez, J. Richard | May 24, July 3, November 26 |
| McCarty, Eric | February 17 |

| | |
|---|---|
| Mills, Frank | February 7, 11 September 27 |
| MoChridhe, Race | June 25, August 14, October 22 |
| Morris, Dawn | March 23 |
| Myhre, J.A. | December 4 |
| Nash, Matthew | January 29, March 21, April 15, May 13, June 10, July 5, August 18, September 9, 10, October 15, November 22, December 5 |
| Norris, Thaine | October 3 |
| Platter, Annie Mae | January 15, February 15, November 15, December 15 |
| Platter, Diane | October 4 |
| Powers, Jerian | May 17, August 24, 25 |
| Powers, William F. | May 17, August 24, 25 |
| Priddle, Agnes | October 9, 10 |
| Prithika | May 21, June 22, September 17, December 11 |
| Redding, Marion T. | February 25 |
| Rice, Alba | January 20, May 4, September 2, December 20 |
| Rushing, Gwen | January 4, July 18 |
| Ryder, Vicki | February 29, March 29, June 29, July 29, September 29, October 29 |
| Sanchez, A.E. | August 5 |
| Schmoll, Zak | September 23 |
| Schuch, Dan | November 11 |
| Schweiger, Kelly | May 20 |
| Scrivens, Dionne | July 14 |
| Shepherd, Laurel | January 7, June 15, September 24, December 19 |
| Sneed, Rennie Marie | February 13, April 30, May 3, July 13, December 14 |
| Speake, B. Daniel | January 11, July 23 |
| Stark, Tegan | August 28 |

| | |
|---|---|
| Storm, Linda S. | March 4, 15, April 22, September 14, October 23, 24, December 9 |
| Strasner, Marjorie | June 24 |
| Thornton, Dottie | January 30, February 9, 22, March 9, 16, 22, April 6, 8, May 10, 18, 29, June 16, July 4, August 19, September 18, October 13, November 6, December 23 |
| Thornton, Karen | January 28, March 7, May 14, July 21, August 6, October 5, November 3, December 30 |
| Tucker, Henna-Marie | April 17 |
| Van Shouwen, Holly | January 1, 16, 31, February 3, 26, March 2, 12, May 15, 19, June 28, July 9, August 13, September 8, 21, October 14, December 29 |
| Vigh, Monte | June 14, 17, 18 |
| Von Bergen, Megan | May 8 |
| Wagner, Bethany | February 12, 14, 20, April 2, July 2, August 7, 8, September 4, November 9, December 27 |
| Williams-Smith, Deborah | January 24, May 12 |
| Wimmer, Carol | January 13, February 10, 24, March 13, April 3, 19, May 25, June 20, July 1, August 21, 23, September 20, October 18, November 18, December 22 |
| Zepernick, Richard | October 17, 28 |

64752262R00226

Made in the USA
Charleston, SC
05 December 2016